The Past That Might
Have Been, the Future
That May Come

CRITICAL EXPLORATIONS IN SCIENCE FICTION AND FANTASY
(a series edited by Donald E. Palumbo and C.W. Sullivan III)

1 *Worlds Apart? Dualism and Transgression in Contemporary Female Dystopias* (Dunja M. Mohr, 2005)

2 *Tolkien and Shakespeare: Essays on Shared Themes and Language* (ed. Janet Brennan Croft, 2007)

3 *Culture, Identities and Technology in the* Star Wars *Films: Essays on the Two Trilogies* (ed. Carl Silvio, Tony M. Vinci, 2007)

4 *The Influence of* Star Trek *on Television, Film and Culture* (ed. Lincoln Geraghty, 2008)

5 *Hugo Gernsback and the Century of Science Fiction* (Gary Westfahl, 2007)

6 *One Earth, One People: The Mythopoeic Fantasy Series of Ursula K. Le Guin, Lloyd Alexander, Madeleine L'Engle and Orson Scott Card* (Marek Oziewicz, 2008)

7 *The Evolution of Tolkien's Mythology: A Study of the History of Middle-earth* (Elizabeth A. Whittingham, 2008)

8 *H. Beam Piper: A Biography* (John F. Carr, 2008)

9 *Dreams and Nightmares: Science and Technology in Myth and Fiction* (Mordecai Roshwald, 2008)

10 Lilith *in a New Light: Essays on the George MacDonald Fantasy Novel* (ed. Lucas H. Harriman, 2008)

11 *Feminist Narrative and the Supernatural: The Function of Fantastic Devices in Seven Recent Novels* (Katherine J. Weese, 2008)

12 *The Science of Fiction and the Fiction of Science: Collected Essays on SF Storytelling and the Gnostic Imagination* (Frank McConnell, ed. Gary Westfahl, 2009)

13 *Kim Stanley Robinson Maps the Unimaginable: Critical Essays* (ed. William J. Burling, 2009)

14 *The Inter-Galactic Playground: A Critical Study of Children's and Teens' Science Fiction* (Farah Mendlesohn, 2009)

15 *Science Fiction from Québec: A Postcolonial Study* (Amy J. Ransom, 2009)

16 *Science Fiction and the Two Cultures: Essays on Bridging the Gap Between the Sciences and the Humanities* (ed. Gary Westfahl, George Slusser, 2009)

17 *Stephen R. Donaldson and the Modern Epic Vision: A Critical Study of the "Chronicles of Thomas Covenant" Novels* (Christine Barkley, 2009)

18 *Ursula K. Le Guin's Journey to Post-Feminism* (Amy M. Clarke, 2010)

19 *Portals of Power: Magical Agency and Transformation in Literary Fantasy* (Lori M. Campbell, 2010)

20 *The Animal Fable in Science Fiction and Fantasy* (Bruce Shaw, 2010)

21 *Illuminating* Torchwood: *Essays on Narrative, Character and Sexuality in the BBC Series* (ed. Andrew Ireland, 2010)

22 *Comics as a Nexus of Cultures: Essays on the Interplay of Media, Disciplines and International Perspectives* (ed. Mark Berninger, Jochen Ecke, Gideon Haberkorn, 2010)

23 *The Anatomy of Utopia: Narration, Estrangement and Ambiguity in More, Wells, Huxley and Clarke* (Károly Pintér, 2010)

24 *The Anticipation Novelists of 1950s French Science Fiction: Stepchildren of Voltaire* (Bradford Lyau, 2010)

25 *The* Twilight *Mystique: Critical Essays on the Novels and Films* (ed. Amy M. Clarke, Marijane Osborn, 2010)

26 *The Mythic Fantasy of Robert Holdstock: Critical Essays on the Fiction* (ed. Donald E. Morse, Kálmán Matolcsy, 2011)

27 *Science Fiction and the Prediction of the Future: Essays on Foresight and Fallacy* (ed. Gary Westfahl, Wong Kin Yuen, Amy Kit-sze Chan, 2011)

28 *Apocalypse in Australian Fiction and Film: A Critical Study* (Roslyn Weaver, 2011)

29 *British Science Fiction Film and Television: Critical Essays* (ed. Tobias Hochscherf, James Leggott, 2011)

30 *Cult Telefantasy Series: A Critical Analysis of* The Prisoner, Twin Peaks, The X-Files, Buffy the Vampire Slayer, Lost, Heroes, Doctor Who *and* Star Trek (Sue Short, 2011)

31 *The Postnational Fantasy: Essays on Postcolonialism, Cosmopolitics and Science Fiction* (ed. Masood Ashraf Raja, Jason W. Ellis and Swaralipi Nandi, 2011)

32 *Heinlein's Juvenile Novels: A Cultural Dictionary* (C.W. Sullivan III, 2011)

33 *Welsh Mythology and Folklore in Popular Culture: Essays on Adaptations in Literature, Film, Television and Digital Media* (ed. Audrey L. Becker and Kristin Noone, 2011)

34 *I See You: The Shifting Paradigms of James Cameron's* Avatar (Ellen Grabiner, 2012)

35 *Of Bread, Blood and* The Hunger Games*: Critical Essays on the Suzanne Collins Trilogy* (ed. Mary F. Pharr and Leisa A. Clark, 2012)

36 *The Sex Is Out of This World: Essays on the Carnal Side of Science Fiction* (ed. Sherry Ginn and Michael G. Cornelius, 2012)

37 *Lois McMaster Bujold: Essays on a Modern Master of Science Fiction and Fantasy* (ed. Janet Brennan Croft, 2013)

38 *Girls Transforming: Invisibility and Age-Shifting in Children's Fantasy Fiction Since the 1970s* (Sanna Lehtonen, 2013)

39 Doctor Who *in Time and Space: Essays on Themes, Characters, History and Fandom, 1963–2012* (ed. Gillian I. Leitch, 2013)

40 *The Worlds of* Farscape*: Essays on the Groundbreaking Television Series* (ed. Sherry Ginn, 2013)

41 *Orbiting Ray Bradbury's Mars: Biographical, Anthropological, Literary, Scientific and Other Perspectives* (ed. Gloria McMillan, 2013)

42 *The Heritage of Heinlein: A Critical Reading of the Fiction Television Series* (Thomas D. Clareson and Joe Sanders, 2014)

43 *The Past That Might Have Been, the Future That May Come: Women Writing Fantastic Fiction, 1960s to the Present* (Lauren J. Lacey, 2014)

44 *Environments in Science Fiction: Essays on Alternative Spaces* (ed. Susan M. Bernardo, forthcoming [2014])

45 *Discworld and the Disciplines: Critical Approaches to the Terry Pratchett Works* (ed. Anne Hiebert Alton and William C. Spruiell, forthcoming [2014])

The Past That Might Have Been, the Future That May Come

Women Writing Fantastic Fiction, 1960s to the Present

LAUREN J. LACEY

CRITICAL EXPLORATIONS IN SCIENCE FICTION AND FANTASY, 43
Donald E. Palumbo *and* C.W. Sullivan III, series editors

McFarland & Company, Inc., Publishers
Jefferson, North Carolina

LIBRARY OF CONGRESS CATALOGUING-IN-PUBLICATION DATA

Lacey, Lauren J., 1976–
    The Past That Might Have Been, the Future That May Come : Women Writing Fantastic Fiction, 1960s to the Present / Lauren J. Lacey.
        p.   cm. — (Critical Explorations in Science Fiction and Fantasy ; 43)
    [Donald E. Palumbo and C.W. Sullivan III, series editors]
    Includes bibliographical references and index.

    ISBN 978-0-7864-7826-2
    softcover : acid free paper ∞

    1. Science fiction—Women authors—History and criticism.
2. Fantasy literature—Women authors—History and criticism.
3. Femininity (Philosophy) in literature. I. Title.
PN3433.6.L33 2014
823'.08762099287—dc23   2013041749

BRITISH LIBRARY CATALOGUING DATA ARE AVAILABLE

© 2014 Lauren J. Lacey. All rights reserved

No part of this book may be reproduced or transmitted in any form or by any means, electronic or mechanical, including photocopying or recording, or by any information storage and retrieval system, without permission in writing from the publisher.

Front cover image © Hemera/Thinkstock

Manufactured in the United States of America

McFarland & Company, Inc., Publishers
  Box 611, Jefferson, North Carolina 28640
  www.mcfarlandpub.com

In memory of my parents,
JOAN R. LACEY
(1947–2010)
and
V. DUANE LACEY
(1932–2010)

Table of Contents

Acknowledgments	xi
Preface	1
Introduction: Fantastic Interventions	5
ONE. Beastly Beauty and Other Revisioned Fairy Tales	21
TWO. Tampering with Time in Historical Narratives	64
THREE. Working Through the Wreckage in Dystopian Fiction	104
FOUR. Becoming-Alien in Feminist Space Fiction	142
Conclusion: Becoming Powerful	174
Chapter Notes	179
Works Cited	186
Index	193

Acknowledgments

Thank you to my intrepid scholarly writing group, the "Wingra Writers," especially Ashley Byock, Laini Kavaloski, Lisa King, and Winifred Morgan, for their willingness to read, re-read, and re-read some more. Also, thank you to Kedar Joyner and Alissa Zimmerman, and to the other colleagues and many students at Edgewood College who have supported me in the writing process.

Since this project originated eons ago in graduate school, I want to thank the faculty members at Rutgers University who helped to shape my original questions and plans. In particular, thank you to Marianne DeKoven, Richard Dienst, and John McClure.

Like every academic work, this one owes its existence in part to the communities that have supported early and revised versions of various chapters. I particularly want to thank the officers and members of the Doris Lessing Society and the Margaret Atwood Society, whose Modern Language Association panels have given me opportunities to try out ideas and to receive invaluable feedback.

I offer my deepest gratitude to my partner, Mike, for his scientific mind and unflagging enthusiasm, and to my girls, Hazel and Violet, for being them. Thanks also to my brother, Duane, for his insights and support. And to Luna, whose furry warmth makes writing so much more fun than it would otherwise be.

For my sake, for my daughters' sakes, and for all our sakes, thank you to the writers whose stories have changed the way I live in the world and inspired the work I do every day, especially Margaret Atwood, Octavia E. Butler, Angela Carter, Tanith Lee, Doris Lessing, Ursula K. Le Guin, Robin McKinley, and Jeanette Winterson.

Some of the points I make in relation to Octavia E. Butler's *Parable* novels in Chapter 3 were originally part of my essay "Octavia E. Butler on Coping with Power in *Parable of the Sower*, *Parable of the Talents*, and *Fledgling*" which appeared in the summer 2008 issue of *Critique: Studies in Contemporary Fiction* (Vol. 49, No. 4, pp. 379–394). Thank you to the readers and editors who helped me to develop my ideas in that essay.

My discussion of Doris Lessing's *Canopus* series in Chapter 4 grew out of ideas that I first published in the Winter 2006 issue of *Doris Lessing Studies* (Vol. 25, No. 2, pp. 18–22) under the title "Genealogy and Becoming in the *Canopus in Argos: Archives* Series." Thank you to the co-editors who helped me to make something of that essay: Phyllis Perrakis, Sandra Singer, and Jeanie E. Warnock.

Preface

In some ways, this book is the result of a long term effort to respond to a single question: do I think fiction can change the realities of our world? Richard Dienst asked me that question during my oral qualifying exams in graduate school. I had just spent two hours responding to complicated inquiries about twentieth-century British and American literature and theories of subjectivity, and describing the project I was getting ready to pursue for my dissertation. Professor Dienst's question shut me up. (Thankfully, I passed the exam anyway.) I am certain that neither he nor the other examiners in the room have any memory of this small moment, but my ongoing struggles to come to terms with the question of the role of fiction in the world have led directly to this project.

At the heart of this book is a fundamental effort to wrestle with the power and potential of stories. Recognizing the power of stories means coming to terms with how they both create and limit the possibilities we see for ourselves. Seeing the potential for stories to expand the parameters of our expectations is easier to do when the stories involved stretch the boundaries of our imaginations. My focus is on texts that help us to see how power functions at the same time as they offer alternatives to those power structures. I argue that a particular method of resistance to dominating and destructive power formations can be seen in a wide range of contemporary fantastic texts, a type of resistance I describe as an ethics of becoming. Working from Gilles Deleuze and Félix Guattari's discussions of becoming, and more particularly with Rosi Braidotti's feminist reinvigorations of those discussions, I demonstrate how fantastic fictions can create an ethical response to power imbalances that are undergirded by concepts of linear time and stable identity. Becoming, in the texts I analyze, is a way of interrupting, revising, and remaking categories like class, gender, and race. Fantastic literary forms can be used to create an ethics of becoming in part because they are themselves narrative modes that interrupt and remake. From revised fairy tales and reworked historical fictions that investigate the socializing tendencies of earlier tales and histories, to dystopian and space fiction narratives that defamiliarize contemporary realities, these texts expose and question the way power works in the world.

This project is organized in a manner that highlights how the fantastic can be used to interrupt linear and closed conceptions of time, rather than strictly according to conventions of genre. Writers including Margaret Atwood, Octavia E. Butler, Angela Carter, Ursula K. Le Guin, Tanith Lee, Doris Lessing, Robin McKinley, and Jeanette Winterson defy simplistic classification. Their narratives can be productively read as ethical responses to the way power operates in the contemporary world in part *through* their insistence upon crossing conventional literary boundaries. In the works of these writers, the fantastic can be read as a narrative performance of disruption that works to unsettle assumptions and to create the potential for new ways of being and thinking. These are narratives that exemplify the kind of work that the very best literature can do in the world — the work of exposing truths and creating space for new possibilities. The imaginative freedom of fantastic fiction allows these writers — who are concerned with dismantling all manner of identity categories including race, class, and sexuality as well as gender — to explore how the world could be different at the same time as they analyze how it *is*.

Those texts that are primarily concerned with the past — revised fairy tales, reinvented myths, and historical fiction — work to reveal the underlying power structures operating in traditional narratives. They also provide examples of alternative narratives by producing new stories and centering previously marginalized forms of knowledge. The future-oriented texts — critical dystopias and space fictions — highlight their own alternative models; however, they also supply criticism of the present and past through revision and defamiliarization. All of the texts self-consciously consider how the past, present, and future might be better understood as interlinked areas of becoming rather than as distinct linear categories. I explore and redefine the category of the fantastic as a way to understand the common work of all the texts. Becoming can be understood as a way to destabilize subjectivity at its most fundamental level, allowing for reconfigurations of the categories upon which subjectivity is built. Fantastic fiction enables contemporary women writers to intervene into and unsettle expectations, and from there to offer an ethics that embraces indeterminacy and possibility.

Doing justice to the wide range of texts explored in this project has meant journeying into scholarship from a number of different fields. Clearly, my poststructuralist theoretical approach informed a lot of the research I undertook, but I found myself learning from scholars from all over academe.

Fairy tale revisions led me to folklore, at least five different brands of feminism, and even psychology. The historical fictions I examine cried out for attention to contemporary historians and to trauma theory. There is an ever-growing and truly exciting body of scholarship devoted to dystopian and utopian fictions, as well as to feminist science fiction, both of which informed my readings throughout this project.

In May of 2004 there was a special issue of *PMLA* dedicated to science fiction, with an introduction by Marleen S. Barr in which she calls for serious scholarship on science fiction — for the creation of such scholarship, and for its acceptance in academic circles. This book is partly an effort to grant fantastic fictions the kind of attention they deserve, and it is an argument not just for the relevance of, but the dire need for, cultural attention to the issues that contemporary writers of science fiction and fantasy force us to consider. Can we learn from mere fictions? Absolutely. Will we choose to learn from them? This project is an attempt to do so.

Introduction:
Fantastic Interventions

This is a book about fiction that refuses to accept the world as it is. All of the texts under discussion are fantastic fictions by contemporary women writers that explore the past, present, and/or future, and most of them work diligently to demonstrate both the problems with our present and the possibilities of our future. Contemporary women writers offer new versions of the myths and histories that form our collective past, as well as explorations of potential futures. The pages that follow will emphasize the ethical dimensions of such writing by focusing on how it can render visible the ways in which past, present, and future are constituted in and through power. Ultimately, the project will argue that certain fantastic fictions by contemporary women writers are engaged in a process of developing an ethics of becoming that both interrupts and revises power structures that support some of the most damaging ideologies of our time, ranging from patriarchal belief systems to environmentally destructive economic policies. Fantastic fiction provides contemporary women writers with the means to critique current conditions and to narratively perform the alternative possibility of becoming.

The oldest texts discussed here were published in the late 1960s (Ursula K. Le Guin's *Three Hainish Novels*, for example), while the most recent are twenty-first century publications. That means that the earliest narratives coincide with the emergence of postmodernist and poststructuralist thinking, as well as with political movements against patriarchal, racist, and heteronormative power. The work of those philosophical, critical, theoretical, and political efforts continues, even as the power structures they address become increasingly complex, and the narratives discussed here reflect that continuing yet shifting and changing work. There are American, British, and Canadian authors represented here, writers with different ethnic and racial backgrounds, and writers with different sexual identities. Yet, all of these women writers employ fantastic literary techniques in ways that allow them to link past, present, and future. Perhaps the most interesting aspect of the shared work of these writers is the degree to which their fictions establish an alternative world view that privileges becoming over being, and process over product. They question the very foundations of identity and self-knowledge by working against essentialized and concretized models of being, and by reimagining subjectivity as open, contingent, and creative. These are narratives that demand a great deal of their readers. There is very little that is easy, comfortable, or reassuring in the works discussed in this book. But there are rewards for engaging with these texts that far surpass consoling familiarity.

Margaret Atwood, Octavia E. Butler, Angela Carter, Ursula K. Le Guin, Doris Lessing, and Jeanette Winterson are the primary writers whose works are considered here, although other writers' works do appear from time to time. From revisionist narratives that reexamine the myths upon which contemporary society is founded to science fictional fantasies that explore the limits of imaginative possibility, these writers make use of the literary fantastic in ways that are both deeply political and, frequently, playful. Indeed, my analyses of the texts will develop ways of reading the fantastic as a mode of interrupting and revising expectations tied to damaging and normalizing power, thereby creating the conditions necessary for alternative ways of understanding. In particular, this book's focus on time emphasizes how fantastic fiction can help us to understand how the possibilities of the present moment are constituted by our understandings of the past and future. In effect, the processes of rewriting the past or of envisioning the future can be read as methods of reconsidering what is possible now. The fact that most of the writers discussed in this book engage in both forms of fantastic writing — revising the past and imagining the future — supports the point that there is a common project underlying both types of writing. While some of the writers mentioned above can easily be labeled as "genre writers," others are more readily recognizable as major figures in late-twentieth and early twenty-first century literature. Lessing, for example, earned a respected slot in the British literary canon before turning to speculative writing. Yet, despite her Nobel Prize for Literature, Lessing's speculative fictions have typically been poorly reviewed and understudied by academics. All of Winterson's works contain elements of fantasy — or, as it is typically termed in reference to her work, magical realism — but she is usually described as a writer of postmodern fiction. (That description adheres despite Winterson's own claims that she is a modernist.)

In other words, genre is a vexed site of analysis within this project because it is unavoidable but far more complicated than it seems. Throughout the chapters that follow genre categories will remain relevant, but the broader notion of the literary fantastic encompasses the formal and thematic work of all of the texts under discussion. As will become clear, the fantastic can be intriguingly linked to the ethical projects of the texts, which are all concerned with investigating, critiquing, and revising problematic and unbalanced power relations. The concept of the fantastic allows for analyses that do not get too bogged down in strict genre definitions. There is much to be gained from looking at contemporary women's writing across genre lines, and from exploring how the fantastic operates in a variety of different texts.

The Fantastic

Ranging from the incorporation of myth into otherwise realistic narratives to science fictional representations of alternate worlds and alien species, the concept of the fantastic is broad enough to encompass a wide range of genres, but narrow in the sense that it refers to specific moments in texts rather than to entire works. In other words, this project sees the fantastic not as a genre but as a literary intervention that can erupt — or simply unfold — in nearly any kind of narrative. Understanding the fantastic in this way is particularly important when looking at contemporary narratives, which so often blur genre boundaries and refuse to fit neatly into any particular category. The term "fantastic" is also deliberately meant to invoke a specific history within literary criticism with which this project engages. Tvetan Todorov's classic structuralist work from the 1970s defines the fantastic as a specific literary interval between the uncanny and the marvelous.[1] According to Todorov, the most important aspect of the fantastic is the way it creates uncertainty. The reader cannot know if the fantastic occurrence in a given text will resolve into realism (the uncanny) or into fantasy (the marvelous). During the interval when the reader does not know if a fantastic event within a text will resolve into something perfectly explicable within our everyday reality (a dream, for example), or if the fantastic event will wind up being a part of an entirely separate alternate reality in the text (as in genre fantasy), there is confusion. The reader's confusion is precisely what Todorov identifies as constitutive of the fantastic; the moment of uncertainty, of hesitation, *is* the fantastic for Todorov.

While the particular categorization Todorov employs is far too narrow for the purposes of this project, his emphasis on the moment of uncertainty created through the insertion of the fantastic is significant. In many of the texts discussed here, fantastic moments enable the writer to unsettle assumptions about the narrative and about the world. In Octavia E. Butler's novel *Kindred*, for example, time travel occurs with no explanation and creates a situation in which the relationship between past and present has to be carefully reconsidered. Doris Lessing's space fiction series revisits our planet's history through the lens of an alien eye. *Oranges Are Not the Only Fruit*, by Jeanette Winterson, integrates fairy tale with realistic first-person narrative in a way that asks the reader to rethink the relationships among memory, story, and history. As these brief examples suggest, the fantastic can provide a way to intervene into expectation. The uncertainty that Todorov finds to be the defining characteristic of the fantastic is still central to how this project uses the term, but here that uncertainty is linked to the work of the text rather than defined in strictly formalist terms.

The fantastic has been a part of storytelling for all of recorded history, but in the latter part of the twentieth-century, women writers reclaimed the fantastic as a way of exploring the possibilities of new modes of thinking and being and doing. In revised fairy tales, the fantastic may create uncertainty about the authority of the text, while in rewritten history the uncertainty might have to do with what counts as historical "truth." Of course, many other important arguments have been made about precisely how the fantastic should be understood, virtually all of which begin with Todorov and go on to share the sense that he was definitely on to something when he identified confusion or uncertainty at the heart of things. Merja Makinen summarizes these various arguments nicely and concludes they "share the sense that the magical trope can indeed uncover or express disturbance, a necessary or valid subversive questioning of the comfort of dominant cultural norms" (153). The fantastic is, at least potentially, a particularly important literary device for critique and for the creation of alternatives to the dominant norms. In the context of contemporary women's writing, the fantastic can be a way to destabilize, denaturalize, and reconfigure problematic power relations. The playfulness, or strangeness, of the fantastic narratives discussed here is precisely what allows them to counter normalizing power and to offer radical alternatives to current systems of thought and action. Identity categories of gender, race, sexuality, and class, as well as political and economic realities of global capitalism and environmental devastation, are just some of the entrenched power structures addressed through fantastic interventions.

Before turning to precisely how the fantastic relates to power, and ultimately to an ethics of becoming, there is one significant counter-argument pertaining to the fantastic that must be considered. Jack Zipes, the eminent fairy tale scholar, has raised some important points about how the fantastic operates in our world — now. The world has changed dramatically since

Todorov's seminal work on the fantastic was first published. Zipes argues that, today, "The fantastic in artworks seems inadequate to deal with the fantastic in our lives. The fantastic is embroidery and embroidered in our daily lives so that perversity and excess appear to be norms" (*Relentless* 47). If one doubts the truth of Zipes' claim, it might be worth remembering that Margaret Atwood's seemingly utterly fantastic fiction *Oryx and Crake* is based almost entirely in reality — which is why she terms it "speculative fiction." Her themes of violence and sex on the internet, abject poverty existing alongside walled-in affluence, corporate-driven technology and education, an international slave/sex trade, and inhumane genetic research are all taken directly from current realities. Zipes is correct to point out that a bit of fictional fancy is unlikely to penetrate the protective shell of the average contemporary global citizen. He goes on to address Todorov's argument by saying, "I do not think we hesitate or are taken aback when we read so-called fantasy literature or watch a fantastical film or see fantastic painting or performance" (*Relentless* 48). Nevertheless, Zipes does argue that the fantastic is important: "We do not need fantasy to compensate for dull lives, but, I want to suggest, we need it for spiritual regeneration and to contemplate alternatives to our harsh realities. More than titillation, we need the fantastic for resistance" (*Relentless* 48). Zipes makes the essential point that fantasy alone is not enough.

The existence of the fantastic within a text does not necessarily mean that the text will cause the reader to rethink her/his basic assumptions; it does not even mean that the reader will pause and feel uncertain or confused. We of the contemporary world happily consume vampire novels after watching films about wizards, pausing to play a round of a smart phone game about zombies. So, while the fantastic is important, it is not enough by itself to offer a different way of thinking about the world. The fantastic *can* create the resistance Zipes desires, but it certainly does not always do so. While this project's focus is almost entirely on texts that do offer a resistant ethics, a few of the narratives discussed in later chapters employ fantastic techniques in ways that seem similar to the resistant texts, but do not develop a critical approach to power or display any real alternatives to the current power structures. So, while the fantastic is well-suited to creating the kind of critical distance that leads readers to hesitate, and to rethink, it is not inextricably linked to such possibilities. In order to do the kind of ethical work that I claim for most of the texts discussed in this project, a fantastic text must address contemporary structures of control — be they models of global power or individual acts of domination, or both — in ways that cultivate critical resistance.

One particularly helpful example of how the fantastic can be understood in relation to large structures of power comes from Marleen S. Barr's works on feminist fiction. Barr defines her concept of "feminist fabulation" as "feminist fiction that offers us a world clearly and radically discontinuous from the patriarchal one we know, yet returns to confront that known patriarchal world in some feminist cognitive way" (*Feminist* 10). The confrontation Barr describes could be understood as a form of critique or analysis of power, and the radically discontinuous world is, in relation to the texts discussed here, a range of possible worlds that all embrace an alternative ethics. Part of Barr's goal in coining the term "feminist fabulation" is to reduce the distinction between "high" literature and popular forms — a goal which this project shares. More importantly, however, Barr's work helps to shift the emphasis of analysis from formal categories to the substance of the texts. In other words, "feminist fabulation" is a category that addresses the work the text does through its uses of the fantastic, which is a helpful example of the focus on power and revisioning that this project will explore more broadly. Ultimately, Barr's work identifies the double process of confronting patriarchal power *and* of creating worlds that portray different conceptions of power.

Nancy A. Walker makes a similar observation about contemporary women's uses of fantasy, arguing that "the frequent use of fantasy —including the utopia and the dystopia — in the contemporary novel by women constitutes both a response to the perceived absurdity of contemporary patriarchy and an impulse to envision an alternate reality that either corrects or intensifies the ills of the present" (147). Those two operations — critique and creation — will come up again and again in the pages that follow, in part because critics have identified them at work in revised fairy tales, rewritten histories, critical dystopias, and feminist space fiction, yet their operations shift a bit in each type of narrative. Walker goes on to describe what she calls "feminist fantasy" as literature in which "contemporary reality continues to exist as a palimpsest on which an alternative reality is superimposed (150). The concept of a palimpsest is useful here because it helps to explain how critique is layered into creation. A revised fairy tale bears the traces of its predecessors and a dystopian future is built on the problems of the present. The fantastic fictions discussed here refer to the past and to the future as spaces for creation, but always also with an underlying emphasis on critique of the present.

Power and Foucault

Complex interrogations of power and subjectivity characterize nearly all of the texts examined here. These texts do not represent power in simplistic terms, nor do they limit their representations to a single temporal frame.

Instead, they render visible the machinations of power at multiple levels and explore how power operates in and through time. My thinking about power springs directly from Michel Foucault's work — and his ideas about power are evident in many of the narratives discussed below. This is not to claim that all of the writers whose works are analyzed here use Foucault directly (although some do, such as Angela Carter), but rather that the kind of analysis of power that Foucault brilliantly demonstrated can be found throughout the fictional texts I address. Which is to say, there is an important affinity between Foucault's philosophy of power and the way power is treated in the literary works examined in this project. Foucault's works invite readers to reimagine contemporary power relations, both to understand how they actually operate in our world and to offer actual ways of resisting. Elsewhere, I have demonstrated how Octavia E. Butler's fiction, in particular, can help to clarify how Foucault's work continues to be relevant — essential, really — to feminist concerns.[2] I also argue that Butler's fiction takes Foucault's ideas a step further than his own work does by integrating critique with creation. Here, I begin from the premise that a Foucauldian understanding of power is central to the work of contemporary women writers who employ the fantastic in ways that force readers to rethink how individual subjects are constituted by and help to perpetuate unequal and damaging power relations. However, this understanding of power is only a first step toward the use of the literary fantastic to construct an ethics of becoming that addresses the kind of power Foucault describes.

It is best to let Foucault speak for himself here in order to maintain an awareness of his specific approach: "[T]here is no power relation without the correlative constitution of a field of knowledge, nor any knowledge that does not presuppose and constitute at the same time power relations" (*Discipline* 27). This mutually constitutive relationship between power and knowledge is an important example of what is at stake in contemporary women's writing about the past and future. The production of knowledge, which occurs in and through power, can be traced in texts that explore modes of historical understanding, and all of the texts in this project are concerned with the nature of historical knowledge to one degree or another. They destabilize accepted narratives of past, present, and future in ways that reveal the problems with the kinds of assumptions those accepted narratives require. Lucie Armitt finds similar emphases in contemporary women's fiction, and her work overlaps with mine not only in relation to some of the texts we read, but also in terms of an awareness of how time is linked to the fantastic in those texts: "It is not just that the contemporary owes a profound debt to the past [...] but that several of these novels explicitly juxtapose past, present and future" (*Contemporary* 12). Armitt ultimately focuses on the tropes of the fantastic and fantasy, while my own project is more focused on how knowledge — of past, present, and future — is analyzed and constructed in the texts. Nevertheless, her project has been influential to this one. Reopening the past to new myths/stories/histories, and providing possibilities for the still open future, these contemporary women writers invest the cultural imaginary with knowledge in ways that reconfigure power in their own terms.

In the first volume of *The History of Sexuality*, Foucault famously undermines the traditional notion of historical progress in relation to human sexuality by arguing that as long as we believe that juridical power is the only (or even the main) type of power, our understanding of the history of sexuality will fail to acknowledge the importance of other forms of control and policing. The alternative construction of power Foucault presents requires a reevaluation of the nature of social control:

> It seems to me that power must be understood in the first instance as the multiplicity of force relations immanent in the sphere in which they operate and which constitute their own organization; as the process which, through ceaseless struggles and confrontations, transforms, strengthens, or reverses them; as the support which these force relations find in one another, thus forming a chain or a system, or on the contrary, the disjunctions and contradictions which isolate them from one another; and lastly, as the strategies in which they take effect, whose general design or institutional crystallization is embodied in the state apparatus, in the formulation of the law, in the various social hegemonies [92–93].

For Foucault power is both positive and negative; it is about coexisting and mutually reliant processes of destruction and production. Power is a "multiplicity of force relations" that are constantly active and changing, and which can — but do not necessarily — take the form of structured hierarchical domination. The complexity of power, understood in these terms, is daunting, yet demonstrably accurate for contemporary subjects. A simple decision like what to eat for dinner is fraught with complicated structures of power — if one pays attention to them. Is it better for the environment to eat locally grown conventional broccoli, or organic broccoli grown on the other side of the country? Whose labor goes into producing the broccoli in each case? Is one choice healthier for you, the consumer? What about imported broccoli? Or, perhaps frozen, prepackaged broccoli is the better choice for the environment, your health, and labor conditions. How are you to know? Foucault's model of power is in evidence in nearly everything the contemporary subject does. But, of course, it is impossible to sustain a thorough analysis of every little action. Part of what is so important about the texts discussed in the project is that they help readers to navigate the terrain of contemporary power relations.

Maintaining a conscious relationship to and with power, which is the only way to resist its pull (and push, and appeal), requires both critical awareness and diligence. That kind of conscious approach to power is precisely what I've found in a number of fantastic fictions by contemporary women writers. The critical possibilities of the fantastic are put to particularly potent use when they are employed as a means of identifying, exploring, and resisting complex power structures. For example, the first chapter explores a number of different revisions of the Beauty and the Beast fairy tale. What is particularly interesting about most of those revisions is their careful attention to the assumptions underlying earlier versions of the tale. As they rework the story, they illuminate the power structures that regulate gender and class, and develop revisionist approaches that require readers to rethink what it means for a young, beautiful, poor, merchant class, educated Beauty to be wed to a rich, ugly, titled Beast. Such reworkings offer ways to see the power structures at work in a given narrative, as well as to rethink how the story *could* go. It would be nearly impossible — paralyzing, even — to live each day in the contemporary world with a full and aware understanding of all (or even many) of the power flows operating in one's life. Survival requires a certain amount of unquestioning adherence to cultural norms, even for those of us who find those norms to be highly problematic. Fantastic fiction can provide an opportunity for distance and perspective; it can help to make visible those power flows that we normally do not see and offer alternatives.

Foucault's analysis of power as not only dominating, but pervasive and containing, is echoed by Gilles Deleuze's formulation of "control societies": "We're moving toward control societies that no longer operate by confining people but through continuous control and instant communication" (*Negotiations* 174). In a control society, power flows on multiple levels and operates through containment — by incorporating resistance and making it ineffective — as much as through suppression. Contemporary women's writing responds to control societies, to increasing conditions of globalization, to enduring forms of patriarchal domination — to power in its various guises — through direct confrontations with the production of knowledge/power. In other words, the fantastic fictions addressed by this project do more than render visible the complexities of power; they also offer models of resistance through their efforts to explore an ethics of becoming that can counter the insidious and relentless pressure of the contemporary control society.

Ethics as Resistance

In confronting how knowledge and power are produced, contemporary women writers use the fantastic to play with the limits of what is possible.

The process of identifying power structures that are frequently difficult to see, exploring those power structures in order to determine their functions and purposes, and developing critiques of the normalizing and/or totalizing operations of those power structures is a way of opening up a space of potential where alternative knowledge/power formations can exist. The particular form that alternative knowledge/power takes is what will be referred to throughout this project as an *ethics of becoming*. Power and becoming are not separate sites of inquiry or analysis here, but rather intertwined elements of the work of the texts. An ethics of becoming is a response to closed systems of knowledge production that create and support normative discourses of gender, sexuality, and subjectivity itself. The use of the term "ethics" is itself a response to moralizing discourses that define actions and/or subjects as either good or bad by applying supposedly transcendental values. An ethical practice embraces multiple, provisional, even contradictory possibilities without resorting to the kinds of good and evil binary thinking that underlie moralistic discourses. Deleuze describes the distinction in the following terms:

> Establishing ways of existing or styles of life isn't just an aesthetic matter, it's what Foucault called ethics, as opposed to morality. The difference is that morality presents us with a set of constraining rules of a special sort, ones that judge actions and intentions by considering them in relation to transcendent values (this is good, that's bad …); ethics is a set of optional rules that assess what we do, what we say, in relation to the ways of existing involved [*Negotiations* 100, ellipses in original].

The Foucauldian notion of ethics that Deleuze finds useful here depends upon an entirely different relation to power than morality. Morality is defined as a negative exercise of dominating power built upon rules that are in turn based on the purportedly transcendent concepts of good and evil. Such a system fails to take into account the specific, contingent, and interested values of those who have the power to define "good" and "evil." Ethics, by contrast, is based upon "optional rules" that are not tied to transcendent or universal notions of right or wrong, but rather to contextual and situated values. While morality functions to restrict — to keep things in bounds — ethics produces open conditions that allow for responses to specific times, places, and situations. The confusion and uncertainty Todorov identifies as central to the fantastic is embraced in an ethical system.

Importantly, an ethical approach is not a slide into relativism. Openness does not mean anything goes; an ethical subject is constituted through its relationships with others, and is always responsible to those others. Feminist poststructuralist philosopher Rosi Braidotti — whose works will be particularly important intertexts in the readings to follow, provides an essential insight into the nature of this kind of ethics: "An ethical life pursues that which enhances and strengthens the subject without reference to transcendental values [i.e., Deleuze's conception of morality] but rather in awareness of one's interconnections with others" (*Transpositions* 162). Interconnection is at the heart of ethical subjectivity, and is a necessary precondition to the process of becoming, which will be discussed shortly.

In the fantastic texts examined in this project, the rules of morality are problematized and an ethics of interconnection, openness, and potential is offered as an alternative to the closure and stagnation of moral choices. For example, in Angela Carter's hands, the "good" father of a fairy tale can easily turn out to be a monster, while the "monstrous" beast can offer an option of living outside social norms that dictate behavior according to gendered identity. Similarly, Margaret Atwood's dystopian near future can demonstrate how quickly moral discourse can turn into repressive domination, at the same time as it portrays alternatives that embrace provisional alliances. (In this case, the reference is to *The Handmaid's Tale*, but *Oryx and Crake* and *The Year of the Flood* contain similar topographies of ethical resistance to moralizing discourses.) The point is to construct a way of reading contemporary women's uses of the literary fantastic so that they may be understood as an effort to appropriate and redirect literary forms. Indeed, the method of reading employed in this project takes the texts' arguments seriously, and therefore works to embrace their critiques and alternatives. Braidotti explains, "Ethics is [...] a discourse about forces, desires and values that act as empowering modes of being, whereas morality is the established set of rules" (*Transpositions* 14). Thought of in this way, ethics is a response to the way power works in our world now. It is therefore crucial that we, as readers, become carefully attuned to how the ethical is represented.

Becoming

Becoming is most readily understood in contrast to "being," as a term that designates subjectivities as open and permeable, rather than closed and static. Subjectivity redefined as becoming rather than being allows for possibilities to resist the power relations found in "control societies." The various flows of power in the contemporary world, as described above by Foucault, assume a static, codified understanding of subjectivity that can be placed, observed, regulated, and produced through normalizing discourses — such as those focused on gender and sexuality. Deleuze and Félix Guattari, realizing that resistance to such structures requires rethinking the very category of subjectivity, describe becoming as a method of ethical, political, and personal resistance. Becoming is, in their terms, a way to destabilize subjectivity at its most fundamental level, allowing for reconfigurations of all the categories upon which subjectivity is built: gender, race, ethnicity, sexuality, and even species. In *A Thousand Plateaus*, Deleuze and Guattari state:

> [B]ecoming is not to imitate or identify with something or someone. Nor is it to proportion formal relations. Neither of these two figures of analogy is applicable to becoming: neither the imitation of a subject nor the proportionality of a form. Starting from the form one has, the subject one is, the organs one has, or the functions one fulfills, becoming is to extract particles between which one establishes the relations of movement and rest, speed and slowness that are *closest* to what one is becoming, and through which one becomes. This is the sense in which becoming is the process of desire [272, italics in original].

Becoming requires something other than identification or empathy. Instead, it is an organic relation that operates through desire and embraces potentiality.

Understood as a method of reworking power relations, becoming offers specific possibilities for reenvisioning and recreating. Braidotti's formulation is particularly helpful here: "Becoming is a question of undoing the structures of domination by careful, patient revisitations, re-adjustments, micro-changes" (*Metamorphoses* 116). Becoming is a positive and productive form of resistance. Instead of pushing back against an ever-expanding power structure, processes of becoming look knowingly into webs of power and tug, undo, remake. It is fairly clear that a postmodern reworking of a patriarchal fairy tale, or a feminist revisioning of Puritan history, could be a site of becoming. In fact, this project will explore the idea that fantastic fiction can be a kind of formal, narrative equivalent or performance of becoming. Those in-between particles described by Deleuze and Guattari bear a striking resemblance to the in-between-ness, the uncertainty, of the fantastic. When a fantastic narrative disrupts assumptions, it undoes narrative expectation and creates potential.

One particular figuration of becoming that occurs throughout the texts to follow is hybridity. Jeanette Winterson's *Sexing the Cherry* takes its title from one of the main character's notions of grafting: "Grafting is the means whereby a plant, perhaps tender or uncertain, is fused into a hardier member of its strain, and so the two take advantage of each other and produce a third kind, without seed or parent" (84). This genetic recombination is a model for creating a monstrous hybrid, and it is a formulation that gets repeated in various ways throughout the texts. Hybrid subjects can be examples of becoming in that they resist classification and codification. They are slippery and difficult to control because they do not adhere to closed categories or to the binary logic that underlies moralizing discourses. The most interesting beasts within the revisions of the Beauty and the Beast tale in Chapter One are human/animal hybrids, as in Tanith Lee's science fiction version. Fevvers, the woman who brings in the future in Angela Carter's *Nights at the Circus*, discussed in Chapter Two, is half-woman, half-swan. In Chapter Three I examine Doris Lessing's *Memoirs of a Survivor*, which includes a particularly intriguing cat/dog figure, and Chapter Four is populated with a variety of human/alien hybrids. These hybrid figures are created through the use of hybrid genres: science fictional fairy tales, autobiographical fairy tales, historical myths, dystopian diaries, the list goes on. The formal hybridity of the texts engenders the creation of hybrid subjectivities within the texts. Becoming is the terrain of in-between-ness, of shifting, moving, changing possibilities, which is precisely the ground covered by the fantastic fictions discussed in this book.

Becoming means a non-unitary, nomadic notion of subjectivity. The hybrid figures that populate the fictions discussed here are one example of how the notion of a nomadic subject aligns beautifully with the fantastic fictions in this project. Braidotti elaborates, explaining that "the theory of becoming aims to reinscribe subversion at the heart of subjectivity and to make it operational" (*Metamorphoses* 145). The promise of becoming is subjectivity's massive potential made manifest. The myth of the unified subject continues to impede the work of resistance to dominant, normalizing discourses. Contemporary women's writing uses the fantastic to transgress boundaries in ways that allow for a proliferation of becomings that are not limited to the stable subject positions that occupy the "real" world. In fact, stability is clearly rejected in favor of provisional, open, shifting, and empowering understandings of subjectivity. Further, the nomadic subject engaged in becoming is part of multiple interrelationships. For Braidotti, "ethics means […] the desire to become," and "becoming is an intransitive process: it is not about becoming anything in particular" (*Transpositions* 163). An ethics of becoming, grounded in the analysis of the production of knowledge/power, but turned toward the potential of the future, is what the texts described here have to offer.

Arguments to Come

The texts examined in this book range from revisionist fairy tales and rewritten history to dystopian narratives and feminist space fiction. Many of the writers — most, in fact — appear in more than one chapter. Rewriting the past and writing the future are both fantastic procedures that tend to engage the attentions of the same writers: Angela Carter, Octavia E. Butler, and Jeanette Winterson, for example. Therefore, the organizational premise of this project is, in part, a function of the interests of the writers themselves.

Chapter One focuses on contemporary versions of fairy tales written by Tanith Lee, Robin McKinley, and Sheri S. Tepper, with a particular emphasis on Angela Carter's "The Courtship of Mr. Lyon" and "The Tiger's Bride" from *The Bloody Chamber* and Jeanette Winterson's *Oranges Are Not the Only Fruit*. Fairy tales privilege the trope of transformation even as they instruct readers in the perils of transgressing social boundaries, making them a suggestive source of material for contemporary women writers who wish to engage with problems of power and possibilities of becoming. Roland Barthes's work on myth is an entry point for the argument in this chapter, which emphasizes a double process of unveiling and revisioning involved in contemporary feminist rewriting of fairy tales. Some of the texts stay very close to the traditional narratives; these tend to prioritize unveiling above revisioning and thus to do the kind of work that Barthes attributes to mythologists. Other texts simply include echoes of traditional narratives while creating fairy tales that are radically new in terms of both form and content. In all cases, the new version of the tale exposes the power relations underlying the traditional tale and creates possibilities for new power configurations. More concretely, some of the fairy tales, particularly those by Angela Carter and Jeanette Winterson, envision specific instances of becoming as alternatives to the traditional trajectory of fairy tales in which otherness is carefully rejected in favor of maintaining restrictive social categories. The revised fairy tales exemplify a process whereby the original narrative is destabilized in order to make room for an emerging ethics of becoming.

An emphasis on the process of rewriting continues in Chapter Two's readings of Octavia E. Butler's *Kindred*, Angela Carter's *Nights at the Circus*, and Jeanette Winterson's *The Passion* and *Sexing the Cherry*, all of which explicitly focus on defining a mutually constitutive relationship between the past and the present. In this sense, the novels under consideration in the second chapter are all examples of what Linda Hutcheon terms "historiographic metafiction," one of the most enduring and productive critical terms to come out of postmodern literary criticism. These texts produce genealogical historical investigations that both denaturalize and revision historical events. Trauma theory is particularly relevant here because it explains that although the past can never be directly accessed, we cannot escape the need to return to traumatic moments in our collective historical heritage. These writers return to the past in order to unveil and confront the power structures that underlie the traumatic cultural histories that they have inherited. Butler's *Kindred*, for example, dramatizes the confrontation between the present and the traumatic past when the protagonist, an African American woman named Dana, is torn out of her life in 1976 and thrust into the world of the antebellum South. Dana struggles first simply to survive in slavery, and later to do what she can to improve the lives of those she encounters in the past. She moves back and forth between the past and the present in the text, and while her existence as a slave foregrounds the need to confront traumatic history, it is her existence in 1976, once she has been physically and emotionally marked by history, that is most intriguing. Dana becomes a slave who must engage in violence simply to survive, and then must reconcile that existence with her comparative freedom in 1976. Butler's novel asks what it would mean for a contemporary subject to become a slave, and what it would mean for that experience of becoming a slave to carry over into contemporary existence. *Kindred*'s focus on what it is to be a subject in and of power is paralleled by similar examinations of power in the other texts in the chapter: the power structures of the past and present, and the ways that those power structures define the relationships between the past and present. These texts incorporate elements of the fantastic (such as time travel, the ability to fly, and even fairy tale figures) in ways that redefine the relationship between the past and present so that the past becomes a site of possibility rather than a closed story.

The fantastic elements of the texts in chapters one and two become more concretely generic in Chapter Three, which explores dystopian narratives that envision speculative futures. Through analyses of a group of texts by Margaret Atwood, Octavia E. Butler, and Doris Lessing that envision grand-scale destruction and the aftermath of that destruction, the third chapter examines how these dystopian narratives — like the texts in the earlier chapters — are engaged in a theoretical process of demystifying and creating. The worlds they depict force us to look more closely at the social structures that are even now creating conditions that could lead to the kinds of terrifying futures envisioned in the novels. In so doing, the texts emphasize the need to analyze, examine, and understand the nature of those structures. Tom Moylan and Raffaella Baccolini have each used the term "critical dystopia" to refer to dystopian texts that offer the kind of dual process of critical inquiry and utopian potential that are to be found in the texts in this chapter. Further, the texts demonstrate an investment in an ethics of becoming as an alternative to more rigid and repressive modes that inevitably lead to disaster. Each protagonist provides a personal narrative that emphasizes the need to understand and to come to terms with large social structures, and to find or to create a different way of existing within and through power, yet the structures and the responses to them vary in each text. The chapter traces the diverse forms that power takes in the texts as well as the various responses of the protagonists to power in order to show that feminist dystopian fiction is a productive site of creation and potential for contemporary women writers. These are genealogies in that they are narratives that trace the ways in which power dissolves and reforms; they are genealogical examinations of the past in relation to a future that does not yet exist.

Through the science fiction device of the alien encounter, the texts in Chapter Four offer alternative structures of gender, race, subjectivity, and even humanity. Perhaps more than any of the other narratives discussed here, those in the fourth chapter are too often dismissed as apolitical or escapist because of their generic label as science fiction. Nevertheless, they offer insightful critiques of real conditions as well as creative responses to those conditions. Their use of space travel and alternate worlds allows for an exploration of the possibilities of posthuman becomings in texts such as Octavia E. Butler's *Xenogenesis* trilogy, Ursula K. Le Guin's *Hainish Cycle* novels, and Doris Lessing's *Canopus in Argos: Archives* series. These stories are dominated by a preoccupation with power structures and emphasize time as a dimension of potential. The past and present are examined through the lens of the speculative futures envisioned by the texts, and thus maintain the genealogical interrogation that occurs in the other narratives in this project. For example, Doris Lessing's series begins with *Shikasta*, a novel that traces earth's history through the eyes of aliens called Canopeans who are particularly alert to power and its shifting constructions over time. In addition to the Canopeans' genealogical depiction of earth's history, the novel offers a specific form of becoming through the Canopeans; they can literally become human. The act of becoming-human, and the resulting construction of a human subjectivity, is a central concern of the text. Read in this way, *Shikasta*, and the other novels in the series, offer an exploration of the relationship between genealogical critique and active becoming. The readings of the science fiction texts in this chapter reveal that there is much to be gained from attempting to cross generic boundaries, and that the ethics of becoming that characterizes the texts in the earlier chapters is given new substance through the device of the alien encounter.

The conclusion offers a discussion of how an ethics of becoming continues to be of paramount importance as writers work to address our complex reality in their fictions. This project transverses the lines that usually close texts off from one another; fantasy, magical realism, postmodernism, and science fiction are all potential sites of the fantastic. Reading across genres means enables the project to expose new veins of common theoretical inquiry and innovation.

One

Beastly Beauty and Other Revisioned Fairy Tales

Why Fairy Tales?

Few narratives are as clearly positioned as socializing tools as fairy tales. Their traditional emphases on cultural norms, closed narrative forms, and truncated "happy endings," particularly in relation to restrictive gender roles, make them ripe for the kind of analysis of power structures with which this project is interested. Near the beginning of *The Madwoman in the Attic*, just before their now-famous reading of the devastating implications inherent in the tale of "Snow White," Sandra M. Gilbert and Susan Gubar explain, "As the legend of Lilith shows, and as psychoanalysts from Freud and Jung onward have observed, myths and fairy tales often both state and enforce culture's sentences with greater accuracy than more sophisticated literary texts" (36). Fairy tales are particularly useful for thinking about how narratives construct, reflect, and enact complex power structures. Nevertheless, fairy tales are not monolithic narratives that can be easily located in a particular time or place. Instead, fairy tales are inherited fictions, passed down through generations and through educational systems. This chapter offers readings of a variety of fairy tales in order to explore how those tales operate in contemporary fiction and to demonstrate how fairy tales can be highly important sites of revisionist rewriting that reveal the possibility of resistance through an ethics of becoming.

This project investigates how narratives by contemporary women writers deploy fantastic literary forms in ways that support an ethics of becoming. As complex, open narratives that invite revision and reinvention, fairy tales have surfaced in the narratives of many of the writers whose works are examined here: Angela Carter, Tanith Lee, Robin McKinley, Sheri S. Tepper, and

Jeanette Winterson are only a small portion of the contemporary women writers whose works treat fairy tales directly. In fact, Margaret Atwood, Octavia E. Butler, Ursula K. Le Guin, and Doris Lessing could all be read through the lens of how they use fairy tales, even though their work appears in other chapters where there is no specific focus on their uses of fairy tales. The point is not to search out examples of fairy tales wherever they may be, but rather to examine how the process of rewriting fairy tales might be understood as a version of an ethics of becoming. Through revision, a fairy tale is remade but still recognizable for what it once was. Revision is central to all of the texts discussed in this book, since contemporary women writers frequently work to rewrite problematic cultural rules and values. This chapter is about more direct efforts to revise that can help to illustrate the very concept of becoming in literature by offering examples of how a cultural narrative can be transformed from one of limitation and stagnation to one of openness and potential. Revisionist rewriting can be read as an ethical practice in that it is a method of engaging with ingrained beliefs and reopening them into alternative possibilities.

In different times and places, and in the hands of various authors, fairy tales mutate, change, metamorphose. Much has already been written about the importance of fairy tales in contemporary fiction, and various theories have been advanced to explain that importance. In *Why Fairy Tales Stick: The Evolution and Relevance of a Genre* (2006), Jack Zipes examines the notion that fairy tales are examples of "memes," or ideas/instructions that follow the same rules as genes in terms of evolution. In *Fairy Tale as Myth/Myth as Fairy Tale* (1994), a much earlier text, Zipes argues that the literary fairy tale actually has its roots in seventeenth-century European proto-feminist thought: "The institutionalizing of the literary fairy tale, begun in the salons during the seventeenth century, was for adults and arose out of a need by aristocratic women to elaborate and conceive other alternatives in society than those prescribed for them by men. The fairy tale was used in refined discourse as a means through which women imagined their lives might be improved" (23). Zipes goes on to argue that fairy tales were later appropriated for use as didactic tools in children's moral training, but the idea that there was a formative moment when the imaginative force of the literary fairy tale held power for women in the seventeenth century suggests that many literary fairy tales still contain elements of earlier subversive potential. There is, in this way of reading, a duality to the fairy tale function: it is both a closed narrative structure that works to define and demarcate social roles, and an open cultural form that retains traces of its oral folkloric heritage in ways that allow it to respond to cultural shifts. That duality makes fairy tales particularly potent subjects for contemporary women writers who seek to address dangerously limiting social norms through critique, and offer a model of nomadic subjectivity in becoming to resist such norms.

A very different kind of approach to fairy tales can be found in a book by Vera Sonja Maass called *The Cinderella Test: Would You Really Want the Shoe to Fit?* Maass is a practicing clinical psychologist, and the book is based on her work with primarily female clients coping with relationship problems. It is, essentially, a book about the damaging effects of the enduring Cinderella story on real women's (and men's) lives. Her themes include the problem of passively waiting for Prince Charming (11), the dangers of believing in happily ever after (10–11), and substantial discussions of body image and the beauty myth (20). Maass writes, "Fairy tales play an important role in early socialization, influencing children's perception of the world and their place in it even before they begin to read. In fairy tales the literature of fantasy and imagination can be tied together to create a new view of the world" (19). In her work as a psychologist, Maass has found evidence for the kind of damaging socialization that Gilbert and Gubar, Zipes, and others have argued can be linked to literary fairy tales. Using examples such as the television show *The Bachelor*, the custom of sending flowers to a woman's workplace on Valentine's Day, and the best-selling dating book *The Rules*, Maass goes on to say that "the socialization process begun by fairy tales continues with modern methods of indoctrination" (22). Maass's book is important in the context of this chapter because it reminds us that fairy tales still have potent cultural power, particularly in relation to heterosexist and patriarchal norms, and they still need to be addressed. Ultimately, Maass claims that the problem with something like the Cinderella story is that it is so culturally powerful that it undermines a woman's self-determination (150). In the narratives discussed in this chapter, the possibility of self-determination — of agency — for female characters is one important way that contemporary women writers revise the old stories and turn them into sites of becoming. However, the most interesting revisioned tales do not end with self-determination, but rather develop a critique of unified subjectivity that goes beyond concepts that rely on identity politics and posits the potential for an ongoing, multiple, subject-in-becoming.

Given current debates about the direction literary studies should follow in the coming years, it seems necessary to pause to consider an alternative assessment of fairy tales from a scholar focusing on quantitative and evolutionary approaches to literature. Jonathan Gottschall, in "Quantitative Literary Study: A Modest Manifesto and Testing the Hypotheses of Feminist Fairy Tale Studies," argues against what he defines as the dominant feminist interpretation of fairy tales, or what he terms the social construction hypothesis:

"The claim that European tales reflect and perpetuate the arbitrary gender norms of western patriarchal societies" (207). Gottschall's analyses of things like the "percentage of male and female main characters" (211) and "personality descriptors of male and female protagonists" (212), taken from tales originating not just in Europe but all over the world, lead him to argue that the social construction hypothesis is wrong because he does not find any significant differences between Western European tales and tales from other parts of the world. Since Gottshcall sees gender roles as consistent across cultures through quantitative analysis, he concludes that "distinct regularities in behavior, psychology, and gender predominate across human populations and are reflected in the world's folk literatures" (218). Evidence of patriarchal norms in different cultures really does not mean that gender identity is not socially constructed, nor does a responsible, scholarly focus on a particular socio-historical context (such as Western European tales) equate with a claim that there are no cross-cultural elements to fairy tales.

Gottschall's claim runs absolutely counter to the argument of this project because it denies the validity of readings that reveal or demystify gendered norms in the tales. It also fails to recognize the way power operates at multiple levels and in various guises. The revisions discussed below lose much of their significance if they are not seen as working against the dominant norms embedded in earlier versions of the tales. Women writers have found it necessary to revise the tales to offer alternatives and this chapter is an exploration of those alternatives. The revisions are, themselves, an indication of the way different versions of the same tale can generate new norms and new subject positions. Gottschall's quantitative approach may help to illuminate how fairy tales function in different cultures at a surface level, but it does not speak to the way revision engages with the layers of a given text.

Many of the writers whose works are explored in this chapter self-consciously exploit fairy tales' potential to adjust to changing cultural conditions in ways that develop an ethics of becoming. Revising the narratives to emphasize the underlying assumptions of earlier versions, the writers alter not just the content of a single tale, but the expectations the reader brings to any fairy tale. In other words, the revisionist rewriting examined below works against uncritical readings of familiar fairy tales at the same time as it posits alternative versions of those tales. The critical revisioning is a combination of confronting the closed-off, socializing function of fairy tales and reinventing the tales so that they remain applicable to the contemporary moment. They speak to the ways that texts circulate and shift. Any power formations, but particularly dominating or repressive forms of power, that reside in earlier versions of the tales must be demystified in order for new configurations, new power structures, to emerge in the revisions. Revisionist rewriting can be understood as both a critical practice and an ethical one. Indeed, this project will develop an understanding of ethics that incorporates a critical stance. In the process of revisioning, contemporary women writers have found the means to disrupt foundational tales without destroying them, and to open them to a process of becoming.

The Work of Revisioning

In *Mythologies*, Roland Barthes argues, "Myth is not defined by the object of its message, but by the way in which it utters this message" (109). His structuralist approach looks at myth as a system of cultural domination, and his emphasis is on process in addition to product; Barthes wishes to study *how* myth works to create whatever object it seeks to create. One of Barthes's priorities is to prove that myths are not universal or eternal. Rather, they are based in human history and constructed for specific goals. The ultimate purpose of myths is to "transform history into nature" (129), and Barthes's project is to reassert the historicity of myths. The work of the mythologist is to demystify and denaturalize even the most mundane tasks, objects, and beliefs of our everyday lives in order to reveal them as constructed through and by myth. According to Barthes, myths tend to support and reify the position of the dominant class, while keeping the working classes and the poor engaged in this support. A mythologist works — through mythology — to "open our eyes": "The unveiling that it carries out is therefore a political act: founded on a responsible idea of language, mythology thereby postulates the freedom of the latter" (156). Resistance to myth requires an awareness of the larger systems of dominance at work in a given society. There is a lot of evidence of precisely that kind of awareness in the works discussed below.

The revisionist fairy tales discussed below engage in mythological projects of unveiling, but also in corresponding remythologizing; they create new myths even as they reveal the ways in which the traditional versions of the tales support repressive dominant discourses. In an engaging discussion of why women writers continue to return to myths and fairy tales, Susan Sellers points out that Barthes encourages the creation of alternate myths as a means of countering the damaging myths. Sellers writes, "Deconstruction or the reading of myth to expose its manipulations and suppressions is not enough, we must counter with our own mythopoeia; as Barthes writes, our best weapon against myth is to mythify in turn" (32). Once myth — or fairy tale — is understood to be inextricably bound up in power relations, once a correlation is made between the narrative structure of a myth/tale and the possibilities for social relations and subject positions surrounding that myth/tale, the need to create new myths and fairy tales becomes paramount. Perhaps the need to create the continuing potential for ongoing myths is even more important. New myths and stories grow from old myths and stories; the process of revision is essential to an ethics of becoming.

In a note, Sellers cites from *Mythologies*: "myth is speech *stolen and restored*" (125, italics in original). She argues that Barthes's description "is empowering for feminist writers since it highlights the constructed nature of myth as well as the disruption caused to the plundered order by the act of theft" (Sellers 32). The obvious patriarchal elements of traditional fairy tales and many folk tales are certainly part of what drives contemporary women writers to revisit those tales. While the "damsel in distress" awaits her prince and the evil stepmother plots against her beautiful young stepdaughter, contemporary narratives describe young women saving themselves and older women helping those young women along the way.

In *Postmodern Fairy Tales*, Cristina Bacchilega studies how postmodern versions of fairy tales work with and against older versions. She focuses on the role of desire in relation to fairy tales in a way that helps to explain how they work on their listeners and/or readers. Gender roles, in particular, are "played out" in great detail in fairy tales. Bacchilega points to the complicated ways in which fairy tales instruct women: "And for girls and women, in particular, the fairy tale's magic has assumed the contradictory form of being both a spiritual enclave supported by old wives' wisdom and an exquisitely glittery feminine kingdom" (5). There is a duality here that is probably already familiar. Fairy tales are always both closed narratives designed to socialize and open narratives ready for revision. On one level, fairy tales perform an insidious kind of naturalizing by conveying the rules of patriarchal society. The roles available to girls and women are severely restricted, but they are couched in the glamour of idealized romance and femininity. The "glittery feminine kingdom" Bacchilega mentions is a particularly potent fantasy that works to entice girls—and women—into accepting their subordinate roles. In reappropriating tales that were originally told by women, but have for centuries been used to socialize children according to patriarchal norms, contemporary women writers are engaging in a practice of reclamation that is partly encouraged by the tales themselves. Sharon Rose Wilson, in *Myths and Fairy Tales in Contemporary Women's Fiction*, explains at the outset of her work that "my major contention is that metafairy tales (texts about myths and fairy tales) generally convey characters' transformation from alienation and symbolic amputation to greater consciousness, community, and wholeness" (1). In her analyses of a wide range of texts including many by Margaret Atwood and Doris Lessing, Wilson emphasizes that "old stories resonate as intertexts in their contemporary work" (5). The power of those older stories is given new life in new, meta-or postmodern tales. Wilson does not, however, emphasize the critical work the revised tales do, which can in part be attributed to the different texts she chooses.

Another way to understand the potential embedded within fairy tales is to focus on the magical — or fantastic — components of the fairy tale form, which is really what links the fairy tales discussed in this chapter to the narratives explored in the rest of the book. Bacchilega usefully points out how the fantastic can operate in fairy tales: "As folk and fairy tale, the tale of magic produces wonder precisely through its seductively concealed exploitation of the conflict between its *normative* function, which capitalizes on the comforts of consensus, and its *subversive* wonder, which magnifies the powers of transformation" (Bacchilega 7). It is this "subversive wonder" that contemporary writers can exploit when they revise fairy tales.

Bacchilega acknowledges, however, that not every postmodern version of a fairy tale manages to create something subversive:

> [S]ome postmodern revisions may question and remake the classic fairy tale's production of gender only to re-inscribe it within some unquestioned model of subjectivity or narrativity. Other postmodern tales expose the fairy tale's complicity with the "exhausted" forms and ideologies of traditional Western narrative [...] Still other tales re-place or relocate the fairy tale to multiply its performance potential and denaturalize its institutionalized power. In every case, though, these postmodern transformations do not exploit the fairy tale's magic simply to make the spell work, but rather to unmake some of its workings [23].

The unmaking Bacchilega describes is a critical procedure. The readings that follow will highlight both strands of feminist revisioning: exposure of the workings of fairy tales and the creation of new possibilities through "subversive wonder." There are important reasons to revisit theses narratives, and the writers involved in rewriting them are always engaged in a kind of recovery, no matter what else they do with the tales. Confronting the power of fairy tales is, in itself, a significant political and aesthetic undertaking. However, most of the narratives described below manage to find new ways of using the very power they expose, and the ethics of becoming they develop takes us beyond subversion to a direct confrontation with normalizing power.

The Tale of Beauty and the Beast

This chapter focuses largely on the tale of "Beauty and the Beast": the story of a young woman's devotion to her father, her encounter with the monstrous, and her ultimate reconciliation with the male other through marriage. In *From the Beast to the Blonde* (1994), Marina Warner demonstrates how the Beauty and the Beast tale has appealed to women writers *and* readers for centuries. Along with its exploration of female sacrifice to patriarchal forces, "Beauty and the Beast" handles complex thematic issues of seeing (particularly of seeing beyond appearances) and unmasking, allowing for a self-conscious examination of how myth operates to conceal — in Barthes's terms — and how rewriting myth can help to reveal what has been hidden. In terms of popular appeal, the subject matter of "Beauty and the Beast" has proven to be engaging to generations of readers; it is about fathers and daughters, wealth and poverty, magic, animality (often in contrast with humanity), and, of course, romantic love. As Jerry Griswold points out, more than any other fairy tale, "Beauty and the Beast" seems to have taken the position of dominant myth in contemporary North American culture (18). The combination of the popular appeal of largely unchanged and unchallenged versions of the tale with its content-driven emphasis on matters of female sacrifice, otherness, domination, transformation, and unmasking, make the Beauty and the Beast tale a productive site for revisionist rewriting that embraces an ethics of becoming.

Before turning to some contemporary versions of the Beauty and the Beast tale, it is necessary to pause to consider what is actually being revised. Since fairy tales can be seen as open narratives that can encompass multiple possibilities, trying to point to a single original tale can be incredibly difficult. In the case of "Beauty and the Beast," the closest thing to a standard version is Madame Le Prince de Beaumont's "La Belle et la Bête," from *Le Magasin des Enfants*, first published in 1756.[1] In this short, familiar version of the tale, Beauty is the youngest daughter of a "very wealthy merchant" (32), and is the object of her two older sisters' jealousy. The sisters "tried to act like ladies of the court" and "went to balls, to the theater, to the park and they made fun of their younger sister, who spent most of her time reading good books" (32). Beaumont sets up her tale to provide a lesson in the virtues of adhering to class rank, but she also begins with a claim for the merits of women's education.

Pausing here, it is already possible to see the two lines of argument that surround Beaumont's "Beauty and the Beast."[2] The first works from the premise that the tale is intended to instruct women in being subservient and mindful of their places in relation to men and class structures. Zipes offers such a reading:

> Beauty is selfless, and perhaps that is why she has no name. She is nameless. All girls are supposed to become "beauties," i.e., selfless and nameless [...] The most

important thing is to learn to obey and worship one's father (authority) and to fulfill one's promises even though they are made under duress [...] Beauty and the beast are suited for one another because they live according to the code of civility. They subscribe to prescriptions that maintain the power of an elite class and patriarchal rule [*Fairy Tale as Myth* 33].

Zipes emphasizes Beauty's selflessness, honor (the need to fulfill promises), and civility, all of which are linked to the larger issue of power preserved and exercised by patriarchal and aristocratic forces. These are the social instructions that Beaumont's early children's tale was designed to convey, and much of the work of later revisions is to unveil precisely such underlying content. However, as Zipes himself acknowledges, there are more positive ways of reading Beaumont's tale that focus on her determination to advocate for women's education as well as aspects of the story that seem to provide Beauty with some power.

Griswold takes the second line of thinking to its fullest extent and argues that Beaumont's Beauty is very much in control:

Although the Beast is a huge and formidable creature, it is Beauty who calls the shots: she is the mistress of the house, the Beast insists, and everything and everyone (including the Beast himself) is at her command. Moreover, the tale dramatically emphasizes Beauty's power of choice: she must come to the Beast's castle of her own free will; she is not to be coerced but must freely choose to marry; she alone holds the power to transform the Beast; and, indeed, through much of the tale he waits upon her decision. In fact, Beauty seems to inhabit a world where males (her father, the Beast) are weak and where women have power [65].

While the outline of Beaumont's plot is much as Griswold describes, Beauty's power is nowhere near so obvious. She is first obligated to go to the Beast by her duty to her father; Beaumont's language betrays the didactic nature of the portrayal of Beauty's choice to leave: "I feel fortunate to be able to sacrifice myself" (36). Later, Beauty is given control over the Beast's fate, yet the implication is that the only truly honorable choice is for her to marry him: "'Aren't I terrible,' she said, 'for causing grief to someone who has done so much to please me? Is it his fault that he's ugly and lacks intelligence? He is kind. That's worth more than anything else. Why haven't I wanted to marry him?'" (Beaumont 40). Why, indeed. Ultimately, Beauty is rewarded for her virtuous, honorable, and self-sacrificing behavior because the beast transforms into a handsome, wealthy, and powerful prince. Griswold is correct to point to the moments in Beaumont's story that leave open the potential for Beauty to take power, but the tale itself is too bound up in the myths of patriarchy and class for anything more than a false sense of choice to be accorded to Beauty. It remains for the revisionist writers to pick up on the potential in the narrative and to give Beauty the power that she has not been granted by Beaumont.

One aspect of Beaumont's story that contemporary critics frequently mention is the way the Beast is transformed at the end of the tale. Beauty revives the Beast with water from a stream running near his castle. Warner reads this moment as a kind of baptism: "He is released from evil to emerge a new man, fit to be loved and to give love in return, like the cleansed soul after the sacrament" (291). In addition to the gender and class prescriptions discussed above, Beaumont's 1756 version of the "Beauty and the Beast" solidified an important civilizing aspect into the narrative. The Beast requires Beauty's ministrations in order to be redeemed. Femininity, although clearly a matter of passivity and obliging acceptance, is also tied to religious and cultural purity. Zipes emphasizes the way in which this part of the tale aligns with the power structures that helped to produce and sustain the new middle class:

> The sentimental if not melodramatic scene of Beauty holding and seemingly rescuing the Beast at the end of the tale is a picture that has been impressed upon our imagination and scripted in thousands of books since Madame Le Prince de Beaumont printed her story in 1756. It was almost immediately frozen as a myth because it complied so "beautifully" with the prescriptions and desires of the male middle class that was solidifying its power in Europe and North America [*Fairy Tale as Myth* 41].

The qualities of the male that might be associated with a lack of civility can all be cured through the purity of his willing, supportive, and submissive female mate. Additionally, the dangerous qualities of the "Beastly" other are neutralized. The limited power Beauty does wield in this early version if the tale is, then, directly tied to her role as an agent of civilizing, patriarchal conventions. At least some of the cultural capital Beauty has accrued over the years must come from the fact that she represents an ideal of femininity that is so far from threatening that it actually reinforces patriarchal conventions. Contemporary women writers find this "mythic" scene to be particularly significant in their reworkings of the tale as they reinvent Beauty's relationship to normalizing power. A number of different contemporary versions of the Beauty and the Beast tale are explored below. Their order is determined not by chronology or author, but rather by how the different revisions offer critical analyses of earlier versions and the extent to which they develop an ethics of becoming.

Subtle Revisioning: "The Courtship of Mr. Lyon," Angela Carter

Angela Carter's collection of fairy tales, *The Bloody Chamber* (1979), is perhaps the most comprehensive example of postmodern revisioning of the fairy tale. It contains versions of a variety of tales, from "Bluebeard" to "Little Red Riding Hood" to "Snow White." These are adult tales that fly in the face of the sanitized Disney versions. Much has already been written about Carter's brilliant tales, so the focus here will be on the versions of Beauty and the Beast in the collection and how they relate to other contemporary revisions of that tale. Carter constantly emphasizes the socializing function of fairy tales, and in ways that do not always please readers: "These stories [in *The Bloody Chamber*] have never ceased to engage — and enrage — their readers, who continue to debate whether Carter's revolutionary handling of European legends contests or colludes with patriarchal values" (Bristow and Broughton 4). So, once again, the dual possibilities for fairy tales come into play, but this time in relation to contemporary revisions.

Are Carter's tales closed texts that reinforce norms, or open texts that create new possibilities? Perhaps both. It is important to consider that Carter does, indeed, at times work from within the restrictive narrative structures that she rewrites. Yet, the presumption that a portrayal of inhibition or problematic norms is always *in support of* those inhibitions and norms is mistaken. This position of working from within is one strategy for turning the power of fairy tales in a new direction. The process of rewriting involves returning to original texts that are often very far from ideal, which is precisely why they beg to be revised. Lucie Armitt recognizes Carter's innovative formal approaches to the tales: "When Carter's collection is simply viewed as a rereading, reworking or revision of the fairy-tale mode, it inevitably has to function within a generic stranglehold that will always (however reluctantly) reduce its stories to closed dream-texts" ("The Fragile Frames" 90). Armitt has an important point regarding Carter's less than rigorous adherence to the fairy tale form, yet the insistence that reading the tales as examples of rewriting is equivalent to de-politicizing them misses much of what the process of revisioning is about. The contention here is that part of Carter's project in *The Bloody Chamber*, and part of the work of revisionist rewriting as it is described in this chapter, is to confront the ways in which power structures are reinforced through both form and content. Therefore, the fairy tale form is essential to Carter's undertaking in the collection. In some stories she chooses to stay close to the original form, and in so doing creates the possibility of interrogating the workings of that form.

In "The Courtship of Mr. Lyon,"[3] the first of the two versions of the Beauty and the Beast tale in *The Bloody Chamber*, Carter tells the story of a devoted daughter who, in order to save her father, throws herself on the mercy of a beast — in this case, a lion. So far everything is familiar. In fact this version of the tale retains much of the plot and the spirit of the Beaumont version. However, Carter makes use of strategic revisions to draw attention to the problematic power structures of patriarchy and class that underlie the original tale. Through these revisions "The Courtship of Mr. Lyon" turns into a story that opens up previously closed structures to critical and ethical questions. In the end an alternative ethics of becoming is merely a hinted possibility in this story, but the revisionist rewriting lays the foundations for such an ethics to begin to take shape.

The first difference a reader notices about this story is that it is set in late twentieth-century England. Beauty's father's financial woes are tied up in court battles, telephones are readily available, and when Beauty leaves the Beast late in the story, she does so by taxi. Sylvia Bryant discusses the significance of Carter's choice to change the historical context of the fairy tale:

> The setting is twentieth-century England, and the tensions which Carter exposes as the modern Beauty confronts the archaic social systems still at work in her contemporary world construct a more overt critique of those systems — represented here more by the Beast than by Beauty's father — than either traditional narrative or dominant cinematic visions have heretofore discovered [89].

The temporal relocation of what is a fairly straightforward rewriting of the Beauty and the Beast tale in "The Courtship of Mr. Lyon" exposes power structures operating in older versions of the tale *and* in the contemporary setting. As Bryant notes, one main point seems to be that little has changed. Beauty's story is not, Carter suggests, only a tale from the distant — and, of course, imagined — past; it is all too relevant today.

In addition, the use of a contemporary setting provides Carter with a way to jar readers out of a complacent reading of a familiar tale. Zipes calls this kind of rewriting "transfiguration," and argues that it "depicts the familiar in an estranging fashion" so that "the reader is compelled to consider the negative aspects of anachronistic forms and perhaps transcend them" (*Fairy Tales and the Art of Subversion* 178). When Carter writes that "the old car stuck fast in a rut, wouldn't budge an inch; the engine whirred, coughed and died and he was far from home" (*Bloody Chamber* 41), the "once upon a time" in which Beauty's father is usually lost in a wood is drastically reframed. The recontextualizing of the story requires the reader to rethink the assumptions upon which the original story is founded.

Class and the significance of both wealth and poverty are always important themes in Beauty and the Beast tales. Beauty's father's loss of his merchant class fortune, the Beast's aristocratic wealth, and Beauty's economic dependence on men are all central to the plot. In "The Courtship of Mr. Lyon," when Beauty's father first walks into the Beast's palace, he is struck by its riches:

> The door behind him closed as silently as it had opened, yet, this time, he felt no fear although he knew by the pervasive atmosphere of a suspension of reality that he had entered a place of privilege where all the laws of the world he knew need not necessarily apply, for the very rich are often eccentric and the house was plainly that of an exceedingly wealthy man [Carter 42].

Wealth and magic are intertwined in the Beast's palace. The extravagance of the Beast's wealth is depicted as unreal or, at least, as capable of creating unreality. In fact, this version of the tale lacks magic of any kind other than that created by the aura of the Beast's money. Griswold misses the point and argues, "In this variation, Carter largely removes fantasy and flattens Beaumont's story in a realistic way; the results are fairly bland" (182). What Griswold reads as "bland" are the realistic details that highlight how the fantastic, romantic versions of the tale actually operate to promote social norms. The correlation between wealth and magic demonstrates how power is really tied to class in the tale; Beauty and her father are not in the same category as the Beast, and do not wield the same amount of power.

Later, when the Beast has helped to restore Beauty's father to prosperity, Carter describes Beauty as being changed by the experience of riches: "She was learning, at the end of her adolescence, how to be a spoiled child and that pearly skin of hers was plumping out, a little, with high living and compliments" (Carter, *Bloody Chamber* 48–49). Beauty's taste of affluence is not described as entirely beneficial: "Her face was acquiring, instead of beauty, a lacquer of the invincible prettiness that characterizes certain pampered, exquisite, expensive cats" (Carter, *Bloody Chamber* 49). Her beauty is compromised by an overly comfortable life. There are two critiques embedded in these brief descriptions. First, Carter is making a point about the nature of wealth and what it does to those who have it. Second, the definition of "beauty" that Carter is promoting is not one of pampered wealth, but rather one of active work. Careful word choice and sentence construction allow Carter to insert a layer of critique into the tale, even as the plot is left unchanged.

As in earlier versions of the fairy tale, Beauty is always economically dependent, either on her father or the Beast. When her father faces financial ruin Beauty does as well. Despite the story's contemporary setting Carter chooses to maintain a plot structure that relies upon Beauty's inability to support herself. Aidan Day sees Beauty's economic dependence as central to Carter's point: "Carter sees the story as summarizing a masculine conspiracy to deny women the chance of ever reaching autonomous, self-responsible adulthood. Carter makes the point not by altering the plot of the original, but through her emphases on observations in the telling of the plot" (136). Carter's choice to remain true to the plot of the fairy tale is a calculated one designed to allow her to reveal those aspects of the narrative that are dangerous for women.

Revisionist rewriting allows Carter to highlight Beauty's economic dependence, among other things, in order to reveal the workings of the older versions of the tale. Unveiling in this manner is similar to what Barthes describes, and it is a productive way to expose the power structures that underlie myths. How we read Carter's version of the tale depends, in part, upon the way we understand its relationship to earlier versions of the tale. For example, Beauty does seem stuck in this story, as when her father first takes her to the Beast and Carter writes, "Yet she stayed and smiled, because her father wanted her to do so" (45). Beauty is caught in a kind of "masculine conspiracy." However, Carter swiftly undermines this reading of Beauty as simply an object to be used: "Do not think she had no will of her own; only, she was possessed by a sense of obligation to an unusual degree" (45). Perhaps Beauty's overdeveloped sense of obligation is itself a symptom of patriarchal indoctrination, but Carter goes out of her way to point out Beauty's complicity if this is the case. Another way to see this description of Beauty as having a mind of her own is as a form of actively rewriting the fairy tale in order to highlight not only its focus on male conspiracy, but also its absence of focus on Beauty's desires.

Maria Tatar reads Beauty's "sense of obligation" against the probable historical implications of earlier versions of the tale:

> That the desire for wealth motivates parents to turn their daughters over to a beast points to the possibility that these tales mirror social practices of an earlier age. Many an arranged marriage must have seemed like marriage to a beast, and the telling of stories like "Beauty and the Beast" may have furnished women with a socially acceptable channel for providing therapeutic advice, comfort, and consolation. Yet what many of these tales seem to endorse in one cultural inflection after another is a reinscription of patriarchal norms, the subordination of female desire to male desire, and a glorification of filial duty and self-sacrifice. Angela Carter's "Courtship of Mr. Lyon" is unique in its effort to demystify these "natural" virtues by subjecting them to grotesque exaggeration. Her heroine, who is "possessed by a sense of obligation to an unusual degree," perceives herself to be "Miss Lamb, spotless, sacrificial" [26].

Tatar points to the social practices of "an earlier age" to demonstrate that most versions of the tale involve an unquestioning reliance on the same power relations that would have encouraged a young woman — or girl — to accept marriage to a stranger as her duty and her only choice. In her rewriting, Carter draws attention to those power relations in ways that encourage the reader to question them. The emphasis Carter places on Beauty's *lack* of self-questioning, which Tatar describes as "grotesque exaggeration," effectively renders visible the underlying assumptions of the tale.

In "The Courtship of Mr. Lyon," Carter sets up the relationship between Beauty and the Beast when the Beast sees a picture of Beauty: "The Beast rudely snatched the photograph her father drew from his wallet and inspected it, first brusquely, then with a strange kind of wonder, almost the dawning of surmise. The camera had captured a certain look she had sometimes, of absolute sweetness and absolute gravity, as if her eyes might pierce appearances and see your soul" (44). Thus, Beauty is described early on as someone capable of seeing past the obvious, of unveiling hidden realities. The Beast's hopes for himself reside with this perceived capacity of Beauty's to see beyond appearances to the reality beneath. Unfortunately for the Beast, in this case, Beauty is not immediately able to see past his appearance:

> Although her father had told her of the nature of the one who waited for her, she could not control an instinctual shudder of fear when she saw him, for a lion is a lion and a man is a man and, though lions are more beautiful by far than we are, yet they belong to a different order of beauty and, besides, they have no respect for us: why should they? Yet wild things have a far more rational fear of us than is ours of them, and some kind of sadness in his agate eyes, that looked almost blind, as if sick of sight, moved her heart [Carter 45].

Beauty recoils when she first sees the Beast, yet her empathy is quickly roused. This first meeting is an important moment in each of the versions of the story examined here, and in this case Carter emphasizes the otherness of the beast: "She found his bewildering difference from herself almost intolerable; its presence choked her" (45). The Beast's otherness is the result of his animal appearance (in this story, he *is* a lion) and also the magic that could create a being that is both lion and man. Beauty is torn between her "instinctual" response to his animal otherness and the rationalized pity she feels for a creature who is clearly unhappy. There is little room in this version of the tale for Beauty to be truly shaken by the otherness she encounters in the Beast. In traditional versions of the tale, and in this rewriting, the plot hinges upon Beauty's ability to see past the Beast's animal qualities to his inner humanity and suffering. The implicit argument being made is that there is an inner self, distinct from appearances. A lion might be a strange form for a man to take, but this beast is still a man, and a recognizably unified and coherent man at that. The idea that the beast is a mask for a "true," inner hero is, of course, central to the original plot of the tale, and in this revision Carter sticks to the basic premise of the originals, even while demonstrating their dangers.

As the narrative develops, Beauty becomes accustomed to her new surroundings. It is not only the Beast that she must get used to, but his whole world. In some versions of the tale, these surroundings can be just as daunting as the Beast himself. However, in "The Courtship of Mr. Lyon," it does not take Beauty long to adjust: "The enchantment of that bright, sad, pretty place enveloped her and she found that, against all her expectations, she was happy there. She no longer felt the slightest apprehension at her nightly interviews with the Beast. All the natural laws of the world were held in suspension" (Carter 47). The Beast is still strange to her at this point, but he is not an immediate danger, and Beauty is happy in the "magic" of the Beast's wealth. Carter's language continues to exaggerate, repeat, and overemphasize in ways that develop a careful critique of earlier versions of the tale.

When Beauty leaves the Beast to go back to her father, she is saddened by his reaction to losing her company: "She was moved almost to tears that he should care for her so. It was in her heart to drop a kiss upon his shaggy mane but, though she stretched out her hand towards him, she could not bring herself to touch him of her own free will, he was so different from herself" (Carter, *Bloody Chamber* 48). Here, Beauty is unable to accept the Beast fully even as she realizes his feelings for her. The power dynamics are striking. We all know that the Beast lets Beauty leave, and that he gives her freedom to his own detriment. This twist in the traditional fairy tale is perhaps the only way the reader can accept Beauty's eventual declaration of love for the Beast. In this version, the weight placed on Beauty's control over the Beast's fate and his need for her to see him as something beyond his appearance is carefully designed to give the reader pause. The Beast's clear need for Beauty — and her inability to fulfill that need right away — emphasize the assumptions inherent in earlier versions of the tale. Just as she felt "a sense of obligation to an unusual degree" (45) to her father, Beauty will of course feel a sense of obligation to the Beast. The implied power Beauty has over the Beast is a misdirection that makes it seem as though she has control when she does not. Carter's revision reveals that traditional versions of the tale carefully construct a link between happy endings and female sacrifice.

If Beauty willingly gives up her independence, she will have a happy ending. Day reads Carter's story in similar terms, pointing out the psychological manipulation the Beast uses to draw Beauty to him: "The Beast is not a certain kind of male ogre: he doesn't imprison Beauty or rape her. But, not content with trading for her with her father, he exploits her sentiment" (Day 138). In this version of the tale, Beauty's overdetermined sense of duty is shown to mark her as having accepted the rules of patriarchal society to "an unusual degree," and the Beast plays upon her need to live up to the role she has been assigned. It would be unfathomable for this Beauty to turn away from a Beast who has shown her such compassion and love, even if he is beastly in appearance. For, of course, it would be exceptionally silly of Beauty to forget that, while her own beautiful appearance is absolutely essential to her embodiment of proper femininity, the rules for men are vastly different and the Beast's wealth and status matter far more than how he looks.

Carter continues to develop a critique of the tale in the scene when Beauty briefly returns to her father in "The Courtship of Mr. Lyon." As in older, more traditional versions of the tale, Beauty finds that she cannot forget the Beast:

> She sent him flowers, white roses in return for the ones he had given her; and when she left the florist, she experienced a sudden sense of perfect freedom, as if she had just escaped from an unknown danger, had been grazed by the possibility of some change but, finally, left intact. Yet, with this exhilaration, a desolating emptiness [Carter 48].

It is the emptiness that drives Beauty to return to the Beast, but Carter's word choice is interesting. In this passage Carter begins to hint at an alternative reading of the Beauty and the Beast tale in which Beauty is altered — "grazed by the possibility of some change"— by her encounter with the other in the form of the Beast. Beauty's choice to return to the Beast could, then, be seen as a choice to challenge her own reality and to accept the other. It could be seen as a choice to *become* other herself.[4] Here, however, Beauty remains "intact." The otherness of the Beast has not destabilized any of the categories upon which Beauty's subjectivity depends.

Similarly, Carter leaves the plot of the original narrative intact, but only after making it clear that this other possibility — the potential for becoming — lies just beyond the bounds of the tale as it has been told. When Beauty does return to the Beast, she finds him — as usual — near death: "His eyelids flickered. How was it she had never noticed before that his agate eyes were equipped with lids, like those of a man? Was it because she had only looked at her own face, reflected there?" (Carter, *Bloody Chamber* 50). In this encounter Carter highlights Beauty's growing awareness of the Beast. Beauty sees past her own response to him for perhaps the first time. When she declares her love for the Beast, Beauty is rewarded with yet another unveiling: "And then it was no longer a lion in her arms but a man, a man with an unkempt mane of hair and, how strange, a broken nose, such as the noses of retired boxers, that gave him a distant, heroic resemblance to the handsomest of all the beasts" (Carter, *Bloody Chamber* 51). When the Beast turns into a handsome hero, Beauty is, in a way, let off the hook. She does not have to find a way to live with the other; he becomes something far more familiar. Of course, if Carter's story is read according to the terms discussed here, the Beast's transformation — restoration, really — back into a man is only the physical manifestation of the underlying logic of the tale that assumes a unitary, human, male subject beneath the façade of a lion. And, in Carter's knowing hands, it is terribly disappointing.

The story ends with a picture of domestic tranquility: "Mr. and Mrs. Lyon walk in the garden; the old spaniel drowses on the grass, in a drift of fallen petals" (Carter 51). For some critics, this ending is nothing less than disastrous: "Ironically, Carter ascribes the last words of this text to Mr. Lyon, rapidly re-inscribing Beauty back into her womanly supporting role" (Bryant 90). Day writes, "A combination of economic dependency and conditioned emotional susceptibility condemns Beauty to continuing impairment and possession by the male. In Carter's reading the fable allegorises the stunting of women's growth to individual, adult identity" (138). The ending is indeed a description of stifled potential. Beauty's growth is not, however, stunted solely through male trickery. Instead, the underlying logic of the tale, which reinforces and reinscribes a limiting notion of unitary subjectivity, wins. The potential for accepting the other, for becoming, is only a shadowy hint, because the tale is closed off into a neat, and socially acceptable, package. Carter's choice to end the story in this manner is in keeping with her choice to remain true to the plot of "Beauty and the Beast," and doing so allows her to focus on carefully undermining the logic of that plot. It is only in her other retelling of this fairy tale that we find a more radical ending.

Reworked and Reworked Again: Beauty *and* Rose Daughter, *Robin McKinley*

Before turning to Carter's second version of "Beauty and the Beast," and to the radical rewriting she provides there, there are other contemporary versions of the tale to consider such as two novel-length versions by Robin McKinley. *Beauty*, her first novel, is often marketed toward an adolescent audience, and was originally published in 1978. *Rose Daughter* is a more mature version of the tale published in 1997. McKinley has explained that "Beauty and the Beast" is her favorite fairy tale, and that it was the only one available to her in the 1950s that did not "have the heroine waiting limply to be rescued by the hero" ("The Story"). So, for McKinley, the potential for Beauty to be a powerful figure was always an important part of what drew her to the tale. Her focus on Beauty's agency is apparent in both revisionings discussed below. Overall, McKinley's fairy tales tend to emphasize updated, positive messages in standard didactic modes. Nevertheless, the kinds of constructive possibilities McKinley writes into the tale do open up space for critique if these tales are read with a focus on how the process of revision operates to reveal the assumptions that ground traditional versions.

Beauty, like "The Courtship of Mr. Lyon," sticks rather close to more traditional versions of "Beauty and the Beast." The most significant difference is that it is narrated in the first-person, from Beauty's point of view, and emphasizes Beauty's inner strength. Both of McKinley's versions of the tale focus on Beauty's relationships with her sisters, and they are always supportive associations. In addition, both versions focus on the merits of hard work as opposed to the idleness that can come with wealth. In *Beauty* the emphasis on productivity leads to a general discussion of gendered divisions of labor: "Grace and Hope [Beauty's sisters] divided the house-work between them, and I did whatever was left over, the odds and ends that were neither house-work nor shop-work; and often thought that it would have been much more convenient if I had been a boy — not least because I already looked like one" (39). Beauty's father has already lost his fortune, and the three sisters have to find a way to survive in the country after leading lives of comfort in the city. In this narrative, "Beauty" is misnamed, as she is the least pretty of the three daughters. However, physical appearance does not bother the heroine a great deal since she distinguishes herself as being the "clever one." Her thought that it would be easier to be a boy is a simple demonstration of the restrictions women must cope with on a daily basis in the "once upon a time" of this tale. In *Rose Daughter*, McKinley takes the gender bending one step further; one of the three sisters in that tale (called Lionheart) actually takes on the identity of a young man in order to work in a stable. Both of these are small gestures, but they do provide instances of demystifying in the sense that Barthes describes; McKinley's insertions of gender-conscious storylines demonstrate how more traditional versions of the tale gloss over a patriarchal system that would not allow the three sisters to provide for themselves.

Economic dependence is, thus, not one of the problems that Beauty faces in either of McKinley's versions of the Beauty and the Beast tale. In both narratives, Beauty is entirely capable of living without the Beast's help, or even without her father's help. The issue of class is also less significant because of this economic independence. Although Beauty's father loses his money at the beginning of both narratives, the new lives the sisters create for themselves in the country are depicted as more satisfying and generally superior to what they experienced before. McKinley updates the tale and, in so doing, eliminates many of the aspects of class and patriarchal power that are problematic in traditional versions. However, McKinley's revisions do not go so far as to probe the underlying logic of the tale, so the degree to which they can provide true alternatives is limited.

At this point, it is best to separate the two narratives. *Beauty* is, as stated above, very close to a traditional version of the fairy tale, but its emphasis on Beauty's capabilities and strengths continues throughout the narrative. Her cleverness and dedication to scholarship are part of what help her to grow closer to the Beast. In his palace library there are enough books to keep Beauty occupied for lifetimes, some of which have not yet been written during the time when the tale is set. When Beauty questions the Beast about books that seem strange to her, he explains, "'Nothing is wrong,' said the Beast; he sounded pleased, which I didn't like, assuming that he was amused at my discomfiture. 'This library is — well —' He paused. 'Most of these books haven't been written yet.' I looked at him stupidly, *Kim* still in my hand. 'But don't worry, they will be,' he said" (148).[5] The Beast is pleased that Beauty is able to see the books at all, since she is sometimes unable to see the purely magical aspects of his existence. Time is not relevant in the Beast's library; all the books that have ever been or ever will be are available there. The emphasis on the future gives McKinley's *Beauty* a sense of potential to be fulfilled that contrasts with earlier versions, which work toward reestablishing a previous balance that has been disturbed. This Beast and Beauty form a habit of reading to one another and forge a relationship primarily through their intellectual connection.

Yet, Beauty's physical reaction to the Beast is as vexed in *Beauty* as in the other versions of the tale. When he does touch her in order to help her, she is frightened:

> I had avoided touching him, or letting him touch me. At first I had eluded him from fear; but when fear departed, elusiveness remained, and developed into habit. Habit bulwarked by something else; I could not say what. The obvious answer, because he was a Beast, didn't seem to be the right one. I considered this. I did not get very far; but I thought I knew what Persephone must have felt after she ate those pomegranate seeds; and was then surprised by a sudden rush of sympathy for the dour King of Hell [170].

This Beauty is immediately aware that there is more to her discomfort than the Beast's otherness. She is already used to his appearance, so there must be more to her reaction to his touch. In this encounter with the other, McKinley creates a situation that speaks of the potential for becoming; the force of the other intimates a kind of latent becoming that Beauty simply does not fulfill here. As in Carter's "The Courtship of Mr. Lyon," Beauty's feelings for the Beast turn out to be the result of her overcoming her reaction to his otherness — and, indeed, his maleness — rather than her embracing his difference. This narrative ends with the Beast turning back into a man as a result of Beauty's acceptance of his proposal of marriage, and she and her family are restored to their former riches. The underlying logic of a beastly mask that hides what is really a unified male subject is, clearly, never really addressed, and certainly not undermined.

Rose Daughter places more emphasis on critiquing traditional versions of "Beauty and the Beast" than does *Beauty*, and it moves closer to a direct representation of the realization of becoming in the encounter between Beauty and the Beast. It is a third-person narrative focusing on Beauty's point of view. The shift from first-person in *Beauty* to third-person here is significant mainly because it indicates a larger perspective. The Beauty of *Rose Daughter* may be just as naïve as her counterpart, but the narrative voice is certainly wiser. A case in point is Beauty's first encounter with the Beast. When she looks into his face, she is stunned into a momentary inability to rationalize:

> The contrasts she found there were too great: wisdom and despair, power and weakness, man and animal. These made him far more terrible than any hungry lion, any half-tamed hydra, any angry sorcerer, terrible as something that should not exist is terrible, because to recognize that it does exist shakes that faith in the foundations of the natural world which human beings must have to bear the burden of their rationality [87].

In this confrontation with the other, McKinley uses the third person to describe both Beauty's temporary loss of her sense of self, and the implications of that loss. This Beast is an uncategorizable hybrid, and Beauty is utterly immobilized by his appearance. The narrator continues, "Whatever — whoever — she was, it was being transformed implacably into something else: *she was being undone, unmade, annihilated*" (87, italics in original). Beauty's loss of self does not last, but this moment is undoubtedly an example of becoming. Her encounter with the other leads Beauty to her own unmaking. There is nothing particularly radical about this passage as far as rewriting is concerned; McKinley is still squarely within the tradition of "Beauty and the Beast," yet the Beast's hybridity is an important choice. Describing the Beast as both human and animal makes it harder to see him as simply a man wearing an animal mask. The inside/outside logic that underlies traditional versions of the tale is undermined in this passage, and Beauty has to cope with something that is truly other.

His animal/human hybridity makes the Beast a potential nomadic subject. This Beast lacks the kind of easy unity that would make the tale resolve into a traditional happy ending. The idea of a handsome prince, and all of the attendant wealth and power of such a figure, lurking beneath the Beast's obscuring appearance is not allowed to persist in this tale. So, in this revisioning, McKinley moves beyond critique to explore the latent possibility of becoming. The force of Beauty's momentary experience of a loss of self, of a becoming-other in response to a hybrid Beast, propels the plot to resolve in a new way.

Beauty is given a choice at the end of the novel. She can either turn the Beast back into a handsome young philosopher/sorcerer and live with riches and power, or leave him as a hybrid Beast and return to a simple life in the country. This Beauty chooses the latter. She embraces the Beast's otherness and invites him into her own world. McKinley changes the terms of the traditional tale by altering the reward; Beauty's prince is the Beast, and her "happily ever after" is a life of simplicity, work, and family harmony that allows for the possibility of hybrid, nomadic subjectivity. Beauty herself is a subject in becoming rather than the catalyst of the Beast's transformation. When the Beast questions whether or not Beauty has made the right choice for herself, she responds, "'But I—I think I will choose to believe that you would miss being able to see in the dark, and to be careless of the weather, and to walk as silently as sunlight. Because I love my Beast, and I would miss him very much if he went away from me and left me with some handsome stranger'" (287). As many critics have pointed out, the beast is generally a much more engaging character than the prince who replaces him.[6] In this revisioning of the tale, McKinley allows the reader—and Beauty—to keep the far more interesting Beast. In so doing, McKinley also privileges a different approach to otherness than traditional versions of the tale; here, otherness is something to be cherished rather than overcome. The otherness of the Beast is preferable to wealth or princely good looks, and it is also the continued condition in Beauty's life that will allow her to constantly encounter opportunities for becoming.

Science Fiction Meets Fairy Tale: "Beauty," Tanith Lee

Another contemporary revision of the Beauty and the Beast tale that uses the Beast as an opportunity to embrace becoming is Tanith Lee's "Beauty" (1983). In this generically complex revision, Lee combines fairy tale conventions with science fictional devices in ways that generate profitable collisions between the two. It is set in the future on an Earth that is inhabited by aliens as well as humans. This version's emphasis is on rewriting and reversal; Lee works from the basic narrative structure of the Beauty and the Beast tale and includes the defining elements of otherness and transformation, yet she shifts the focus of the narrative to make the *human* other in a way that is more commonly found in science fiction. "Beauty" follows the basic trajectory of the traditional tale of "Beauty and the Beast," but it establishes a fundamental difference from the first line: "His hundred and fifty-first birthday dawned aboard the sleek ship from Cerulean, high above the white-capped ocean that was the Earth" (149). The line refers to Mercator Levin, Beauty's father (Beauty's name is Estár here), but he is placed in a spaceship orbiting Earth rather than on horseback in the woods.

Lee depicts a utopian future in which poverty has been eradicated, war is something that happened in the past, weather is controlled, and the arts are highly valued. The comfort of life on Earth is due to advanced technologies brought by an alien race that is reported to be unbearably ugly; these aliens choose to remain covered so that they are hidden from the view of the humans with whom they interact. Lee gives the setting of the story the kind of primacy and explanation that science fiction generally demands, but never at the expense of the more dominant thread of the tale. As the reader might expect, when Levin returns to Earth he is intercepted on his way home. He is summoned to the office of someone who is referred to only as "the commissioner," and in an interaction that is entirely official and diplomatic, Estár's father is presented with a green rose that — the reader later learns — is to indicate that a member of his family must be sent to live with an alien. Estár is chosen, not because she is the most selfless, but rather because she has much less to lose than her two sisters. Estár goes to the alien's home and, after a month of living in isolation she finally asks to meet with the beast/alien, who is completely covered. Estár grows increasingly comfortable with the alien before returning home for a scheduled visit. The alien does not languish in her absence as in traditional versions of the tale, but Estár returns readily and this time asks to see him uncovered. Her encounter with the alien in his actual form — which comes much later in Lee's story than in most versions of the tale — is the climax of the story, and it sends Estár fleeing back to her father's house. When she does return to the alien, she learns that she is not properly human herself and that she is actually a member of the alien's race. Estár and the alien have grown to love one another, and the story ends with her finding a home and happiness with the alien.

Lee's revision of the Beauty and the Beast tale brings the past and the future together in the encounter between Mercator Levin and the commissioner. Beaumont's beast demands that one of the unlucky traveler's daughters die in his place, and Disney's piteous — and somewhat ludicrous — beast roars in anger at the arrogance of the theft of a rose; the interchange that takes place in Lee's novella is utterly different. Levin is greeted by an assistant: "The attendant was human, a courteous formality that boded ill" (150). Presumably, the usual attendant would be a robot or machine of some kind. Levin asks this human attendant if there is something wrong with his cargo, and once he is assured that his meeting with the commissioner is about another matter, he is offered a variety of "wines, teas, coffees, and other social stimulants" (150). Finally, the commissioner appears and says, "'Depending on how you see your situation, Mercator Levin, it is my duty to inform you that either a great honor, or a great annoyance, is about to befall your family'" (150). The commissioner gives Levin a green rose, which Levin understands to mean that one of his children will have to leave to live with an alien, and which he clearly does not see as an honor.

The entire exchange is polite, formal, and utterly antithetical to the standard fairy tale versions. This is a subtle but highly effective insertion of the future world into the fairy tale narrative. Power functions differently in this world. There is no need for the father to encounter the alien/beast in any dramatic or violent way. The aristocrat/merchant class distinction is irrelevant here and instead of a horrifying encounter in the wooded lands of a powerful beast, Levin faces an official who is simply delivering the unfortunate news that he has no choice but to accept. The reader learns that some had tried to ignore the roses that were sent to them, but battles had broken out. Lee writes, "Without their gifts [those from the aliens to the humans], humanity would not thrive quite as it did. Gradually, persuaded by their own kind [...] those who had hidden and fought and stood alone, crumbled, gave in, let go" (155). Levin knows that he cannot ignore the rose, and that he must choose a daughter to send to the aliens. Like the aristocratic beast of earlier versions of the tale, the alien beasts in this story wield status and power. However, their power is organized and distributed through various mechanisms of control that, taken together, make the requirement of turning a daughter over to the beastly other seem a part of a citizen's duties. Yet, as the story unfolds it becomes difficult to know if the aliens' power and control is to be viewed negatively.

Lee's story creates a number of reversals as it rewrites "Beauty and the Beast." From the beginning, Estár, meaning "psyche"—a clear reference to "Cupid and Psyche," which is considered to be the earliest version of "Beauty and the Beast"—is not a typical Beauty.[7] Her father describes her as having an "unrested turbulent spirit" (149), and it turns out that her request for a humble rose, which is a generous gesture in most versions of the tale, is not a simple matter in this world. "Natural" gifts are not easy to come by in this future, and asking for a rose means requiring her father to go out of his way. Lee positions Estár as an outsider in her own family who "had been born with no creative skills and had learned none" (157). Beauty as an outsider is not a new approach, but Estár's family is nothing but kind to her so her outsider status is not the result of cruelty or exclusion. She does not feel herself to be a part of what goes on around her, and when she learns that she must leave her family to live with the alien, her thought is that "those who must live with the aliens were finally estranged from all humanity that was well known. So, she had lost her own chance at becoming human" (158). Before she ever encounters the alien, the beast, Estár struggles with the otherness within herself. In reference to the way otherness operates in Beauty and the Beast tales, Warner argues that "at a fundamental level, 'Beauty and the Beast' in numerous variations forms a group of tales which work out [a] basic plot, moving from the terrifying encounter with Otherness, to its acceptance, or, in some versions of the story, its annihilation. In either case, the menace of the Other has been met, dealt with and exorcized by the end of the fairy tale" (276). Lee's version of the tale does not eliminate the conflict with the external other, but it redirects the essence of the encounter.

When Estár arrives at the alien's home, she is catered to by "a luminous bead [that] came to hover in the air like a tame bird" (159). It is not quite the dancing candelabra of Disney, but the point is the same and the substitution of science fiction for fantasy hardly registers here. The house is so technologically advanced that it is in effect telepathic, and Estár lives in complete comfort without having to encounter the alien until she is ready to do so. When she does meet him — fully covered — it is because he has responded to her thoughts: "She looked up, and an extraordinary sensation filled her eyes, her head, her whole torso. It was not like fear at all, more like some other tremendous emotion. She almost burst into tears" (161). She still has no real idea of what he looks like, and she spends some time resisting his efforts to connect with her, but Lee establishes that there is an immediate response to his otherness. It is only after the alien convinces Estár that her resistance to him is based in what she imagines she should feel rather than what she does feel that she is able to accept him. To return to Warner's description of "Beauty and the Beast" tales in general, she explains that by the end, "the terror has been faced and chased; the light shines in the dark places" (277). Estár clearly feels this kind of illumination after she has come to know the alien: "She knew herself enveloped in such a glow, a light penetrating her resistance" (165). The sense of otherness that had plagued her before she arrived at the alien's house, when in the company of other humans, has begun to leave her.

Still, Estár has yet to see the alien as he actually is beneath all of the covering he always wears when he is with her. When she does see him without barriers he is swimming, and her first reaction is to feel othered, as she has her entire life, once again: "With very little effort, Estár might imagine it was his planet she saw before her, and that dark swift shape was the indigenous thing, not the *alien* thing at all. Instead, she herself was the alien, at this instant" (175). Lee creates another reversal so that the beast is no beast at all, and it is Estár who feels herself to be alien. Estár is overwhelmed by the full sight of the alien out of the water, and she escapes back to her father's house without any real explanation, but the alien is unsurprised by her reaction. Lee does not offer a detailed elaboration of Estár's thoughts as she views the alien. In fact, the reader does not get a full description of the alien until she returns to him, at which point the reader learns that his appearance is not ugly at all, but rather painfully beautiful, at least to Estár.

At this late point in the story, his description takes up an entire page. To summarize, he is a statuesque figure with fine fur, lionesque eyes, and an overall appearance that is described as "neither like a man nor an animal. He was like himself [...] Utterly and dreadfully beautiful" (180). As in McKinley's *Rose Daughter*, the beast is a human/animal hybrid. Lee's emphasis on the point that the alien/beast "was like himself" also further pushes against the more traditional idea of an inner, coherent male subject hidden beneath a beastly mask. Remembering that the aliens are responsible for highly advanced technologies, the alien/beast becomes representative of a kind of posthuman possibility that is both more animal and more advanced than humanity. In addition, the alien/beast's beauty indicates, clearly, that there will be no transformation of the beast into a prince in this version of the tale, just as there was none in McKinley's *Rose Daughter*. Bacchilega reads the fact that the beast is beautiful and need not be transformed as meaning that "there is no Beast in 'Beauty,' a narrative move that exposes xenophobia as a defensive mechanism grounded in misunderstandings and blind superiority" (87). Clearly, the human assumption that the aliens are ugly is being undermined, but in this case it is also important to note that Lee is drawing on the oldest version of the tale in which Psyche beholds Cupid or Eros, who is a god and so stunning that he is beyond human beauty. In Lee's version, Estár learns that she is herself an alien who was born to a human mother because the aliens are facing a problem with sterility, and that is why she has been summoned.

The established pattern of the tale is for Beauty's love to break the spell that holds the beast, thereby returning him to his true princeliness. In this case, the beast/alien remains as he is and Estár is the one who finds herself transformed. Bacchilega reads the ending differently: "If the alien is no beast, then Estár has no need to change him, but neither must she change herself, needing instead simply to acknowledge her nature — her reason to be, and to be with the alien" (88). Understandably, Bacchilega finds this to be a conservative and disappointing ending. There is a point to be made about the restoration of order here; Estár being revealed as an alien is, as Bacchilega suggests, much like Cinderella being revealed to have been a princess all along in a maneuver that is typical of the fairy tale function. Nevertheless, Lee's novella emphasizes Estár's internal transformation long before she finds out that she is actually an alien. In that sense, it is a modified version of the kind of transformation that Warner describes as always taking place in "Beauty and the Beast" tales: "In her encounter with the Beast, the female protagonist meets her match, in more ways than one. If she defeats him, or even kills him, if she outwits him, banishes or forsakes him, or accepts him and loves him, she arrives at some knowledge she did not possess; his existence and the challenge he offers is necessary before she can grasp it" (Warner 318). The challenge the beast/alien offers is perhaps not as radical as that posed by the Beast in *Rose Daughter*; Estár turns out to be risking her sense of self in her encounter with the beast only to have a different, but possibly stable, identity provided for her. Nevertheless, the way in which Lee constructs Estár's movement from human to alien focuses attention on the tale's potential to examine the process of becoming; the fact that Estár was actually always already an alien cannot erase that process. In addition, Lee's particular creation of an alien/beast who is something more than but suggestive of a human/animal hybrid, is a provocative change to the traditional depiction of the beast as a seeming animal other but really just a human male in disguise.

Beauty the Beast: "The Tiger's Bride," Angela Carter

While McKinley's and Lee's beasts are tantalizingly hybrid, the beast can be a more traditional animal and still create the conditions for an ethics of becoming to take shape. Angela Carter's second revision of the tale in *The Bloody Chamber*, "The Tiger's Bride," is a dramatic revisioning that, at times, bears little resemblance to more traditional versions of the tale. The story opens with the line, "My father lost me to The Beast at cards" (51). This is not a story about a daughter's loyalty or a father's love; this is a story about a degenerate and irresponsible father who gambles his daughter away in a fit of drunkenness.[8] Emphasizing the process of revision as a method for revealing the power configurations at work in earlier versions of the tale, this can be read as Carter's take on the "real" situation in "Beauty and the Beast": a daughter is sold as property in order to cover a father's debt. There is no "Beauty" in this story, only a female protagonist/narrator who is completely incensed at her situation: "I watched with the furious cynicism peculiar to women whom circumstances force mutely to witness folly, while my father, fired in his desperation by more and yet more draughts of the firewater they call 'grappa,' rids himself of the last scraps of my inheritance" (51–52). The astute "Beauty" narrating this version of the tale provides a critique of the power systems at work from *within* the narrative itself. Rather than offering subtle manipulations of older versions of the tale designed to demystify the underlying power dynamics, this rewriting literalizes and confronts the forces that create a character such as the Beauty in "The Courtship of Mr. Lyon."

Bryant helpfully emphasizes the importance of the narration in "The Tiger's Bride": "By appropriating the personal voice, the girl in this second tale not only takes charge of telling the narrative of her life, and consequently of the narrative traditions of the fairy tale, but she also makes clear from the start that what blame there is to be assigned lies not with her but with the dominant systems to which she is only a bargaining chip" (90). As Bryant notes, this narrator is more than a pawn in a male game, although that is exactly the position in which she finds herself at the beginning of the story. The point is that she can see what Beauty in "The Courtship of Mr. Lyon" could not; this narrator *knows* where she stands in relation to the men around her. When the Beast's valet comes to "collect" her, the narrator dryly comments, "The valet sat up on the box in a natty black and gold livery, clasping, of all things, a bunch of his master's damned white roses as if a gift of flowers would reconcile a woman to any humiliation" (55). She sees nothing romantic in her situation, and through her critical eyes Carter emphasizes the treachery of earlier versions of the tale which do romanticize such a predicament.

As in all versions of the Beauty and the Beast tale, the encounter between the two title characters is a crucial moment in the narrative. Here, the narrator's initial description of the Beast is just as candid as her other observations:

> I never saw a man so big look so two-dimensional, in spite of the quaint elegance of The Beast, in the old-fashioned tailcoat that might, from its looks, have been bought in those distant years before he imposed seclusion on himself; he does not feel he need keep up with the times. There is a crude clumsiness about his outlines, that are on the ungainly, giant side; and he has an odd air of self-imposed restraint, as if fighting a battle with himself to remain upright when he would far rather drop down on all fours. He throws our human aspirations to the godlike sadly awry, poor fellow; only from a distance would you think The Beast not much different from any other man, although he wears a mask with a man's face painted most beautifully on it [53].

She is more disposed to pity the Beast than to fear him. This Beauty is too knowing and too self-aware to succumb to the guilt that plagues other "Beauty" characters, who must first pass through stages of terror and fear. Perhaps part of the narrator's reaction has to do with this Beast. Bryant writes,

"Not only is this girl not your typical Beauty; neither does she face the typical Beast. Just as she is entrapped in an unfamiliar land — demographically, and also socially, sexually — so he is encased in an unfamiliar skin; and, ill-fitted for traditional roles, both are outsiders because of their differences" (91). The Beast's anachronistic clothing, delicate mask, and efforts "to remain upright" combine for an overall image that is hardly imposing in the same way as traditional representations of the Beast. In fact, his attempts to pretend to be human make him seem both vulnerable and a bit ridiculous. While none of the versions of the Beauty and the Beast tale examined here go so far as to illuminate the Beast's point of view, Bryant is correct in pointing to this Beast's particular situation. He is, in comparison to the narrator's father, an alternative to the degenerate and male-dominated world that the narrator already knows. Indeed, even at this early stage in the story, Carter suggests that the Beast might offer something outside of, or at least resistant to, the economic and patriarchal structures that circumscribe the narrator's life.

The Beast's status as an actual alternative to the existence she has always known becomes clear to the narrator herself as she rides out with The Beast and his valet. Her understanding of her own position as an object of male control becomes a way for her to find common ground with The Beast. In a thoroughly revisionist passage, Carter describes the narrator's shrewd analysis of her situation, and of the Beast's:

> A profound sense of strangeness slowly began to possess me. I knew my two companions were not, in any way, as other men, the simian retainer and the master for whom he spoke, the one with clawed forepaws who was in a plot with the witches who let the winds out of their knotted handkerchiefs up towards the Finnish border. I knew they lived according to a different logic than I had done until my father abandoned me to the wild beasts by his human carelessness. This knowledge gave me a certain fearfulness still; but, I would say, not much ... I was a young girl, a virgin, and therefore men denied me rationality just as they denied it to all those who were not exactly like themselves, in all their unreason. I could see not one single soul in that wilderness of desolation all around me, then the six of us — mounts and riders, both — could boast amongst us not one soul, either, since all the best religions in the world state categorically that not beasts nor women were equipped with the flimsy, insubstantial things when the good Lord opened the gates of Eden and let Eve and her familiars tumble out. Understand, then, that though I would not say I privately engaged in metaphysical speculation as we rode through the reedy approaches to the river, I certainly meditated on the nature of my own state, how I had been bought and sold, passed from hand to hand [63].

They are all "other." The narrator finds that she can relate to the existence of The Beast because she lives in a world in which she is defined as other because she is a woman. Both rationality and religion have passed judgment on the narrator; she is less than (hu)man in a power structure that works diligently to demarcate, describe, and categorize according to a fixed notion of unified and coherent identity. The alternative logic The Beast represents begins to appeal to the narrator because it is utterly different from the logic represented by her father and the world as she knows it. In combining "mounts and riders" in her reflections, the narrator further asserts the bond among all creatures excluded from the system of rationality that denies her, as a woman, a soul. In aligning herself with The Beast, and the animals of the party, the narrator finds a way to oppose the system that has denied her a legitimate role.

Eventually, because the narrator will not undress for him first as The Beast requests, The Beast disrobes for her, making it a reciprocal act. The narrator then sheds her connection to the social structures that have oppressed her and tastes another possibility. At the end of the story, the narrative describes the narrator's experience of becoming-other. Rather than return to her father, the narrator offers herself to The Beast. The moment is nuanced and complex. Carter's story does not imagine the process of becoming as simple or easy, nor does it erase the fear that must attend the loss of identity — even if the narrator already sees that identity as fluid and constructed rather than fixed: "Nursery fears made flesh and sinew; earliest and most archaic of fears, fear of devourment. The beast and his carnivorous bed of bone and I, white, shaking, raw, approaching him as if offering, in myself, the key to a peaceable kingdom in which his appetite need not be my extinction. He went still as stone. He was far more frightened of me than I was of him" (67). The narrator has to overcome the socialization process that is here directly linked to the nursery, and to nursery rhymes, in order to become-other, to become-animal. The beast/tiger's response is perhaps even more interesting than the narrator's actions, in that his fear of her signifies his awareness of what she brings with her from the world. However, he does accept her, and the story ends with the narrator's transformation, or becoming: "And each stroke of his tongue ripped off skin after successive skin, all the skins of a life in the world, and left behind a nascent patina of shining hairs. My earrings turned back to water and trickled down my shoulders; I shrugged the drops off my beautiful fur" (67). The Beast licks away the confines of social structures that have defined the narrator as an object for male consumption; he is the agent who causes a kind of change that was denied to the Beauty in "The Courtship of Mr. Lyon." The narrator is reborn as a furred beast without a fixed identity — a truly nomadic subject open to the possibilities of continuous becomings.

In her discussion of how revisions of the Beauty and the Beast tale have shifted over time, Warner points out that late twentieth-century revisions tend to privilege "[t]he attraction of the wild" (307) through the figure of the Beast. According to Warner, the Beast "no longer stands outside [Beauty], the threat of male sexuality in bodily form, or of male authority with all its fearful amorality and social legitimacy [...] but he holds up a mirror to the force of nature within her, which she is invited to accept and allow to grow" (307). In this account, the Beast signifies an idealized animal other through his link to the natural world. Certainly, the beast/tiger of Carter's "The Tiger's Bride" is representative of an alternative to the "civilized" order of the human world. The fact that Carter constructs an opposition between The Beast and the logic of the patriarchal structure also demonstrates that The Beast is depicted in a way that could be seen as problematically romanticized. Bacchilega argues, however, that Carter's story is not about a simplistic return to an idealized notion of nature: "[T]hroughout the telling, the eye-work makes it uncomfortable to view this magic as 'natural.' No return to nature, no simple reversal of the human/beast dichotomy" (99). Bacchilega's insistence on the more complicated nature of the transformation at work in the story seems correct. While Lee's science fictional version of the story seems to hinge upon a series of reversals in order to create the possibility of an alternative to normalizing structures, this narrative moves beyond binary logic so that the narrator's becoming is truly beyond the bounds of any simple set of categories.

The narrator becomes-other through her choice to discard her attachments to the structures of the world she has always known. This is a different choice from that made by the Beauty character in most versions of the tale. Typically when Beauty returns to the Beast, it is not to embrace the possibility of becoming, but rather to submit to the dictates of the world in which she lives. In "The Tiger's Bride," it is crucial to understand that The Beast does not wish to be returned to a human state; he is simply curious about the narrator. There is nothing desirable about being human for The Beast or for the narrator. Carter reimagines the terms of transformation in such a way as to install a new set of ethics into the tale that privileges the process of becoming-animal instead of revealing a stable human subject underneath a beast's mask.

Multiple Retellings, but One Narrative: *Beauty, Sheri S. Tepper*

While the Beauty and the Beast tale is, obviously, a particularly fruitful narrative for writers interested in power and becoming, contemporary fiction contains a wide range of approaches to blending and incorporating fairy tales. Sheri S. Tepper's novel offers multiple examples of revised fairy tales, and it is an interesting text to explore here because it is ultimately a very different kind of story from those discussed above. Like Lee, Tepper combines genres in her rewriting. Her *Beauty* (1991), however, offers a very different approach to bringing the mythical past of the fairy tale into contact with the future world of science fiction. Tepper retells "Sleeping Beauty," "Cinderella," "Snow White," and "The Frog Prince" (a cousin tale to "Beauty and the Beast"), but includes the science fictional device of time travel and offers a dystopian future alongside the magical past.

The novel is almost entirely comprised of the title character's journal, with some brief insertions from her Aunt Carabosse, the fairy of clocks. When the novel opens, Beauty is a duke's daughter in fourteenth-century England who is facing the double threat of a new stepmother and her sixteenth birthday, which is supposed to mark the date of a curse placed upon her when she was a baby. She escapes the curse and her stepmother, leaving her father's house with everyone else in it sound asleep and a rose hedge growing up around it. She winds up encountering time travelers from the twenty-first century just outside the hedge who are recording what they believe to be the end of magic. Beauty spends some time in a horrifying vision of the twenty-first century, and then a few years in the 1990s when she is accosted and raped. Fortunately, she has magical boots (a gift from her real mother, a fairy) to take her back to 1350, where she is able to dupe a nice nobleman into marriage. When Beauty's baby begins to look like her rapist, she spends some time with her mother the fairy in imaginary worlds, and then goes back to England where she encounters her baby as a young woman. Beauty's daughter turns out to be a version of Cinderella, and Beauty plays the role of her fairy godmother.

Eventually, Beauty meets her granddaughter who is Snow White, and plays a part in her tale as well. There is a trip to Faery, a grueling stay in Hell, and finally a trip back to her father's home in England where she encounters her great-grandson, the Frog Prince, whom she kisses back into a prince. At the end of the novel Beauty and the newly restored Frog Prince bring genetically viable pairs, herds, and seeds of every living thing on the planet to the duke's house where they can sleep for as long as might be necessary. Beauty intends to try to save everything in some form. She has already tried to do something about the destruction of the world in the 1990s through activism, and it made no real difference. Therefore, she will attempt to keep everything safe for a possible alternate course of history in some possible future. As it turns out, her fairy Aunt Carabosse had already thought of all of this and had shrunk samples of everything in the world down to a size that could be carried in Beauty's own body, which is why she had been so important to her aunt in the first place. The end of the novel finds Beauty finally going to sleep, the very thing she has resisted doing from the beginning of the narrative. Saving the world, or, rather, preserving the world for the possibility of the future when humanity may be able to try again — hopefully, with better results — is the end goal of Tepper's novel. Fairy tales, fantasy, and science fiction are no match for the onward march of history. It is a novel that, even as it reconsiders individual tales, closes them down into a larger monolithic narrative in a manner that is inconsistent with either a revisionist critique, or the creation of an ethics of becoming. However, it is useful to explore how this novel operates in order to clarify how it differs from the works described above and below.

When Beauty arrives in the twenty-first century, she finds an enormous hive-like building with no windows, no comfort, no real food, and absolutely no beauty: "I learned very soon that there was nothing beautiful in that place. Even the things they watched were not beautiful. There was no contrast between beauty and ugliness. There was only ugliness" (83).[9] Because the novel takes the form of Beauty's journal, the reader knows no more than she does about why things are so bad at this point, but there are hints about all of the free space going to a program called "Fidipur," which obviously sounds like "Feed the Poor." Tepper later inserts a more detailed explanation of programs designed to feed an ever-growing population. Beauty languishes in confinement in the twenty-first century, but she is not there long; the travelers who bring her there do not wish to stay either, and they escape with her back to the 1990s. There are other time-travelers in the 1990s whom Beauty and her companions encounter in the homeless shelter where they first stay. Beauty learns that the future only gets worse and worse after the time she experienced in the late twenty-first century; she meets a mother and daughter from the twenty-second who had tried to kill themselves — as part of a mass attempt, apparently — but who couldn't fit into the chutes. Beauty later finds the mother holding a bloody knife, sitting next to her dead daughter singing, "'Down ... down ... down ... to happyland'" (97). Thus, Tepper's narrative is built around the idea that the world is doomed and headed for the destruction that Beauty glimpses. Unlike the dystopian narratives examined in the third chapter of this book, Tepper's novel does not offer anything like a critical framework in which to understand the social disintegration she describes. Instead, the losses of magic and beauty are treated as inevitable outcomes of an unstoppable march of progress, and only a return to the past is offered as a potential solution.

The fairy tales in Tepper's narrative all take place in the past; there seems to be no room for them in the present or the future. Yet, even in the past her heroines are not exactly what the reader might expect. Beauty's daughter turns out to be a sex-crazed version of Cinderella who murders one of her stepsisters in cold blood before she marries Prince Charming. Her "happily ever after" is short-lived because she dies in childbirth, and her husband's only reaction to her death is relief. The child turns out to be Snow White who is, unfortunately, incredibly stupid, and while she does marry her prince with Beauty's help, there is no satisfaction for the reader in her story either. Making Snow White obviously stupid is, nevertheless, a kind of revisionist rewriting; it highlights the fact that the original tale assumes she is both passive and overly credulous. ("Oh, why, yes, I'd love an apple, strange old woman to whom I should not be speaking.") Similarly, Cinderella's scheming and sex-crazed behavior is not that strange considering the basic premise of her story. Still, Tepper's approach to retelling the narratives leaves their problematic underlying assumptions (about gender roles, stable identities, heteronormative behaviors, class structures, etc.) intact.

Snow White's son shows up at the end of the novel in the form of a frog, and at last we have a hero who is worth something. Beauty — now very old — kisses him back into a prince, and he finally seems to be an heir worthy of her legacy. Perhaps the most interesting aspect of the way that Tepper constructs the tales in this novel has to do with the thread that holds them together: Beauty. She is part of each one of them, her role changing from heroine to fairy godmother to ancient grandmother. Even more interestingly, she is aware of them *as* fairy tales that she has come across in various forms in the 1990s. When she tracks down her daughter and recognizes her as Cinderella, Beauty has already aged a great deal due to all of her time traveling and the time she has spent in Faery where she learned how to perform the magic she was capable of as a result of being half fairy herself:

> I had figured out who I was that morning. Even I, who had never cared for children's stories, could not have failed to notice what role I was playing. In the twentieth I had seen Disney, after all. Though Elly and I were not privileged to be attended by singing mice, it did not surprise me greatly that this segment of my life had gained a spurious immortality, a glossy, oversimplified and untruthful half-life [263].

There is a sense of narrative destiny about the story of Cinderella, and Beauty simply helps the process take shape. The same is true of her granddaughter's coughing up of the poison apple. Beauty plays her part in each tale, occasionally even creating moments of interesting demystification, but the overall effect is one of closure.

The one place where there is a sense of potential in this novel is in its treatment of the experience of love. The narrative creates a contrast between the "glossy, oversimplified" fairy tales that Beauty encounters and the actual love that Beauty feels for Giles. He had been a man-at-arms when she was a duke's daughter, and was sent away for his clear preference for her. Throughout the novel Giles and Beauty try to find their way to each other, and they do have a brief but passionate encounter outside the ball as Cinderella is capturing Prince Charming. However, it is not until they are very old that Beauty finally finds Giles for more than a few days. Beauty explains, "Our love, mine, was made of such little things [...] he would bring me something and sit on the side of the bed while I drank it and call me Beauty, though I was an old, white-haired hag with pouches beneath my eyes and lines around my mouth even then" (405). A familiar contrast is set up here between romanticized fairy tale love and the kind of love that is constituted by everyday gestures. The point seems to be that it is this more ordinary, mundane, and much more significant form of love that Beauty must attempt to save from the future that she has seen. The novel links Beauty's love for Giles with a kind of awe and respect for the natural world when Beauty writes, "And the love would come up from inside me like water rising in a well. Not lust, not romance, but something kindlier than that. The feeling one has watching a sunrise sometimes. The feeling one has watching kittens at play. The feeling one has seeing a rose bloom beside the window[...] A perfection of being" (405). A sentimental, idealized vision of what is worthwhile in life is set apart from the despair of the future, and even the carelessness of the 1990s. Interestingly, the fairy tales in the novel also seem to be part of the larger category of things that are problematic; at least, they do not contribute to the more perfect love that Beauty finds with Giles.

Tepper's *Beauty* contains many of the elements present in the other revisionist works discussed in this chapter, but her focus on bringing the tales together rather than on encouraging the proliferation of their possibilities leads to a damaging sense of narrative closure. Still, there are playful moments in the novel that could be redeemed by their removal from the larger narrative, and the pairing of revised fairy tales with time travel could be a useful device. In terms of creating ways of confronting the normalizing power structures that are perpetuated by the original tales, however, Tepper's novel simply has its protagonist go back to sleep.

A Fairy Tale of Becoming: Oranges Are Not the Only Fruit, *Jeanette Winterson*

Jeanette Winterson's *Oranges Are Not the Only Fruit* (1985) is a semi-autobiographical novel that challenges readers to rethink the status and position of a given story. Proliferation and the creation of new possibilities mark every page of this text. The narrative is loosely structured according to the first eight books of the Bible, and a fictionalized autobiographical storyline constantly collides with Winterson's versions of fairy tales, quest narratives of the Arthurian variety, and internal dialogues — often involving a friendly demon. Winterson uses the Bible as both a structuring device and a counternarrative to her own story. The debate about whether the Bible is history or myth underlies Winterson's project in the novel by forcing the reader to question if those two things are really all that different. Within the main storyline of *Oranges*, fairy tales are a source of disquiet for a young Jeanette who hears adults referring to the fact that the "right man" would eventually surface (72).

In particular, Jeanette is critical of the tale of "Beauty and the Beast," which she finds in a book of fairy tales at the library:

> In this story, a beautiful young woman finds herself the forfeit of a bad bargain made by her father. As a result, she has to marry an ugly beast, or dishonour her family forever. Because she is good, she obeys. On her wedding night, she gets into bed with the beast, and feeling pity that everything should be so ugly, gives it a little kiss. Immediately, the beast is transformed into a handsome young prince, and they both live happily ever after.
>
> I wondered if the woman married to a pig had read this story. She must have been awfully disappointed if she had. And what about my Uncle Bill, he was horrible, and hairy, and looking at the picture transformed princes aren't meant to be hairy at all.
>
> Slowly I closed the book. It was clear that I had stumbled on a terrible conspiracy [72].

Reading and storytelling are central to Winterson's text, and the postmodern metanarrative she employs is one way of revealing and undermining the assumptions of traditional tales. Jeanette's adoptive parents have not included fairy tales in the stories they have read to her; in fact, Jeanette's mother has altered the ending of *Jane Eyre* whenever she reads it to Jeanette so that Jane marries the young missionary St. John Rivers and chooses a life devoted to God. Therefore, when Jeanette encounters the Beauty and the Beast tale she is both uninitiated in the *usual* romanticized myths of patriarchy, and old enough to see the ways in which it does not reflect the realities of the lives of the women around her. Jeanette's analysis of the story continues:

> There are women in the world.
> There are men in the world.
> And there are beasts.
> What do you do if you marry a beast?
> Kissing them didn't always help.
> And beasts are crafty. They disguise themselves like you and I.

One. *Beastly Beauty and Other Revisioned Fairy Tales*   57

> Like the wolf in "Little Red Riding Hood."
> Why had no one told me? Did that mean no one else knew?
> Did that mean that all over the globe, in all innocence,
>   women were marrying beasts? [72–73]

Clearly, the narrative structure of the Beauty and the Beast tale is unacceptable to Jeanette. The humor of the passages quoted above helps to establish Jeanette's distance from discourses of heterosexual romance grounded in patriarchal exchange. She never accepts the idea that she could or should marry a beast; instead, she begins from the premise that there must be an alternative to such a fate.

The inserted fairy tales in *Oranges* are, in part, a vehicle for questioning the status of stories. It is difficult to think of any kind of story which is more easily identifiable *as* a fictional story than a fairy tale. Winterson uses both the legitimized status of fairy tales and their self-referentially fictional status in order to provoke more questions about the traditions that form the reader's world view. In the novel, fairy tales both follow prescribed formats and break with them. They are undoubtedly fairy tales, but they mirror Jeanette's story in ways that destabilize the conventions of competition among women, the knight in shining armor, and the happy marriage at the end. Laurel Bollinger describes Winterson's rewriting as a form of parody: "Postmodern parody, no longer a strictly comic genre, enables parodists to repeat material we define as (capital L) Literature with ironic difference in order both to explore and to confront their position within the tradition — a possibility particularly valuable for members of oppressed or marginalized social groups" (375). Jeanette's story has no place in the traditions of fairy tales and the Bible, so Winterson must create a new tradition in which Jeanette may be located as a subject with a voice. But perhaps constructing a clear subject position is not the point. Perhaps the new stories are meant to offer a more troubled notion of subjectivity — even a nomadic subjectivity.

In the chapter entitled "Genesis," the reader learns of Jeanette's early life with her adoptive mother. As in the Bible, the chapter deals with creation, and specifically the creation of Jeanette as a socialized subject. The chapter also provides information about Jeanette's mother, and how her mother's earlier adventurous life led her to the church. Here a fairy tale breaks the autobiographical narrative for the first of many instances:

> Once upon a time there was a brilliant and beautiful princess, so sensitive that the death of a moth could distress her for weeks on end. Her family knew of no solution. Advisers wrung their hands, sages shook their heads, brave kings left unsatisfied. So it happened for many years, until one day, out walking in the forest, the princess came to the hut of an old hunchback who knew the secrets of

magic. This ancient creature perceived in the princess a woman of great energy and resourcefulness [9].

The princess decides to take the hunchback's place rather than go back home. This story deals with Jeanette's mother's conversion, but it also foreshadows Jeanette's departure at the end of the novel. Obviously, the princess is not to be condemned. It would have been easy for Winterson to fit Jeanette's mother neatly into the archetypal role of "evil step-mother," but that is not how fairy tales work in this novel. Instead, the story presents a somewhat refreshing change from the autobiographical narrative which is strictly limited to Jeanette's point of view. This first fairy tale intrusion is an example of one of the functions the fantastic stories serve in the novel as a whole; it is both an elaboration of and an alternative to the autobiographical narrative. It is also a way to destabilize traditional fairy tale narratives which foster competition rather than cooperation among women.

Sir Perceval, an Arthurian knight in pursuit of the Holy Grail, appears at a few different moments in the text: "Sir Perceval has been in the wood for many days now. His armour is dull, his horse tired. The last food he ate was a bowl of bread and milk given to him by an old woman. Other knights have been this way, he can see their tracks, their despair, for one, even his bones" (134). This particular passage occurs just after Jeanette's mother has committed the betrayal of going along with the pastor and blaming Jeanette's lesbianism on the notion that women have been given too much power in the church. Like Perceval, Jeanette is truly on her own and struggling to find her way. She too knows that others have had to face similar challenges, but at the moment she is still alone. With Perceval's story, Winterson plays off of a traditional foundational narrative for England, and one that is particularly masculine. Perceval's story also serves to bring up one of the oldest narrative archetypes: the quest. Jeanette's quest is made to parallel Perceval's, so that one is not privileged over the other. The multiple, sometimes conflicting, stories surrounding Jeanette's life give the narrative an unstable core that reflects an ethics of becoming. Nowhere is that ethics more pronounced than in one of the inserted tales — in Winnet's story.

Winnet's story appears in the last chapter of the novel, entitled "Ruth." In effect, it provides an allegorical retelling of Jeanette's whole story. Although readers will have become accustomed to Winterson's particular brand of fairy tales at this point in the narrative, the revisionist aspects of Winnet's story are of a new order. There is no royal birthright (that we know of), no "true" family that has been lost, and, perhaps most importantly, no happy marriage at the end. Possibly the most glaring lack is the absence of any romantic narrative at all. It is a story built on the foundations of fairy tale and quest, but developed in a postmodern mode that focuses on language, representation, and subjectivity.

For example, at one point Winnet leaves her studies (with a sorcerer) behind in order to make her own way and finds herself in a different culture with unknown rules, but she remains conflicted about her past:

> The woman tried to teach Winnet her language, and Winnet learned the words but not the language. Certain constructions baffled her, and in an argument they could always be used against her, because she could not use them in return. But mostly this didn't happen. The villagers were simple and kind, not questioning the world. They didn't expect Winnet to talk very much. Winnet wanted to talk. She had left her school and her followers far behind, she wanted to talk about the nature of the world, why it was there at all, and what they were all doing on it. Yet at the same time she knew her old world had much in it that was wrong. If she talked about it, good and bad, they would think her mad, and then she would have no one [153].

Winnet wants to confront the big questions, but how? And with whom? Winnet's dilemma in her new life is more than we find out about Jeanette's new life. This particular passage explains a great deal about the sort of struggles Jeanette has, and is itself an important example of the difficulties of language and representation. Winterson, the author, has written a story about a character named Jeanette, whose experiences are clearly related to Winterson's own experiences as a child and adolescent, yet *Oranges* is definitely a fictional narrative. And within that fictional narrative, Winnet becomes a kind of hyper-fictionalized Jeanette, struggling through fairy tales and quests in a way that mirrors Jeanette's experiences in a world that is much like our own — much like Winterson's own. Story-telling is linked to a notion of multiplicity, but not just multiple versions of one story. This is not the same thing as Carter revising the Beauty and the Beast tale in two different ways. Here, Winterson uses fantastic fairy tale narratives in a manner that destabilizes the expectation of unified subjectivity. Is Jeanette a version of Winterson? Is Winnet a version of Jeanette who is a version of Winterson? If we can't trace the relationships among the different versions it soon seems silly even to try. They are related but distinct, proliferating possibilities.

Similarly, the way the narrative is constructed works against a simplistic relativism that might advocate for each of us to write our own stories. The more important point has to do with what kinds of stories we choose to tell about ourselves. In the spirit of embracing a nomadic subjectivity that is open to continuous becomings, Winterson offers a narrative that multiplies possibilities instead of pinning them down. Jan Rosemergy points out that "[i]n the Winnet fantasy and in the Perceval myth, the quest is not completed; both end with the quester still searching, suggesting that the individual's quest for identity is likewise incomplete" (251). Perhaps the issue is not really whether or not Winnet or Jeanette or Perceval reach a stated goal, and the notion of a "quest for identity" is in itself a problematic idea in the context of this novel. The open-ended fairy tale of Winnet is suggestive of tales to come, of further possibilities. Rather than remain in a stable location, Winnet leaves the village described in the passage above and heads for open waters and new adventures. A fixed identity seems to be the last thing Winnet is after; her tale demonstrates a clear emphasis on becoming rather than being.

Still, it must be noted that there is a way in which the larger narrative structure of *Oranges* can be read as closing down certain possibilities, rather than providing opportunities for their proliferation. Laura Doan argues that "Winterson clearly presents lesbianism as the only viable and intelligible alternative for Jeanette; yet, on a fundamental level, Winterson remains (albeit unwillingly) in the realm of parody, of imitation, in the unproblematic reversal of binary terms" (146). While Jeanette's world view includes a complete reversal of the usual categories of what is "natural" or "unnatural"—consider her response to the Beauty and the Beast tale—Doan does not see any evidence that *Oranges* gets beyond the kind of binary logic that requires such terms. Many critics puzzle over how to read the fairy tales and quest narratives in *Oranges*. As I mention above, Bollinger, like Doan, sees postmodern parody as the primary explanation. In contrast, Lauren Rusk sees the use of multiple genres as a formal strategy for handling the deeply complex autobiographical material of the text: "A generically unstable work may [...] better convey the experience of being shunned for loving someone you cannot [...] introduce to your mother or walk with, arm in arm" (110). Through the complex intermingling of genres, Winterson evokes a narrative instability that represents the lack of a familiar, recognizable generic or narrative structure for describing Jeanette's experiences. Unlike Doan, Rusk argues that "as she grows, Jeanette engages in an ongoing struggle with [...] dualistic thinking and more often than not subverts it" (121) and points out that "the author subverts binarism by declining to identify either the younger protagonist or the older narrator as the originator of the fantasy interludes" (122). The binary structure that Doan sees as limiting for *Oranges* can be reevaluated when the focus is placed upon the alternative narratives within the text. Isabel C. Anievas Gamallo examines the inserted tales of Perceval and Winnet against critical work on myth, folklore, and fairy tales—including work by Zipes—and comes to the conclusion that "[t]hese fantastic tales comment on, explain, displace, condense, and/or allegorize some of the crucial elements displayed in the linear progression of realistic events, subverting the possibility of a single authoritative reading of her fiction" (126). Ultimately, even if the character Jeanette is unable to think outside of the binary logic that requires her to think in terms of "natural" or "unnatural," the inserted tales provide Winterson with the means to offer alternative narratives that need not adhere to the logic of the world Jeanette inhabits.

Along with the many critical views, in the chapter entitled "Deuteronomy," the narrator seems to add her own instructions as to how to read the novel:

> Of course that is not the whole story, but that is the way with stories; we make them what we will. It's a way of explaining the universe while leaving the universe unexplained, it's a way of keeping it all alive, not boxing it into time. Everyone who tells a story tells it differently, just to remind us that everybody sees it differently. Some people say there are true things to be found, some people say all kinds of things can be proved. I don't believe them. The only thing for certain is how complicated it all is, like a string full of knots. It's all there but hard to find the beginning and impossible to fathom the end. The best you can do is admire the cat's cradle, and maybe knot it up a bit more. History should be a hammock for swinging and a game for playing, the way cats play. Claw it, chew it, rearrange it and at bedtime it's still a ball of string full of knots. Nobody should mind [93].

The novel is concerned with history, time, and story-telling. Winterson knots up the string of history in her own ways, and plays with our conceptions of reality in the process. However, one point about the passage above falls short of the novel itself. History may continue to be a ball of knots, but it is altered when old narrative structures must give way to new constructions. As a coming-out narrative, the novel confronts and critiques heteronormative ideologies, as well as male-centered myths and structures. In order to achieve alternatives to the problematic power structures being critiqued, Winterson creates her own modes of representation. She asks the reader continually to readjust to different notions of reality. Rewriting fairy tales is one way to rebuild our sense of the world and how we live in it. When the autobiographical narrative is broken by fairy tales, the reader is forced to confront the concept of representation in a way that is not necessary when reading a more traditional narrative. On another level, the fairy tales offer possibilities for alternatives in a way that the autobiographical narrative cannot. Winterson uses the fantastic mode of fairy tale in order to play with possibilities that do not exist in the more realistic narrative, producing sites of becoming that resist the heteronormative discourses associated with the "reality" of the narrative.

Near the end of the novel, Jeanette discusses her conception of art, and of what art can accomplish:

> If a potter has an idea, she makes it into a pot, and it exists beyond her, in its own separate life. She uses a physical substance to display her thoughts. If I use a

metaphysical substance to display my thoughts, I might be anywhere at one time, influencing a number of things, just as the potter and her pottery can exert influence in different places [169].

Winterson rewrites foundational myths in her own way, and on her own terms, highlighting the idea that art can open up worlds, that we each have the power to recreate our own worlds in ways that embrace nomadic subjectivities and the potential for becoming. Writing — particularly rewriting — is a way to redefine the world. Winterson gives us stories that re-inscribe meaning so that we may understand the world in new ways. These new ways of understanding are sites of rupture, sites of possibility, opened up through Winterson's creative play with stories and storytelling, and developing an ethics of becoming.

Tales of Becoming

Fairy tales provide contemporary women writers with the opportunity to critique entrenched power relations, but also with the means to reimagine those relations in terms that replace moralizing discourse with possibilities for becoming. While readers immediately recognize the didactic purposes of most fairy tales, their socializing functions are not always as recognizable as the more overt morals embedded within the tales that are usually designed for children. Contemporary revisionist rewriting is a way of focusing the reader's attention upon aspects of fairy tales that may previously have gone unnoticed so that the socializing function is demystified, and the values that the tales pass on to future generations are made more obvious. In Carter's "The Courtship of Mr. Lyon" and McKinley's *Beauty*, for example, the reader is asked to reconsider Beauty's economic dependence upon her father and then the Beast. Although the two versions of the tale treat Beauty's economic status in utterly different ways, they both demand that the reader reconsider assumptions about how more traditional versions of the tale portray her dependencies. Once the power structures that underlie fairy tales have been exposed, it is possible for contemporary women writers to create alternative tales with different ways of conceiving of relationships and power.

An example of an alternative version of the Beauty and the Beast tale is portrayed by both McKinley, in *Rose Daughter*, and Lee in "Beauty." In these contemporary revisions, the Beast is not transformed at the end of the tale. This seemingly small change is a drastic shift in the ethics of the tale. If the Beast remains a Beast, he remains other, and the kind of order that is supposed

One. *Beastly Beauty and Other Revisioned Fairy Tales* 63

to be restored at the end of the fairy tale is suspended. Beauty does not only fall in love with a Beast, she marries and lives with one. An even more drastic example of a revision that undermines the traditional function of the tale is Carter's "The Tiger's Bride," in which Beauty transcends any fear of the other and actually embraces the possibility of becoming-beast. Finally, there is also the fairy tale of Winnet, which is Jeanette's chosen alternative to the Beauty and the Beast tale in Winterson's *Oranges Are Not the Only Fruit*. Winnet's story is outside the bounds of any available fairy tale narrative; it is a model for a kind of make-your-own fairy tale, in which the restrictions are loosened and the individual is given license to decide his or her own place in the larger social structure. In both Carter's and Winterson's reinvented fairy tales, the emphasis is on a proliferation of possibilities. Importantly, Tepper's lengthy novel *Beauty* demonstrates that not all contemporary women's revisions of fairy tales lead to an opening out into new narrative structures. By utilizing embedded fairy tales according to a concept of narrative "destiny," Tepper prevents her tales from making any truly significant break with traditional versions. In addition, the overall structure of the novel leads to a formal closure in which the individual tales cannot — and do not — matter in any significant way.

In the revisionist fairy tales of Carter, McKinley, Lee, and Winterson, the need to reexamine the narrative structures that inform contemporary women's lives is clear. Also clear is the way in which rewriting can work to destabilize the power formations that rely on coherent, unified notions of identity and that that underlie traditional versions of narratives or tales. The revised tales examined in this chapter work toward new possibilities for the kinds of stories that women writers can tell by revisiting, remaking — and in the process, unmaking — the stories that we have all been told. The new stories privilege becoming over being, and the need to embrace rather than to fear the other. The underlying logic of a tale like Beauty and the Beast, which is mired in restrictive social norms, is dismantled and replaced by an ethical model of potential. There is a movement away from binary thinking and toward hybrid beasts, open-ended quests, and new tales. Ultimately, these revisioned fairy tales demonstrate that contemporary women writers have found ways to make use of the stories they have inherited. The emphasis placed on past, present, and future throughout the revisions in this chapter — from the closed off past of "once upon a time" to fairy tales set in the future libraries of books yet to be written — linear, circumscribed concepts of time are consistently replaced with a concept of openness to revision and rewriting throughout different times. Storytelling itself is revealed as an open process of becoming, and revisionist rewriting is an ethical approach to stories that have latent potential and continue to be important parts of our cultural imagination.

Two

Tampering with Time in Historical Narratives

History and the Fantastic

Fairy tales are not the only type of narrative contemporary women writers revise. Historical events — both momentous and overlooked — frequently provide writers with material for revision. Like fairy tales, history is often written to be instructive; we learn what it means to be who we are through our histories. Narratives that define us in such direct ways are particularly ripe for contemporary revision. Unlike fairy tales, however, the history we learn as children is regularly defined as official, objective, or otherwise unassailable. Rewriting history is, then, a fundamentally different process from offering the latest revision of a fairy tale or myth; revising history requires that a writer either dismiss the possibility of "real" or "true" history, or that she question the need for such a construct in the context of her work. In either case the writer's revisionist history will question not just the dominant version of an historical event, but the manner in which history is recorded in the first place.

This chapter explores novels by Octavia E. Butler, Angela Carter, and Jeanette Winterson, focusing on their interventions into history in order to analyze their use of historical facts in the creation of fictional worlds. The choice of texts is informed not simply by their focus on history, but also — and crucially — by their integration of the literary fantastic into representations of the past. The novels examined below incorporate elements of the fantastic (such as time travel, the ability to fly, and even fairy tale figures) in order to redefine the relationship between the past and present. Fantastic intrusions into historical narratives serve to clarify the extent to which what happened in the past is constituted in the present. By demonstrating how the past is created through/in/by the present, the texts in question here offer new hope for the future. If the narratives we have of the past can be reworked and rewritten, it is no longer possible to see history as the march of progress — or as in any way inevitable. Reopening the past to new understandings and new possibilities means that nothing is closed to the potential of an ethics of becoming.

As we are often reminded, historical knowledge is the property of those who have the power to make their stories heard. Cultural memories are shaped by the dominant forces of the past and present; current discursive formations will have at least as much control over what constitutes "history" as those responsible for recording it in the moment. There is, of course, an enormous body of work that addresses these issues. In this context, what is important is to consider how contemporary women writers use the fantastic to address the production of historical knowledge — and, crucially, to understand the relationship between subjectivity and that knowledge. One method employed to reopen historical narratives by the writers discussed in the chapter is the recovery of unheard, silenced, and subjugated voices so that they are included in our cultural memories. Feminist historian Jane Haggis describes the kind of historical work that aims to reintegrate lost "voices" as mistakenly "placing them within a past presumed knowable and transparently reconstructed in the historian's narrative" (162). And here is where the fantastic becomes so important. Through the incorporation of the fantastic, the narratives in this chapter resist metahistorical claims of "Truth" or "authenticity," and thus allow new histories and stories to be told.

In order to decenter historical metanarratives and open space for alternative narratives, it is necessary to expose the machinations of historical knowledge. Indeed, Haggis describes an alternative approach to history that embraces the poststructuralist emphases on "meaning and discourse rather than experience and voice" (162). The texts discussed below engage in a critique of the procedures whereby history is cut off from the present so that it solidifies into something that seems unified and coherent — something that is about static being rather than becoming. This solidified object of the past — created by closed historical narratives — is broken open in the process of revisionist rewriting which requires a new, multi-directional understanding of the relationship between past and present.

In "Nietzsche, Genealogy, History," Michel Foucault describes a form of historical investigation that is meant to challenge Western metanarratives of linear progress. The narratives discussed below engage in similar practices of disturbance and fragmentation, making them examples of the kind of genealogical histories for which Foucault advocated. They are not interested in leaving history intact, nor are they content to fabricate alternative worlds and/or pasts that would allow the actual events of our collective past to remain untouched. Instead, they focus on the "sentiments, love, conscience, instincts" (153) that Foucault lists in ways that reimagine the association between the past and present. In other words, they reopen historical narratives by telling stories that engage with the constructions of individual subjectivities.

One of Foucault's particular emphases in his discussions of genealogy and history is the process whereby history is inscribed on the body. Importantly, the novels considered in this chapter share Foucault's concern with the body as a site of historical construction, and they demonstrate that concern through different uses of the fantastic. In *Kindred*, Butler's protagonist bears the physical marks of history when she travels into the future. Winterson's *The Passion* begins with a description of Napoleon's size and appetite and of the horrible cold that bores into the bodies of the men in his army. Her *Sexing the Cherry* dwells in descriptions of outrageously violent acts perpetrated in the name of historical justice. Carter's *Nights at the Circus* is obsessed with circus bodies, freak shows, and even the bodies of women consigned to a panopticon. The point is that, in all of the novels, the historical production of bodies is central to the understanding of history being developed; bodies are defined by normative discourses, and regulated by the various power structures at work in the social settings of the narratives. By focusing on the existence of bodies in time, in history, the narratives in this chapter challenge the dominant historical narrative of history as the march of ever increasing freedom. Understanding how bodies, and subjectivities, are constructed in and through their historical contexts helps to illustrate power's productive and constraining operations. However, as shall become clear, the historically produced bodies of the novels are not entirely defined by the histories with which the reader is familiar, leaving room for new possibilities.

By concentrating on the details of everyday life and the production of the body through historical conditions, genealogical investigation is highly attuned to the power structures that influence historical knowledge. Butler, Winterson, and Carter reappropriate the past in their novels in ways that allow them to reopen, or even to reverse, what Foucault might call "relationship[s] of forces" ("Nietzsche" 154). Within the novels, characters engage in varying degrees of rebellious activity: teaching slaves to read, plotting to overthrow the occupying forces in Venice, murdering hypocritical Puritans when they visit a whorehouse, and aiding Marxist terrorists. These politicized activities on the part of individual characters relate to the novels' larger engagement with genealogical historical investigation. All three writers use the device of historical fiction in order to engage in genealogical investigations that then open up space for "reversals" at the level of undoing the hard line between fact and fiction, undermining heterosexist and patriarchal norms, and recoding the relationship between past and present.

Trauma and Becoming

Trauma has been an important site of inquiry related to the analysis of cultural and literary representations of the past, in part because it is located at the crossroads between poststructuralism and psychoanalysis. An understanding of some of the key elements of the discussions surrounding trauma and trauma theory can help to make sense of how fantastic fiction can be a particularly important way to rethink history. A traumatic experience wounds or injures at an emotional level to the extent that the experience itself may be repressed in order to safeguard against further psychological damage. In Freudian terms, as Cathy Caruth explains, a trauma "is experienced too soon, too unexpectedly, to be fully known and is therefore not available to consciousness until it imposes itself again, repeatedly, in the nightmares and repetitive actions of the survivor" (4).

The unknowable nature of traumatic experience is precisely what interests Caruth in her work on trauma. However, the notion of *repressed* memories has become less prevalent in trauma theory. Work with victims of what is now classified as Post Traumatic Stress Disorder (PTSD) has led to the proposal that traumatic experiences are not actually repressed memories. Instead, the belief is that a traumatic experience is so overwhelming to the body's systems that the brain is unable to record the experience as a memory at all.[1] The individual's understanding of history — if historical trauma is the subject — is then limited by the body's ability to process what it experiences. If Foucault emphasizes that the body is produced by history, trauma theory teaches that the body defines what constitutes history. There is no "true" history outside of or beyond the way individual subjects perceive and record their experiences. So, just as the power structures of a given time and place produce particular bodies (and the subjects that are tied to those bodies), individual bodies interpret and create the narratives that constitute history. Understanding the construction of historical knowledge as bound up in the way individual subjects and collective systems of power operate helps to clarify how fantastic fiction can intervene into assumptions about the past.

Kirby Farrell, whose emphasis is on *Post-Traumatic Culture,* relocates trauma in social and collective rather than specifically individual experience: "Post-traumatic culture registers the dissonance — the shock — of meeting long-denied realities that threaten our individual and collective self-esteem" (Farrell

15). Unfortunately, or perhaps inevitably, history is full of events and deeds that could easily be termed "traumatic." The need to return to these historical moments is symptomatic of trauma. Indeed, the *denial* of history is precisely how trauma is perpetuated. An individual relives a brush with death over and over in dreams; a society relives its darkest moments over and over in films, television shows, history books, etc. Thinking further along these lines means conceiving of history as a process of return and reevaluation — a model that bears much in common with the genealogical approach Foucault advocates.

In fact, some trauma theorists discuss cultural/historical trauma in terms of its ability to reflect, refract, and even resist power structures. Laurie Vickroy, through studying fictional representations of trauma, concludes that

> trauma, and the literary writers from various backgrounds, challenge power relations, subjectivity and institutions as they have been formulated in Western culture. The fact that trauma [...] is often created out of cultural conflicts and attempts to efface certain cultures (and by extension the identities of individuals therein) makes it especially important to understand the nature of these conflicts and the mistakes of the past [221].

Traumatic events — at least those that occur on a cultural scale — are frequently the result of shifting power formations and the attendant struggles such shifts produce. Importantly, trauma itself can be read as a "challenge [to] power relations" in that it leads to an examination of the processes through which the traumatic event was created. The emphases on critical analysis of social structures and the possibility of challenging such structures through historical inquiry are central concerns in trauma theory and in genealogical history. Dominick LaCapra is troubled by the emphasis on repetition and rewriting, especially in Caruth's work, to which he contrasts the concept of "working through." For LaCapra, "[n]arrative at best helps one not to change the past through a dubious rewriting of history but to work through posttraumatic symptoms in the present in a manner that opens possible futures" (121–22).[2] LaCapra fears a totalizing or sacralized concept of trauma (123), which would certainly be problematic. The use of the term here is meant to highlight the aspects of trauma that are akin to becoming — to the process of responding to a past that seems unknowable.

At least part of the reason for rewriting the past may be tied to the nature of trauma, which suggests that although the traumatic experience can never be directly accessed, it requires that we return to and attempt to "come to terms with" the trauma itself. For an individual, such a return is a psychological phenomenon that may take the form of dreams or flashbacks. On a larger, cultural scale, returning to traumatic moments means confronting events — although always in a mediated fashion — that have helped shape the present. The nature of the trauma may be obvious in some cases. *Kindred*, for example, is a novel in which Butler contends with slavery in the antebellum South and explores how the present continues to be bound up in a past that so many Americans refuse to confront. In other cases, the traumatic quality of the history or event may be less apparent. According to Farrell, "Because cultural memory is necessarily overdetermined, past injury can be ambiguous or even apocryphal and still be damaging" (24). Regarding the revisionist works considered in this chapter, traumatic events include large nation-changing events such as the beheading of King Charles II in Winterson's *Sexing the Cherry* and the Napoleanic Wars in her *The Passion*, as well as the rise of Marxist thought in Russia in Carter's *Nights at the Circus*.[3] However, traumatic cultural memory in those works also extends to the gendered division of labor, heterosexist and Puritan sexual codes, and normalizing power structures of various sizes and mechanisms.

Representing the Past

Formally, returning to historical traumas requires complicated confrontations with the very notion of representation. How do we reveal/revisit/reopen something that we cannot access? Caruth and other trauma theorists suggest that trauma is a way into the problem of representation and that history's inaccessibility is exactly the condition we must accept. Linda Hutcheon discusses how postmodern writers deal with the problem of representing history with her now famous and often-quoted concept of historiographic metafiction, which "self-consciously reminds us that, while events did occur in the real empirical past, we name and constitute those events as historical facts by selection and narrative positioning. And, even more basically, we only know of those past events through their discursive inscription, through their traces in the present" (Hutcheon 97). In order to represent the past, a postmodern writer must also find a way to, simultaneously, represent the problem of representing the past. Each historical event is embedded in ideological and discursive constructions that have created meanings for that event. Part of the nature of a postmodern rethinking and revisioning of traumatic cultural memories is precisely its ability to point out their embeddedness and to suggest that they can be known and understood in different ways. In terms of the novels discussed below, this means linking the present and the past in provocative ways that demystify and reopen the historical past.

In her description of historiographic metafiction, Hutcheon further explains that the work of maintaining a vital awareness of the processes through which historical knowledge is produced is linked to a form of complicitous critique. She writes, "Postmodernism marks a challenge to received ideas, but it also acknowledges the power of those ideas and is willing to exploit that power in order to effect its own critique" (Hutcheon 209). The *trope* of trauma is one such idea. Traumatic history as a process of repetition, rewriting, and reopening is a parallel model in that it acknowledges the power of ideas, concepts, and events but also can create reversals. The model of historiographic metafiction is, then, useful to keep in mind. However, Hutcheon's term and analysis do not extend to the fantastic literary elements that are central in the texts discussed below. These fantastic elements are crucial in linking the past and the present, so that time travel and imaginative fantasies within the novels work to develop the theoretical relationship between the past and the present. The point is that these texts break with realistic narratives in ways that produce alternative realities. They do not take us out of history, but they do reopen it to new possibilities that are perhaps beyond the scope of what Hutcheon has in mind when defining historiographic metafiction.

While many writers emphasize a return to traumatic moments in history, their tendency is to privilege a highly realistic model of representation. The narratives I have chosen do occasionally choose realism to depict historical events, particularly Butler's *Kindred*, but they also employ fantastic literary techniques. Avishai Margalit argues that "modern shared memory is located between the push and pull of two poles: history and myth" (63). The genre choices Butler, Winterson, and Carter make are entirely valid if Margalit is correct. Traumatic cultural memories provide an even stronger case because the "unreality" or unrepresentability of trauma requires something more than what can only be a failed attempt at direct representation.[4] Science fiction, magic realism, postmodernism — generic definitions aside — fantastic literary techniques enable these writers to depict traumatic events and encounters in history in such a way that the mechanisms by which trauma becomes traumatic cultural history are also examined. Those mechanisms include normalizing power structures that define both history and subjectivity as closed off and solidified rather than as processes in becoming. In contrast, the fictions discussed below offer nomadic subjectivities that enable an ethics of becoming to replace fixed, sterile notions of past, present, and future.

Subjectivity and Time

An ethics of becoming makes sense only if subjectivity itself is understood as multiple, instead of unitary. The notion of a non-unified — or nomadic —

subject is furthered by an emphasis on subjectivity in time in the narratives discussed in this chapter. Butler's protagonist, Dana, literally travels to the past and back to the present over and over, and much of *Kindred* focuses on how Dana has to cope with learning that she is part of both times simultaneously. She experiences the process of becoming through her travels in time. In Winterson's novels, narration becomes central to an understanding of subjectivity. Her narrators move forward and backward in time and memory and fantasy, taking the reader along on their boundary-blurring journeys. Finally, in Carter's novel, time literally stops as the main characters come to terms with history itself. *Nights at the Circus* asks the reader to consider time itself as multiple, comprised of memory, material history, fantasy, and foretelling all at once. In all of these novels, the reader can see nomadic subjectivity at work across time. And, to reiterate one of the main points of this project, as the narratives reconfigure our understandings of time and subjectivity — of the relationships between past and present — they develop hopefulness for the future. Rosi Braidotti ties these concepts together: "Hope for change and transformations for mobility and becomings are the key to ethics. To bring about an empowering present, however, is a project and a process which requires the reorganizing of the entire time structure of subjectivity" (*Transpositions* 153). The ethics of becoming emerging in the texts discussed in this book is itself hopeful because it engenders awareness of potential and possibilities for alternative ways of acting/reacting to dominant and/or normative power structures. But such an ethics is only possible if subjectivity is understood as nomadic, both in time and in space. Revisionist rewriting of history allows women writers to explore subjectivity in time.

The Brutality of Becoming: Kindred, *Octavia E. Butler*

Octavia E. Butler's *Kindred* (1979) is a complex narrative about a young black woman — Dana — living in California in 1976, who finds herself violently snatched out of her own world and into the world of the antebellum South. The mechanics of her travel through space and time receive a good amount of speculation within the text, but they are never fully explained. In other words, the fantastic in this novel is both inevitable and unfathomable; it literally erupts into everyday life without explanation. Although most of Butler's writing falls into the category of science fiction, *Kindred* barely fits that label because the time travel within the novel is unexplained, and certainly never scientifically examined. However, in terms of examining the relationship between the present and the past, Butler's choice to leave the mechanism of Dana's travels unexplained is an interesting one. By avoiding any easy (or not so easy) explanations for Dana's experiences, Butler foregrounds the ways in which history can disrupt any of our lives; the past, *Kindred* seems to say, is never really safely closed off from any of us. The trauma of slavery is part of our cultural heritage, and coping with that trauma may not be a choice; it may be the only productive or hopeful option. The fantastic in this novel is an interruption into expectations that undermines assumptions about the relationship between past and present, thereby creating conditions of openness and instability necessary to an ethics of becoming.

There are, however, some rules for the fantastic time travel Dana experiences. She returns to her life in 1976 whenever her own life is in danger in the past, but she is recalled to the past whenever the life of a specific ancestor — a white slave-owner — is in jeopardy. Aside from the time travel upon which the narrative is based, Butler's representation of Dana's existence in both 1976 and on a Southern plantation in the early nineteenth-century is thoroughly realistic, employing narrative techniques familiar from slave narratives. Within *Kindred*, Dana must constantly negotiate between her two lives in order to survive and to maintain her sanity. She literally becomes a multiple subject, defined in and through both the past and the present. The narrative begins at the end, multiplying the complications of time in the telling of Dana's story by adding a layer of personal memory. We meet Dana as she recovers from the loss of an arm after her final trip to the past. History has taken a piece of Dana's body. She narrates her story, and begins with her first experience of being pulled across space and time on her twenty-sixth birthday. While she unpacks books in a home she has recently moved into with her husband, Kevin, she finds herself getting dizzy and blacking out. She awakens in a strange place on the edge of a river, and proceeds to rescue a drowning boy. In order to save the boy, she administers C.P.R., and winds up staring down the barrel of a rifle for her trouble. At that point, she becomes dizzy again and regains consciousness in her own home, but not in the exact spot where she had been before she got dizzy. From her husband's perspective, she has completely disappeared for only a few seconds, and then reappeared a few feet away. There is no explanation for the occurrence.

As the narrative progresses, Dana returns to the past whenever the little boy, Rufus, is in mortal danger. Rufus is the son of a slave-owner in Maryland in the early nineteenth-century, and Dana quickly realizes that he must be an ancestor whose name she has seen in the family Bible.[5] Dana is usually in the past for months at a time, although no more than a few hours pass in 1976 while she is gone. At one point, her husband is taken to the past with her

Two. *Tampering with Time in Historical Narratives*

because he holds onto her when she begins to get dizzy. As a white man, he has privilege and power in the past that he tries to use to protect Dana, and sharing the journey back and forth to the present allows Kevin to bear witness to Dana's experiences. Functionally, Kevin's experiences are important because knowing that he too travels to the past means that Dana is not hallucinating or imagining, but really experiencing time travel. Without his corroboration of her experiences, the reader would likely find ways to rationalize Dana's claims, but Kevin's experiences confirm Dana's story.

Butler uses the device of time travel to create a narrative that absolutely refuses to see past and present as discrete, closed off, or even formal categories. Dana's life — her home, her life with her husband — are caught up in the demand to see the relationship between past and present as mutually constitutive. Throughout the novel, Butler emphasizes how difficult it is for Dana to "leave the past behind." Early in the narrative, after Dana has been pulled out of her life in the present with her husband for the first time, she attempts to explain her new fearfulness to him: "I moved uncomfortably, looked around. 'I feel like it could happen again — like it could happen anytime. I don't feel secure here'" (17). Her safety and comfort have been breached, and although she is not yet aware of exactly where she was, the past has broken into her present. Through the lens of trauma theory, Dana experiences a surfacing of repressed or ignored history; the usual distance that allows her to live her life is no longer dependable. Dana's fear turns out to be justified, and her existence in the present, in 1976, is always tenuous because she can find herself called back to the past whenever Rufus needs her. The physical symptoms Dana experiences when she is time-traveling are important to note here. Dizziness is an early indicator: "I felt sick and dizzy. My vision blurred so badly I could not distinguish the gun or the face of the man behind it. I heard a woman speak sharply, but I was too far gone into sickness and panic to understand what she said" (14). After a brief black-out, Dana is back at home with her husband Kevin.

Not only do the unplanned — and unwelcome — trips to the past evoke a traumatic response from Dana, the actual events are framed by bodily reactions that mimic the symptoms of traumatic flashbacks. Butler compels the reader to connect Dana's experiences to issues of cultural memory, repression, and trauma. Lisa Long connects *Kindred* to Caruth's explanation of trauma as an event/experience that was never truly known in the first place. She goes on to say that Butler offers "a theory of history —*always* mediated by a particular modern consciousness" (463). This is, in fact, what a genealogical or traumatic model of historical inquiry is designed to do, and it is a required shift of perspective in order for an ethics of becoming to be possible. Making use of the fantastic device of time travel allows Butler to create a narrative that offers such an alternative.

One of Dana's first experiences of the brutality of the time to which she travels occurs when she is summoned, along with the other slaves on the plantation, to witness a beating. She does not know the slave being whipped, but she begins to realize how utterly unprepared she is for the world she now inhabits: "I had seen people beaten on television and in the movies. I had seen the too-red blood substitute streaked across their backs and heard their well-rehearsed screams. But I hadn't lain nearby and smelled their sweat or heard them pleading and praying, shamed before their families and themselves" (36). History is now reality for Dana. Although she has read about slavery and seen it depicted in film and on television, those representations have not prepared her for actual witnessing of the violence of slavery. In this passage Dana experiences the difference between becoming-other (in time and space) and simply watching and trying to sympathize with the other. Dana becomes a slave here, part of the system of slavery that has defined race relations in this country from the beginning.

The comparison Dana draws between her experience as a witness and the inadequate representations of history available to her in 1976 resonates with many critics' complaints about how easily we are numbed by over-representation in contemporary culture. It is in moments like these that Butler draws the reader's attention to the production of historical knowledge in the contemporary world, and pushes the reader to ask what it would mean to react to history in a truly ethical manner.

As time goes on, Dana will not be fortunate enough to escape becoming a victim of that racist violence herself. A white patroller attacks Dana as she attempts to flee the plantation. Sandra Y. Govan argues that "in order to bring her readers closer to the immediacy of the horror we have just seen, Butler moves Dana rapidly from witnessing slavery to experiencing it, from watching, to feeling, to testifying what life was like for a Black woman, even if she were nominally free" ("Homage" 90). The idea that literary representations of violence can give readers access to a more immediate or more authentic experience is one that some trauma theorists adopt as well. Vickroy, for example, believes writers of trauma fiction use "narrative to try to make readers experience emotional intimacy and immediacy, individual voices and memories, and the sensory responses of the characters" (xvi). Such an approach to literary depictions of trauma clearly does not take into account the *mechanisms* of representation to the extent that a genealogical history would. *Kindred* is not a simple attempt to "absorb readers into personal and historical trauma" (Vickroy xvi); it is, instead, a complex treatment of the possibilities for representing historical trauma in the present. Dana does, indeed, become a victim of the violence of slavery, but not in order to give the reader a vicarious sense of what that violence would feel like. Butler's emphasis on Dana's own inability to relate the images she has seen of slavery in the present to the experience of it while she witnesses the whipping is evidence of the difference here. Dana's becoming-slave is, instead, a literary enactment of the conflict between present and past.

It is not long before Dana is forced not only to be a victim of violence, but to enact it. In one of the more poignant passages in the novel, Butler offers the thoughts of a woman from the late twentieth-century who finds herself accused of being a runaway slave and fighting for her freedom:

> His eyes.
> I had only to move my fingers a little and jab them into the soft tissues, gouge away his sight and give him more agony than he was giving me.
> But I couldn't do it. The thought sickened me, froze my hands where they were. I had to do it! But I couldn't....
> The man knocked my hands from his face and moved back from me — and I cursed myself for my utter stupidity [42].

Dana is, at first, unable to respond to the brutality with which she is treated in the past. The well-learned rules of social behavior in 1976 make an act like sticking her fingers into a man's eyes too difficult, even when it seems her life may be at stake. Butler's inclusion of this moment of hesitation helps to demonstrate that Dana will have to change in order to survive in the past; she has to become-other than the person she is in 1976 in order to exist in the American South during slavery. Fortunately, like almost all of Butler's female protagonists, Dana is quick to adapt. When her attacker retaliates for the scratches that did not actually penetrate to his eyes by attempting to rape her, Dana grabs a large stick: "I grasped it with both hands and brought it down as hard as I could on his head. He collapsed across my body" (43). When Dana returns home immediately following her defeat of her pursuer, she sees a blurred male face and begins to attack again. Her husband Kevin has a very difficult time calming her down, and winds up with some scratches of his own.[6] Dana has had to become a different kind of subject in order to see herself through the eyes of a white male patroller in the past, and the transition to the present is not particularly simple. Kevin's status as a white male is newly complicated for Dana by her experiences in the past.

The interplay between Dana and Kevin comes to occupy a larger role in the narrative when Kevin manages to get himself dragged back in time with Dana. Dana fears how the past will affect him: "A place like this would endanger him in a way I didn't want to talk to him about. If he was stranded here for years, some part of this place would rub off on him" (77). Since they have no control over when they travel to the past, or back to 1976, Dana worries that an extended stay in a time and place that automatically privileges Kevin over her — a time/place that cannot conceive of an equal marriage between them — will change Kevin in ways Dana does not want to consider. Kevin is, understandably, skeptical about Dana's announcement that she has been traveling back in time before he experiences it for himself. He comes around relatively quickly, however, and has his own fears about how her experiences in the past will impact their relationship. He asks her: "'Do I really look like that patroller?'" (51) in reference to the attacker she mistakes him for. Neither one of them can escape the ways they are defined in the past. Ultimately, both Dana and Kevin have to come to terms with nomadic subjectivity, with existences that are multiple and changing and frequently defined in ways that are beyond their control. The narrative's depictions of their struggles is an example of how the texts discussed throughout this project explore the way coming to terms with nomadic subjectivity, with an openness to becoming, can often seem as something far from desirable. Nevertheless, as the circumstances of Dana's and Kevin's story make clear, it is better to embrace becoming than to resist it.

It is important to note that Butler chooses to make use of the fantastic device of time travel in order not only to explore how the past impacts us in the present, but how we might wish to change the past if we could. Kevin is completely skeptical about any such attempt: "'We're in the middle of history. We surely can't change it'" (100). To which Dana replies, "'Maybe.... But I can't close my eyes'" (100). Kevin's words are similar to Margalit's description of the worldview associated with history, when history and myth are opposed to one another: "In the disenchanted world of critical history, there is no backward causality. We cannot affect the past; we cannot undo the past, resurrect the past, or revivify the past. Only *descriptions* of the past can be altered, improved, or animated" (66). It is precisely this hardened, closed notion of history that is broken open through the mingling of history with myth; the literary fantastic provides writers with a way to enact the dismantling of the binary that closes history off from myth, as well as from the present.

Dana's unwillingness to allow history to "take its course," her desire to make whatever small improvements she can, constitutes an alternative to a passive approach to history.[7] She tells Kevin that she "can't maintain the distance. I'm drawn all the way into eighteen nineteen, and I don't know what to do. I ought to be doing something though. I know that" (101). She has already begun to teach one of the young slave children how to read, and she continues to do so. Her teaching does, eventually, get her into trouble, but

Butler makes the point that Dana cannot simply witness the past without wishing to do something to change it. Not all of Dana's efforts to educate those in the past are successful. Many critics point out that all of Dana's attempts to teach Rufus a different way, her efforts to counter the dominant discourses of his time, wind up failing. Govan writes, "Try as she might, she is unable to teach the maturing Rufus enough about respect, responsibility, or compassion to prevent him from adopting the behavioral patterns of his class and race" ("Connections" 86).[8] There are limits to what can be done to change the past. Butler maintains a genealogical awareness of the power structures of history even as she argues for the need to *want* to create change. And it is the desire to change, to see history as open to change, that underlies an ethics of becoming.

Along with emphasizing of Dana's moments of conflict about the two periods she travels between, another tactic the narrative employs to readjust the reader's sense of how the past and present relate is to further destabilize the boundary between those two terms. In other words, Dana's story is not allowed to settle into a time-travel narrative about two distinct worlds. Each time Dana returns to 1976 she brings marks of slavery with her. One of Foucault's key points about genealogical history is that it understands the body to be produced in and through history. Dana's physical wounds are more than symbolic of psychic trauma; they are actual markers of history's effects. Butler literalizes Foucault's argument through the bruises, cuts, and welts that Dana carries with her from the past into the present.[9] Every time she comes home to 1976, she returns with more scars and more fresh wounds to clean and dress. Her *pain* is a constant throughout the narrative. During her final trip to the plantation, Rufus — now a grown man who has lost the woman he loves — attempts to rape Dana, and she kills him. When she kills Rufus, Dana is transported back to 1976. However, Rufus grips Dana's arm as he dies, trapping it in the past; when she arrives in her own time, the same arm is trapped within a wall of her home. Dana loses her arm and will bear a permanent bodily imprint of history, and of her experience of history.

Kindred is an incredibly unsettling novel about the relationships between the past and present, between trauma and culture, between history and the individual. Dana becomes-other through her travels to the past, requiring the reader to explore the conflict between present and past in her experiences. Butler examines the nature of how we, in the present, perceive the past, and forces the reader to reconsider the assumed distance from the traumas of the past. While the narratives discussed below offer more obvious examples of fantastic interventions into conventional historical knowledge, *Kindred* delivers a significant alternative model of history through its ambiguous construction of a relationship between the past and the present. Dana and Kevin become nomadic subjects that exist simultaneously in different times. Their experiences are terrifying, but also liberating because there is hope for all of us if we can learn to see ourselves in similar terms.

Nomadic Narration: The Passion, Jeanette Winterson

Butler's use of time travel in *Kindred* redefines subjectivity in nomadic terms, providing a necessary, and arguably hopeful, reworking of the relationship between past, present, and future. Winterson's fictions, which are in many ways very different from Butler's, offer a similar reworking of subjectivity and time. Aside from the time travel that is the subject of *Kindred*, Butler's novel is mostly realistic and linear. None of Winterson's novels can be described in those terms, particularly not the two novels read here as examples of revisioned history. *The Passion* (1987) uses a variety of fantastic techniques in the service of critical — or genealogical — historical investigation as it returns to the traumatic events of the Napoleanic Wars.

The novel tells the story of the wars through the perspectives of Napoleon's cook, Henri, and the woman that he comes to love, Villanelle.[10] The (highly unorthodox) love story between Henri and Villanelle is the central focus of the text, but Winterson's choice to tell that story in the context of Napoleon's campaigns is at least as important as the story itself. On a broad scale, the historical subject matter of the novel provides an opportunity to analyze war and the drive behind war, which the narrative works to supplant with the drive toward love: passion. More particularly, including Napoleon as a character and retelling his story is a direct intervention into traditional history. Winterson sets her novel against those histories that focus on battles, dates, and numbers rather than on everyday conditions and emotional lives. Henri narrates the first part of the narrative; he tells the story of how he came to be part of Napoleon's army, as well as his experiences once he is there. The second section in narrated by Villanelle, who tells the story of her life as a child in Venice, and her passionate love for another woman when she gets older.[11] Henri and Villanelle meet in the next section, and Henri promptly falls in love. They journey together from snow-covered battlegrounds back to Villanelle's home in Venice. The final chapter finds Henri locked away, writing his life story, his sanity highly suspect.

Throughout the novel, fantastic elements interrupt narrative expectations. Christy L. Burns sees Winterson's use of the fantastic as a way of creating a narrative link between reality and the imaginary: "Fantasy is at best an unstable term in Winterson's writing, but she often uses it (and art) to bridge the gap between harsh reality and a more hopeful construction of the social imaginary. This social imaginary includes the constant possibility of resistance and alternative realizations of identity, in that fantasy can offer far more potentialities than reality" (304). The instability of fantasy in Winterson, to which Burns refers, is partly due to its multiple functions within her works. In *Oranges Are Not the Only Fruit*, discussed in Chapter One, Winterson inserts fantastic episodes into a realistic narrative in a manner that works to destabilize assumptions of unified subjectivity, and thus allows for the emergence of an ethics of becoming. It is absolutely imperative to remember, however, that Winterson's use of fantasy is never itself without critical implications. In *Oranges*, Winterson revises Arthurian legend and creates an alternative fairy tale; she rewrites even the fantastic texts she employs. Therefore, the creation of "potentialities" through fantasy, which is undoubtedly a large part of what is at stake in Winterson's use of the literary fantastic, is not a simple matter of imagining any possibility. In *The Passion*, there are many fantastic interruptions, including boatmen and women who can walk on water, a stolen heart that has to be literally rescued and replaced into Villanelle's chest, and, perhaps most interesting of all, the city of Venice which is more of a living organism than a static location. These moments of the fantastic that occur throughout the narrative are linked to critiques of normalizing power, including official or authentic history, gender roles, and sexuality.

The Passion is intricately woven through a variety of narrational perspectives. The narrative begins with Henri's description of his duties as Napoleon's cook and with his memories of serving in the Russian campaign. The first paragraphs are in the past tense, and the novel opens with a reference to Napoleon's appetite: "It was Napoleon who had such a passion for chicken that he kept his chefs working around the clock. What a kitchen that was, with birds in every state of undress" (3). The use of past tense within the first sentence of the novel produces the possibility that it could be read as an historical narrative. In other words, until Henri adds his first-hand knowledge of the disarray in Napoleon's kitchen, the first line reads like a contemporary account of one of the quirks of one of the most notorious — and most often written-about — historical figures in the Western world. The novel opens with a slide from historical narrative into individual memory; these two terms — history and memory — resurface throughout the text. If "[m]emory is usually contrasted with history" (63) as Margalit contends and daily experience seems to bear out, genealogical inquiry would seem to require that such a distinction be undone. Yet, the inclusion of memory in relation to history in the novel creates more questions than answers. Even if memory is included in a larger genealogical history, does it hold the same status as statistical fact or critically weighed evidence? How is a memory to be critiqued, particularly a traumatic memory, without doing violence to the one who remembers?

It is only a matter of paragraphs before Henri's first-person narration shifts into the present tense as he recounts a specific encounter with Napoleon. The telling of the memory — its narrativizing — is enough to create a conflict between the present and the past:

> There is no heat, only degrees of cold. I don't remember the feeling of a fire against my knees. Even in the kitchen, the warmest place on any camp, the heat is too thin to spread and the copper pans cloud over. I take off my socks once a week to cut my toe-nails and the others call me a dandy. We're white with red noses and blue fingers.
> The tricolour.
> He does it to keep his chickens fresh.
> He uses winter like a larder.
> But that was a long time ago. In Russia [4–5].

In memory "[t]here is no heat," but then — in the present of the narrative — Henri does not "remember the feeling of a fire." Even as Winterson's narrator revises history from an individual's embodied perspective, it questions itself as a site of truth or authenticity. How can the reader trust that Henri's memories are accurate? As in *Kindred*, the physical reality of pain is central to the revisioning of history. Henri's experience of the extreme cold of war is an example of how history has imprinted his body.[12] To further dissuade the reader from seeing Henri's story as an authentic representation of trauma, Winterson continues to complicate the relationship past and present. Just as the narrative begins to take on a clear tense in the time of Henri's service to Napoleon, Winterson inserts a line — the last quoted above — referring to the fact that the narrative is actually located in Henri's memory. In the small shifts between sentences, Henri's sense of his own location in time seems to be fluid. He is a nomadic subject, in multiple times and places but still one subject. As a story-teller, he locates himself in the past to tell his own story and to explain just how cold it was in Russia, but he is also in the present telling the story.

Within the narrative, Henri's personal memories are put into stark contrast with official history. His nomadic subjectivity makes him a particularly intriguing narrator who takes on the usual dichotomy between official and personal history:

> Nowadays people talk about the things he did as though they made sense. As though even his most disastrous mistakes were only the result of bad luck or hubris.

It was a mess.
Words like devastation, rape, slaughter, carnage, starvation are lock and key words to keep the pain at bay. Words about war that are easy on the eye.
I'm telling you stories. Trust me [5].

Henri's experiences of war are incompatible with the words used to describe that war. His concise analysis of the disjunction between his memories and the representations that were already solidifying into official narratives demonstrates that Henri is an astute narrating voice. The last lines quoted above, however, remind the reader that this is not history, or even memory, but fiction. Winterson's novels refuse to subordinate fantasy or fiction or storytelling to "official" narratives. Henri's self-conscious, nomadic narration is one way that Winterson uses the fantastic not only to trouble readers' expectations about time, but to dismantle those expectations, making room for new possibilities.

Henri's early statement about the ways in which historical events come to be recorded is both a critique and an invitation. The narrative calls attention to the dangers of attempting to write the past, of attempting to use words to describe traumatic experiences. However, it also invites the reader to consider the text as an alternative to the histories that perform the kind of oversimplification that Henri describes. Hutcheon argues, "It is one of the lessons of postmodernism that, while all knowledge of the past may be provisional, historicized, and discursive, this does not mean we do not make meaning of that past" (Hutcheon 149). The meanings we make of the past are the result of how we exist in the present. Even as she rewrites the past, Winterson emphasizes the gap between representation and reality—much like Butler in the early scene in *Kindred* when Dana first witnesses a slave being whipped. Revisionist rewriting here is not about erasing or revising in order to eliminate other representations; rather, rewriting works to focus attention on the processes of history making, and on the possibilities of different, multiple representations of a given event.

This history/memory dichotomy mentioned above is evoked in the line at the end of the quote from Henri: "I'm telling you stories. Trust me" (5). Both Henri and Villanelle use this line repeatedly throughout the narrative.[13] It is central to the text's methods of interrogating representations of history. The stories, although at times thoroughly fantastic, are presented as no more or less trustworthy than any other historical text. In fact, by drawing attention to the issue of trusting the story-teller, Winterson's narrative approaches a kind of honesty that more "objective" accounts lack. Henri explains how he and Villanelle survived their long journey from the Russian battlefields to Italy after losing their companion, Patrick: "He [Patrick] was always seeing things and it didn't matter how or what, it mattered that he saw and that he told us stories. Stories were all we had" (107). The implication is that, when they have nothing else, Henri and Villanelle do have the possibilities inherent in the stories they are told. And those stories, along with all of the possibilities and potential they offer, are missing from "official" history.

One of the ways *The Passion* further develops a model of history that could be called genealogical is by addressing dangerous aspects of normalizing power, particularly dominant discourses of gender and sexuality. Villanelle works in a casino, and she explains that cross-dressing is part of making a living for her: "I dressed as a boy because that's what the visitors liked to see. It was part of the game, trying to decide which sex was hidden behind tight breeches and extravagant face-paste" (54).[14] Villanelle is often mistaken for a young man, but at other times she is easily recognized as a woman. Her story is a complex treatment of gender from the beginning, when the reader finds out that she was born with webbed feet, a distinction normally reserved for boat*men* in this fantastic version of Venetian history. As Villanelle's story unfolds in the second chapter, she falls deeply in love with a married woman. At first, Villanelle thinks that the woman believes Villanelle to be a man because of how she is dressed, but it turns out that the woman knows Villanelle is also a woman, and they have a brief, agonizing, and very passionate love affair. Other than the confusion over Villanelle's sex, the idea that it might be out of the ordinary for Villanelle to love a woman never enters her consciousness. Like Henri, Villanelle is a nomadic subject who is aware of the workings of normalizing discourses, but she is not bothered by them. Winterson's revisionist rewriting proliferates the possibilities of the past by offering a narrative without any trace of transgression to stigmatize Villanelle's love.

The city of Venice itself is one of the most fantastic element of the narrative, and it is in the descriptions of Venice that Winterson's narrative most directly engages with an ethics of becoming. Villanelle describes Venice in the following way: "The city I come from is a changeable city. It is not always the same size. Streets appear and disappear overnight, new waterways force themselves over dry land" (97). Nothing is fixed, and everything is open to change. The geography of Venice, with its infinite potential, provides a seductive image.[15] However, within the text Venice can be a difficult place to navigate. Villanelle's section of *The Passion* begins:

> There is a city surrounded by water with watery alleys that do for streets and roads and silted up back ways that only the rats can cross. Miss your way, which is easy to do, and you may find yourself staring at a hundred eyes guarding a filthy palace of sacks and bones. Find your way, which is easy to do, and you may meet an old woman in a doorway. She will tell you your fortune [49].

The changeability of a city that is constantly engaged in a process of becoming is both dangerous and full of future potential. Along with being a fantastic site of infinite becomings, Venice is, of course, a real city with a history with which Winterson is engaging. As Villanelle explains: "Since Bonaparte captured our city of mazes in 1797, we've more or less abandoned ourselves to pleasure. What else is there to do when you've lived a proud and free life and suddenly you're not proud and free any more? We became an enchanted island for the mad, the rich, the bored, the perverted" (52). Winterson juxtaposes her fantastic depiction of Venice with the historical reality of the city just after it lost its independence. One implication is that the positive qualities of the fantastic can be trivialized and co-opted for the pleasure of others. The power of Venice is diminished by those for whom it is simply a place of enchanted entertainment. Another important point Winterson makes here is that the fantastic city and the historical city are the same. Instead of inserting an alternate world or fairy tale with a fantastic city, Winterson makes Venice itself fantastic.[16] Winterson does not dismiss the distinction between history and story, between truth and fiction, but she does insist that we trouble the lines in order to reconsider how we might better understand the interconnected lines of potential. An ethics of becoming can embrace history and memory and story because it does not require privileging one or setting them up against one another.

Ultimately, the repetition of "I'm telling you stories. Trust me" is part of a larger pattern of doubling, mirroring, and repeating in the narrative that evokes a sense of traumatic historical process. One example is the cook whom Henri replaces in Napoleon's army. Early in the narrative, Henri witnesses his violence toward a prostitute and is sickened by it (14–15).[17] Once Henri and Villanelle have traveled all the way to safety in Venice, the cook resurfaces in Henri's life. In a scene that parallels the one earlier in the narrative, the cook — now Villanelle's husband — slaps Villanelle and Henri recognizes him, and is presumably reminded of the earlier moment in the brothel. He and Villanelle are unable to escape the former cook, and Henri turns on him and stabs him to death (128). Judith Seaboyer points out that Henri managed to survive Napoleon's army without ever killing another person, but "now stabs his enemy Other again and again" (503). The violence of the battlefield is not, ultimately, what resurfaces for Henri. Instead, it is the violence of sexual predation which becomes linked to that of war. Rosemergy explains the text's analysis of gendered behavior in relation to war, concluding that "as Napoleon brutalizes his soldiers, so the soldiers brutalize women, trapped in their gender role of 'meat' for men" (253). Henri's murder of Villanelle's husband is not the end of the story, for he proceeds to cut out the man's heart and offer it to

Villanelle. That last act lands him in an insane asylum at the end of the novel, but is the reader meant to question his sanity? He hears voices that Villanelle cautions him to fight against, but Henri thinks to himself, "There are voices and they must be heard" (142). The recurrence of events within the narrative stages a kind of traumatic memory, but it does not "work-through" (as LaCapra might put it) the trauma in any conclusive manner. Susana Onega reads Henri as suffering from "bouts of schizophrenia or post-traumatic stress disorder" (74), a reading that would seem to be supported by the fact that he refuses to escape when Villanelle gives him the opportunity to do so.

Perhaps, however, writing is meant to be a way of working-through trauma, or of confronting traumatic history. A highly self-conscious approach to writing marks all of Winterson's texts, and *The Passion* ends with a meditation on writing. The end of the narrative finds Henri in prison for murder, and coming to terms with the fact that Villanelle does not return his love. While in the insane asylum, Henri asks Villanelle for "writing materials and seemed intent on re-creating his years since he had left home and his time with me" (146), as Villanelle explains. As time goes on, Henri loses all contact with his former life and lives only in his own world in jail and through his memories. He explains, "I go on writing so that I will always have something to read" (159). The only version he is comfortable with at this point is his own.

Henri's need to write his own story can be read as alternative production and becoming. He takes his story into his own hands and makes the past what he wishes it to be. Alternatively, Henri's writing represents the danger of becoming in a way that requires a rethinking of the model of imaginative revision described in this chapter. Burns writes, "Whether one finds oneself through fantasy or loses oneself in madness becomes the closing question of *The Passion*" (Burns 289–90). Perhaps finding or losing *oneself* is not the central issue at stake here, although it is the gamble that one takes when one becomes-other. The central issue, the point that marks Winterson's texts as creatively resistant, is the gamble itself. Villanelle is warned by an old woman who tells fortunes: "'Beware the dice and games of chance'" (54). She loses her heart — figuratively and literally — because she fails to heed the old woman's advice, but the gamble does seem to be worth the price in a novel entitled *The Passion*.

Journeys of Becoming: Sexing the Cherry, Jeanette Winterson

In *Sexing the Cherry* (1989), as in *The Passion*, historical facts within the text serve both as grounding devices — as in standard historical fiction — and

Two. *Tampering with Time in Historical Narratives*

as invitations to the reader to reconsider the status and position of history itself. *Sexing the Cherry*, however, offers a more direct confrontation of the relationship between the present and the past by linking contemporary England to Puritan England. Additionally, although there are fantastic qualities about the main narrative, Winterson also includes more obvious breaks with that storyline and returns to the approach she employs in *Oranges Are Not the Only Fruit* of punctuating the narrative with folk and fairy tales. The narrative's blending of the fantastic and the historic provides another important case for examining how the relationship between the past and the present can be made theoretically and politically productive.

The novel begins with Jordan, and the woman who finds and raises him. It is narrated alternately from each of their points of view and develops chronologically in the main narrative, but frequently detours into fairy tales, imagined journeys, and metafictional speculations. Jordan grows up under the care of a gigantic being known to us, and to him, only as Dog-Woman, as she has forgotten the name she was originally given. Dog-Woman is an enormous figure who loves Jordan as a mother but also periodically kills and disembowels others in the name of justice. The nonlinear narrative fluctuates between historical events and fantastic or mythical narratives. Cromwell's rise to power and the beheading of King Charles I are significant pieces of the plot in *Sexing the Cherry*, but so are the story of Twelve Dancing Princesses and Jordan's description of a city in which words take on material substance and clog up the air. Finally, the novel performs a narrative slide between past and present in the last section when it shifts from the seventeenth century to 1990 and introduces characters who have uncanny links to those in the earlier sections.

The historical setting of *Sexing the Cherry* is made evident early in the narrative, but not in the first lines as in *The Passion*. Instead, this novel begins with a direct address to the reader: "My name is Jordan. This is the first thing I saw" (1). Perspective is crucial to the narration of this novel, and to its contents. A drawing of a pineapple precedes the passages narrated by Jordan, while a half-peeled banana signals that what follows will be narrated by Dog-Woman. The frequent shifts in perspective prevent the text from settling into any single, coherent narrative. In addition, Jordan explains at the beginning that "Every journey conceals another journey within its lines: the path not taken and the forgotten angle. These are the journeys I wish to record. Not the ones I made, but the ones I might have made, or perhaps did make in some other place or time" (2). Winterson begins the novel with a narrator who promises alternative "journeys"; the basic premise of the narrative, at least when Jordan's voice is dominant, is fixed in an imaginative discourse rather than a realistic one. There is a way in which the opening of *Sexing the*

Cherry mirrors the opening of *The Passion*; Henri asks for the reader's trust even as he clearly blurs the line between his present and past, making him a difficult narrator in which to have confidence. Here, Jordan establishes his unreliability by informing the reader of his intention to focus on "the other life" (3). In both cases Winterson begins the novels with direct assaults on any notion of objective history.

Just as the reader becomes accustomed to Jordan's fanciful narration, Dog-Woman's voice intercedes with a more pragmatic approach to storytelling. A few paragraphs into her first section, Dog-Woman locates the narrative in time and space: "When Jordan was three I took him to see a great rarity and that was my undoing. There was news that one Thomas Johnson had got himself an edible fruit of the like never seen in England. This Johnson, though he's been dead for twenty years now, was a herbalist by trade" (4). Johnson, a medical apothecary who died in 1643, is an actual historical figure whose presence grounds the text in time. He is known for having displayed bananas in his shop window in 1633. Given the argument of this chapter, it is worth noting that Thomas Johnson's status as the man who introduced bananas to England has been thrown into doubt since Winterson's novel was published in 1989. In 1999, archeologists working at a site on the Thames in London recovered a shriveled, black banana peel that seems to date to the middle of the fifteenth-century (Kennedy). History — and historical knowledge — is, indeed, always evolving, and keeping an open relationship to the past is a necessity.

The oscillation between fantasy and history continues when Jordan picks up the narrative to relate his story of a city he visits "[t]o escape from the weight of the world" (11). The peculiarities of that city will be discussed below, but the point here is that Dog-Woman's interruptions into Jordan's fantasies redirect the narrative. Jordan's journey into the fantastic wanders further and further away toward fairy tale and myth: "Then I saw her. She was climbing down from her window on a thin rope which she cut and re-knotted a number of times during the descent. I strained my eyes to follow her, but she was gone" (16). Just as Jordan's fantasy loses its grounding, a half-peeled banana appears on the page, and Dog-Woman's voice asserts: "It must have been in about 1640, when Jordan was something close to ten, that he met John Tradescant on the banks of the boiling Thames" (16). The historical reality of the text does not close down Jordan's fantastic tale, for it will continue in a matter of pages, but it does interrupt it in a way that requires the reader to redirect focus on the material conditions of Jordan's life. Tradescant, gardener to Charles I, becomes a role model for Jordan who has no men in his life. Through the movement between Jordan's journeys and Dog-Woman's memories, the narrative insists that the reader think carefully about the relationship between official and unofficial, or traditional and personal, narratives. The narrative only makes sense if Jordan's journeys are given equal weight with Dog-Woman's memories.

Tradescant's entry into the text also provides Winterson with an opportunity to allow Dog-Woman to assert her political views: "It is true that the ferment in the city is due not only to the heat, but also to the King seeming to turn Papish on us, and Parliament being in uproar, and Cromwell with his lump-shaped head stirring it and stirring it" (16–17). The uncertainty of the political situation — the instability of the historical moment — is a crucial element of the novel, and one of the ways the narrative links the past to the present. Dog-Woman's response to the Puritans' rise to power is less than welcoming. She is a staunch supporter of the King, and while this political stance can be read as conservative,[18] the more important issue at stake has to do with Dog-Woman's personal experiences of historical events:

> I went to a church not far from the gardens [of King Charles]. A country church famed for its altar window where our Lord stood feeding the five thousand. Black Tom Fairfax, with nothing better to do, had set up his cannon outside the window and given the order to fire. There was no window when I got there and the men had ridden away.
> There was a group of women gathered round the remains of the glass which coloured the floor brighter than any carpet of flowers in a parterre. They were women who had cleaned the window, polishing the slippery fish our Lord had blessed in his outstretched hands, scraping away the candle smoke from the feet of the apostles. They loved the window. Without speaking, and in common purpose, the women began to gather the pieces of the window in their baskets [65–66].

History has happened *to* these women. The church they love and care for is caught up in a conflict in which they have no voice, and the men who destroyed the window have already left. Dog-Woman is struck by their loss and their careful collection of the window shards, which they tell her they will put back together in a different place. This passage is about the traumatic experiences of those who survive — unnoticed — the events that are recorded as history; the women who have to piece their window back together with bloodied hands are subjects in and of history. Winterson offers a genealogical model of historical story-telling here which looks to the small "scenes" within the larger narrative, and in so doing questions the validity of that larger narrative. Indeed, the larger narrative of traditional history is also linked to a patriarchal, normalizing power. Dog-Woman is a witness to an alternative historical narrative that runs counter to normalizing discourses.

An ethics of becoming is, however, about more than a counter-discourse or a single alternative. The experience of the women in the church is one of many different stories that come together to make up one of the central points of the text: there is always more than one possible story, more than one journey, more than one experience. When Jordan is found as a baby, he is in a river. Dog-Woman explains that he was so covered in mud that she had to wash him down to find out his sex (7). In recounting this event, she goes on to describe the pain and heartache that Jordan will bring into her life; we know where we are going before the narrative has really even begun. She says, when describing the old woman who helped her clean Jordan off and warned her of the pain he would cause here, "Truth to tell, I could have snapped her spine like a fish-bone. Had I done so, perhaps I could have changed our fate, for fate may hang on any moment and at any moment be changed. I should have killed her and found us a different story" (7). The multiplicity of possible stories is precisely what is at stake in this novel — in all of the novels discussed in this chapter. There are, inevitably, limits, but those limits are far, far less restricting than the limits of traditional history and unified subjectivity. Mother and son are told by Tradescant, "that the sea is so vast that no one will ever finish sailing it. That every mapped-out journey contains another journey hidden in its lines" (18). There is always potential for something new if subjectivity is understood as nomadic. There is never just one way to do or to see things in the world of this novel, and imagination is given the same attention and status as "reality."

Maps come up again later in the narrative in one of the more self-conscious sections. Jordan explains "The Flat Earth Theory":

> The earth is round and flat at the same time. This is obvious. That it is round appears indisputable; that it is flat is our common experience, also indisputable. The globe does not supersede the map; the map does not distort the globe.
> Maps are magic. In the bottom corner are whales; at the top, cormorants carrying pop-eyed fish. In between is a subjective account of the lie of the land. Rough shapes of countries that may or may not exist, broken red lines marking paths that are at best hazardous, at worst already gone. Maps are constantly being re-made as knowledge appears to increase. But is knowledge increasing or is detail accumulating? [87–8]

Jordan's description of the world as both round and flat is an ethical understanding with far-ranging implications. Our common experience, our common perspective, is of a flat, mappable world. For Jordan, the two contradictory descriptions of a flat world or a round world need not exclude each other; they are simultaneously valid and real. (His ability to move beyond binary thinking is, it should be noted, in sharp contrast to Dog-Woman's hatred for all things Puritan.) The "magic" of maps is that they contain potential; each

Two. *Tampering with Time in Historical Narratives* 89

line represents a possibility. Official narrativizing, or mapping, is questioned here in an effort to force the reader to rethink what actually should qualify as knowledge. While the accumulation of details allows us to fill in empty places on maps, does it really qualify as an increase in knowledge? A true increase in knowledge requires something more than the gathering of facts; it entails a rethinking of the ways in which knowledge is created, which in turn creates the possibility of alternative forms of knowledge.

Jordan goes on to explain how maps can be useful starting points for the creation of alternatives:

> A map can tell me how to find a place I have not seen but have often imagined. When I get there, following the map faithfully, the place is not the place of my imagination. Maps, growing ever more real, are much less true.
> And now, swarming over the earth with our tiny insect bodies and putting up flags and building houses, it seems that all the journeys are done.
> Not so. Fold up the maps and put away the globe. If someone else has charted it, let them. Start another drawing. [88]

Realism and fantasy are given equal consideration in this account. Multiple subject positions, multiple stories, multiple possibilities: Jordan is describing an ethics of becoming. The colonizing impulse that prefers to claim space and use force is supplanted by imaginative potential. These potentialities have their own truth. The limitations that seem so solid — including those of time and space — are precisely those which the narrative text questions. Jordan refuses to be disillusioned by the difference between his imagination and reality; instead, he argues for the creation of new journeys.

All of the concerns over planting flags and swarming the globe are historically linked to Puritan England. However, Winterson's use of the fantastic tends to disrupt the historical narrative in interesting ways, particularly when Jordan's emphasis on the equal importance of reality and fantasy are kept in mind. The city Jordan imagines early in the text, referred to above, is a place where language has literal material substance; the people's "words, rising up, form a thick cloud over the city, which every so often must be thoroughly cleansed of too much language. Men and women in balloons fly up from the main square and, armed with mops and scrubbing brushes, do battle with the canopy of words trapped under the sun" (11). At first glance, this fantasy is a witty comment upon the hazards of linguistic representation. The literalization of the materiality of language, and its dangerous tendency to clog up the free space in the sky, are particularly potent images for a writer who plays with language as freely as Winterson does. A shift in the nature of the fantasy changes its role in the narrative from a distanced commentary upon the main action to another strand in the dominant narrative of the text. Jordan does not simply imagine the city of material words; he becomes part of it when he states "I once accompanied a cleaner in a balloon" (12). It is while he is in that city — the fantastic city of material language — and visiting a family that lives without floors (only winches and tightropes) that Jordan sees the woman who becomes the target of his quest in the rest of his fantastic voyages. Jordan occupies his fantasies; he becomes an actor in them, becomes-other through them.

Significantly, the fantastic elements of the novel are not limited to those sections that Jordan narrates. The very figure of Dog-Woman exceeds realistic boundaries:

> I was wearing my best dress, the one with a wide skirt that would serve as a sail for some war-torn ship, and a bit of fancy lace at the neck, made by a blind woman who had intended it to be a shawl. I had given her some estimate of my dimensions, but she would not believe me and so, although I have nothing to go round my shoulders save a dozen blankets sewn together, I do have a fine-worked collar [67].

Her grotesque size, capacity for violence, and utter lack of femininity make Dog-Woman both a powerful and a fascinating character: "Dog-Woman is the exaggeration of everything earthly; she is the grotesque personification of culture's symbolic connection of nature and woman" (Farwell 184).[19] The figure of Dog-Woman is a hyperbolic reversal of normalizing gender discourse. In keeping with Winterson's tendency to rewrite and revise normative discourses, the women in the seventeenth-century of *Sexing the Cherry* do not lead stagnant lives. Dog-Woman is a case in point. She raises and races dogs, making her economically self-sufficient, and Jordan is the child of her choice rather than of any social requirement. Nevertheless, Dog-Woman also seems to be a lonely character, who from the beginning laments the loss of her grown son. The narrative does not over-romanticize her position as an outsider — an important choice that allows the reader to see Dog-Woman as a complete character rather than a grotesque anomaly. She is, among other things, a witness to the major historical events of her place and time. Although it requires a disguise, she witnesses the trial and beheading of King Charles, after which Jordan leaves on a real journey with Tradescant.

Dog-Woman's sections of the text take on a new violence after Jordan leaves her. She murders virtually any Puritan who crosses her path, and — taking the Law of Moses literally — arrives at a Royalist meeting with a sack of "119 eyeballs ... and over 2,000 teeth" (93). Her feelings are genuinely hurt when she is asked to be "less zealous," but Dog-Woman soon finds a kindred spirit in the form of a prostitute who requests help disposing of the bodies of the Puritans that she and her colleagues have been murdering at their brothel. As Lucie Armitt points out, Dog-Woman's violence is often humorous, stating that Dog-Woman "victimizes others in a horrifying and ruthless manner, but does so in a way that makes us laugh and, in the process, question why we laugh" (*Contemporary* 20). Humor here seems to be, at least in part, an effect of the reversal of power relations. Recalling and inverting the brothel scene in *The Passion* in which a terrified Henri witnesses Napoleon's cook beating a prostitute, the whorehouse in *Sexing the Cherry* becomes the site of women's power and men's victimization. Dog-Woman's violence toward the men in the brothel, particularly the hypocritical Puritan men she knows, is beyond grotesque. The extremity of these scenes, in which Dog-Woman lops off limbs and heads, only to have other patrons of the brothel scramble in "to disport themselves amongst these ruins" (98), once again falls outside the bounds of realistic narrative. Violence beyond realism — fantastic, grotesque violence — may be another reason for the humor of many of the incidents. However, it is difficult to ignore the fact that homosexual love between men is punished by murder in the text, even if the rationale is that those men are hypocrites.[20]

Lesbians do, however, fare better in the text. If the gender politics involved in writing about the seventeenth-century are intriguing, the fact that Winterson returns to the device of inserted fairy tales — a device that works well in *Oranges Are Not the Only Fruit*— is even more interesting. Perhaps the most obvious example of a fantastic narrative within *Sexing the Cherry* is the inserted revision of "The Story of the Twelve Dancing Princesses." Jordan encounters eleven of the twelve princesses who share their individual tales with him; Fortunata, the woman he seeks, turns out to be the twelfth. In the Grimm Brothers' version of the tale, the twelve princesses would deviously sneak out of their father's castle every night in order to meet twelve princes.[21] Their father — the king — naturally offers a reward to the man who can figure out where his daughters disappear to every night; the reward being, of course, one of his daughters as a wife.[22] In Winterson's revisionist rewriting of "The Story of the Twelve Dancing Princesses," which is introduced as such by a title page within the novel (45), the twelve sisters had enjoyed nightly flights (for they do fly rather than escape through a hatch in the floor as in older versions) to a city where everyone simply dances all the time. There are no romantic entanglements associated with their flights, just the desire to fly and dance. After a prince catches them one night, he and his eleven brothers become husbands to the twelve princesses. It is here where Winterson begins to make drastic changes. In traditional versions of the tale, the princes are the object of the princesses' desires and their dancing partners. Here, the princes are their punishment. The eldest sister explains to Jordan: "we were all given in marriage, one to each brother, and as it says lived happily ever after. We did, but not with our husbands" (48).

In the case of the first sister, she fell in love with a mermaid with whom she ran away, eventually finding most of her other sisters and setting up a home with them — and many of their partners. The second and third princesses both killed their husbands; the first for his refusal to allow her to collect religious memorabilia, and the second because although she loved him, he loved another man. Similarly, the fourth princess simply waits for her adulterous husband to die of venereal disease. Inserted in the middle of the revised tale is a version of Rapunzel; the fifth sister is the "older woman" (52) with whom Rapunzel chooses to live rather than marry the prince. Her husband had turned into a frog when she first kissed him. The remaining princesses relate tales of stagnant married life that they simply had to leave, Bluebeard-like husbands who had to be murdered to be escaped, and lesbian love thwarted by social disapproval. Realism, fantasy, and fairy tale intermingle in the various lives of the eleven princesses Jordan meets. However, none of them found happiness in traditional heterosexual marriage. Laura Doan writes,

> None of the twelve dancing princesses ... finds ultimate happiness with a prince. When the prince isn't homosexual himself and when princely husbands aren't murdered in a surprising and grotesque manner, the princesses explore, in richly poetic imagery, a startling array of unconventional liaisons, from "salty bliss" with a mermaid to a happy lesbian arrangement in Rapunzel's tower [138].

The story of the princesses further illustrates *Sexing the Cherry*'s emphasis on an ethic of exploration and potential, even as it undermines normative constructions of gender and sexuality. Revisionist rewriting is, in this narrative, a method of reopening closed discourses and creating a space for becomings. Angela Marie Smith puts it in familiar terms: "These tales' strategies of reversal and humor reconfigure power structures: the women violently reclaim their right to freedom and to self-narrative, and their narratives question mythical norms" (28). In *Oranges*, Winterson creates an entirely new fairy tale. "The Story of the Twelve Dancing Princesses" within *Sexing the Cherry* is, itself, a collection of revised and new tales that redefines love and happiness outside of dominant male and heterosexual ideologies. Staging her revisionist rewriting within Puritan England, along with being particularly cheeky, is a way for Winterson to stress that the stories we tell about the past are due, in large part, to the way we see ourselves in the present.

The last section of *Sexing the Cherry* provides the most overt treatment of the strength of the relationship between the present and the past that is so central in all of the texts discussed in this chapter. After a page break in the text, the reader is introduced to two new characters whose story takes place in 1990. They are clearly linked to Jordan and Dog-Woman; one is a young sailor named Nicolas Jordan and the other is a female environmental activist whose self-image is bound up in a childhood battle with obesity. She daydreams about being a gargantuan woman who engages in grotesque violence — just like Dog-Woman.[23] As a child Nicolas was obsessed with *The Boys' Book of Heroes*, and as an adult he goes back over the stories of the heroes that had been most important to him: William the Conqueror, Christopher Columbus, Francis Drake, and Lord Nelson (131–32).[24] Nicolas, like Henry and Jordan, is an astute reader. He decides that the stories can be summarized to mean: "If you're a hero you can be an idiot, behave badly, ruin your personal life, have any number of mistresses and talk about yourself all the time, and nobody minds. Heroes are immune" (133). History is full of heroic figures that boys are meant to worship, but who — as men — are failures in life, love, and any measure of ethical behavior.

Still, Nicolas joins the Navy and returns home to be entranced by a picture of a woman who is trying to stand up to a large chemical corporation for polluting. The line between Jordan and Nicolas is blurry at best, providing another model for understanding the idea of nomadic subjectivity. Like Jordan, Nicolas sets out in pursuit of the woman. This time, the environmentalist Nicolas seeks is having her own difficulties with fantasies of being an enormous woman whose size enables her to take over the World Bank, the Pentagon, and so on, so that she can force all of the world leaders to "line up for compulsory training in feminism and ecology" (139). Since she is not actually a monstrous giantess capable of picking grown men up by the scruffs of their necks, she settles for burning down a polluting chemical factory with Nicolas Jordan's help. Jordan and Dog-Woman exist in 1990 as well as in the seventeenth century, because subjectivity here is fluid, multiple, and changing.

Smith, who offers an important reading of *Sexing the Cherry* alongside Walter Benjamin's historiography, makes the intriguing point that it seems to be Nicolas's and the young woman's "awareness of an intimate relation to the past" which "prompts a reconsideration of relation to the present and the future" (30). Their political actions are, in Smith's estimation, motivated directly by their link to history. Such a reading helps to clarify the link between revisionist rewriting and an ethics of becoming. The ability to think and act in an ethical manner is tied to an awareness of how the past is constituted in the present, which is in turn necessary for an understanding of the potential of the future. Is burning down a chemical factory guilty of polluting waterways an ethical act? A better question might be, is such an act consistent with an ethics of becoming? While it is difficult, and unnecessary, to read the action of burning down the plant as a particularly wise or ethical choice, it does make sense to see it as an action that embraces potential and possibility, and thus becoming. As Butler demonstrates in *Kindred*, becoming can be a brutal and violent process, which is part of why it is such a difficult concept to sustain, both in fiction and in life.

In one final narrative slide, the text returns to the past and to the characters who have occupied most of the book; Dog-Woman and Jordan leave as London burns in the Great Fire of 1666. Fire is the trope of choice at the end of the novel; it erases the damaging pollution of chemicals and discourses, leaving space for rebirth and reconstruction. The consuming image of the fire is tempered by Jordan's hopeful final words:

> As I drew my ship out of London I knew I would never go there again. For a time I felt only sadness, and then, for no reason, I was filled with hope. The future lies ahead like a glittering city, but like the cities of the desert disappears when approached. In certain lights it is easy to see the towers and the domes, even the people going to and fro. We speak of it with longing and with love. *The future.* But the city is a fake. The future and the present and the past exist only in our minds, and from a distance the borders of each shrink and fade like the borders of hostile countries seen from a floating city in the sky. The river runs from one country to another without stopping. And even the most solid of things and the most real, the best-loved and the well-known, are only hand-shadows on the wall. Empty space and points of light [167].

Hope lies in the understanding that "[t]he future and the present and the past exist only in our minds," because coming to terms with that knowledge means accepting the possibility of being able to create the past, present, and future. A non-unified subject, multiple in time and space, is capable of such things. *Sexing the Cherry* argues that, in order to have hope for the future, we need to conceive of new potentialities in the present and past.

Fact and Fiction: Nights at the Circus, *Angela Carter*

The last novel considered in this chapter is one in which the border between history and fantasy is not only blurred, but threatened on multiple fronts: Angela Carter's *Nights at the Circus* (1984). In this text, Carter imagines a history in which a woman with wings takes the English public by storm and travels through Russia with a circus containing intelligent apes, depressingly philosophic clowns, a mute musician who trains tigers to dance, and a strong man whose sensibility and intellect are engaged in rapid development. In the midst of this fantastic voyage, a young American reporter finds himself losing track of the difference between fact and fiction, and not really minding the loss when it happens. There are countless ways in which the narrative undermines normative discourses about gender boundaries, sexual restrictions, and class structures throughout the novel, which takes place in the final months before 1899 becomes 1900. Fevvers, the winged *aerialiste* whose story is central to the narrative, is interviewed by Jack Walser, an American reporter, in the first section of the novel. Walser's intention is to expose Fevvers as a fraud.[25] As the narrative develops, Walser joins the circus to which Fevvers belongs and travels with it through St. Petersburg and into Siberia. The story of the growing love between Walser and Fevvers takes place during the chaotic journey of the circus and the changing lives of the people and animals that make up the circus.[26]

Carter's choice to explore the daily scenes, power structures, and forms of knowledge of 1899 could be read as an attempt to reopen a moment of potential in history that has been closed down in the present due to traditional historical narratives. Farrell's study of *Post-Traumatic Culture* is divided into two sections. The first part analyzes late Victorian writers in an attempt to explore what he sees as post-traumatic imagination at that time. In that context, Farrell points out that "Men in particular shuddered that modern life would prostrate Western civilization at the feet of barbarian hordes and domineering women" (4). While there may be some hyperbole involved in Farrell's phrasing, the point is that 1899 was a time of potential for women in certain ways that Carter's novel seems to recall. Women's efforts to mobilize for equality in the nineteenth century are rarely discussed. Students in undergraduate women's studies courses are frequently astounded at how much they never learned about women's political activities in that era. Carter's choice to write about 1899 is similar to her work with fairy tales; in both cases, she creates revised narratives that uncover latent possibilities. For example, the brothel where Fevvers is raised is simply crawling with suffragists.

The early concern of the narrative is the difference between fact and fiction, or fantasy and reality. Walser contemplates the truly fantastic tale that Fevvers provides of her own history, and he finds himself wondering if all that he knows about the rational world is, indeed, faulty. He begins to try to understand the experiences Fevvers relates from the point of view of a woman with wings: "For, in order to earn a living, might not a genuine bird-woman — in the implausible event that such a thing existed — have to pretend she was an artificial one?" (17).[27] Walser's need to determine the fact or fiction of Fevvers's anatomy is undermined by his actual experience of Fevvers herself. He maintains a kind of journalistic distance for most of the interview, but he has moments in which the possibility of Fevvers actually having the wings of a swan growing out of her back becomes reasonable. Those are moments of becoming for Walser, when his world view and sense of unified subjectivity are thrown into doubt.

The unstable binary division between fact and fiction that is set up early in the novel carries over into the narrative's complex treatment of historical knowledge and time. Fevvers's adoptive mother, Lizzie, is present for almost the entire interview between Walser and Fevvers, and, as we find out later in the narrative, Lizzie has certain abilities that transcend the ordinary, one of which involves being able to play with time itself. Thus, Walser makes the following observation far into his interview of Fevvers: "Big Ben had once again struck midnight. The time outside still corresponded to that registered by the stopped gilt clock, inside. Inside and outside matched exactly, but both were badly wrong" (53). Walser, of course, has no idea why time seems to be stuck at midnight, and he is disconcerted when Big Ben repeats the chimes.

Beginning with the choice to set the narrative in 1899, Carter's approach to history in *Nights at the Circus* takes various forms ranging from Lizzie's Marxist beliefs to a Siberian Shaman's experience of the world as occurring entirely in the present. When the circus arrives in St. Petersburg, the knowing narrator points out the convoluted relationship between history and the narrative at hand: "Beauty of a city, stirs and murmurs, longing yet fearing the rough and bloody kiss that will awaken her, tugging at her moorings in the past, striving, yearning to burst through the present into the violence of that authentic history to which this narrative — as must by now be obvious! — does not belong" (97). This narrative, while touched by and involved in history, does not belong to the specific "authentic history" that will soon reinvent St. Petersburg.[28] The logical question is, then, to what history — if any — does it belong? The variety of formulas of historical knowledge Carter rehearses in the text suggest that this novel, much like the others in this chapter, is less likely to fit one model of history than it is to require that the reader rethink the necessity of a single, monolithic model of history.

Memory, or personal history, is one important form of historical knowledge in *Nights at the Circus*. Fevvers's long narrative describing her life history to Walser takes up a large portion of the text. A young woman named Mignon has a past in which she has been the victim of a series of abusive situations. In the novel she is involved in two violent relationships, with the circus ape trainer and strong-man, respectively. When the drunken ape trainer throws her out, Walser takes her to Fevvers and Lizzie. The narrative recounts her painful history, but it is unclear about how that history is told. Mignon does not tell her own story; the narrator has to tell it for her and interpret her lack of a voice for the reader: "She had the febrile gaity of a being without a past, without a present, yet she existed thus, without memory or history, only because her past was too bleak to think of and her future too terrible to contemplate; she was the broken blossom of the present tense" (140). Mignon's existence in the present is the direct result of an unspeakable past, and a future lacking in hope. Her personal history is one of traumatic memories that she has either repressed or failed to record, and which she cannot or will not access. Mignon's lack of a personal history is interpreted by the narrator as being directly linked to her hopeless future. Fortunately, Mignon finds a new course for her life through Fevvers's aid.[29] The causality of the relationship between personal history and future potential is not entirely clear; a promising future does seem to alter the status of Mignon's present, and perhaps even her past since it is in the company of Fevvers's and Lizzie that her story is told at all.

Another model of historical understanding Carter works with in the novel has to do with a variation on the story of "Sleeping Beauty." Chapter One explores how Carter's revised fairy tales from her collection *The Bloody Chamber* work to expose the power structures inherent in more traditional versions and to offer alternatives that embrace an ethics of becoming. Like Winterson, Carter integrates rewritten fairy tales into her historical fiction in productive ways. Fairy tales surface throughout *Nights at the Circus*; in fact, Fevvers explains her own conception as the result of an illicit meeting between her unknown mother and "the King of the Fairies" (65). Therefore, it comes as no surprise when Fevvers describes a sleeping woman who, like herself, is on display at an illicit freak show for wealthy male patrons. This Sleeping Beauty — unlike the fairy tale princess — only wakes once each day to eat and void, will never be awakened by a dashing prince, and dreams feverishly as she sleeps. Fevvers explains to Walser, "'And, sir,' concluded Fevvers, in a voice that now took on the somber, majestic tones of a great organ, 'we do believe ... her dream will be the coming century. And, oh God ... how frequently she weeps!'" (86). Sleeping Beauty is consigned to a terminal sleep in which she dreams the future, complete with tears for the horrors to come. The inclusion of the reference to Sleeping Beauty serves to further complicate the astoundingly muddled range of ways of understanding fact, fiction, past, present, history, and memory. What role do stories play in how we understand the past — and, perhaps more importantly, the future?

Further complication develops as Carter's narrative explores more rationalized systems of historical knowledge. Lizzie provides a different perspective on history. Early on the reader is given hints about Lizzie's political involvements, and it soon becomes clear that she is working directly for Marx. In an exchange with a young would-be revolutionary, Lizzie explains, "We live, always, in the here and now, the present. To pin your hopes upon the future is to consign those hopes to a hypothesis, which is to say, nothingness" (239).

Her view is that any focus on the far too fuzzy future is doomed to ignorance of the material conditions of the present. The emphasis on future potential that marks so many of the texts under discussion would be seen as empty hope to Lizzie. She prefers direct action to alter the course of the present. As for the past, she goes on to say, "What we have to contend with here, my boy, is the long shadow of the *past historic* ... that forged the institutions which create the human nature of the present in the first place" (240). Instead of seeing the past as open, it is by definition the source of pain in the present.

Carter's inclusion of Lizzie's political speech at this late point in the text is interesting in that, along with providing another model of historical knowledge, it gives voice to a particular critical stance that Carter maintains in much of her work. Lizzie sees history — at least, as it has operated to date — as something from which to escape because of its confinements. Carter is similarly critical of containing power structures and normative discourses, but she is nowhere near as prescriptive as Lizzie about how to proceed. Clare Hanson reads Lizzie's speech in direct relation to Foucault's theory of power, which makes a certain sense considering Lizzie's emphasis on institutionalized structures of power (64–65). However, Hanson goes on to conflate Marx and Foucault and to assume a reading of Foucault in which power is deterministic. The point Hanson wants to make is that Lizzie's speech undermines a certain kind of freedom in the text. Such an argument requires that the reader assume Lizzie's voice is somehow authoritative, and that would be completely inappropriate within the context of the narrative. Lizzie's model of historical knowledge is merely one among many offered by the text. Although he complicates a simplistic application of the term in other contexts, Linden Peach uses the "carnivalesque" to describe the lack of a "single, unified utterance" in the novel (149). He goes on to say that "Between them, Fevvers, Kearney, Walser, Lizzie all express different attitudes and ideologies so that, typical of the carnivalesque, the novel appears to proclaim to relativity of everything" (149). Or, it can be read as offering a proliferation of possibilities that need not break down into binary logic. Similarly, it is interesting that the novel is described as magical realism (Armitt), postmodernism (Michael), and the "carnivalesque." Carter herself defined the work as "picaresque" (Haffenden 87). Genre slippage is another way in which Carter refuses simplistic categorization.

As the possibilities for understanding the past multiply, *Nights at the Circus* also develops specific critiques of discourses that normalize, simplify, or otherwise reduce possibilities. For example, at one point the novel includes discussion of a panopticon, a device of power analyzed in detail by Foucault. In Siberia, a Countess who has killed her husband and gotten away with it builds a prison for other women who have killed their husbands. Carter writes:

> It was a *panopticon* she forced them to build, a hollow circle of cells shaped like a doughnut, the inward-facing wall of which was composed of grids of steel and, in the middle of the roofed, central courtyard, there was a round room surrounded by windows. In that room she'd sit all day and stare and stare and stare at her murderesses and they, in turn, sat all day and stared at her [210, italics in original].

According to the Countess, the women should come to terms with their crimes while they are constantly watched, and learn to claim responsibility. However, her plans backfire and none of the women manage to satisfy the Countess. Instead, eventually, they revolt. One of the prisoners manages to communicate through a touch with one of the guards, who are also prisoners of the panopticon because their jobs offer no escape. That brief communication changes the nature of the entire prison, and "desire, that electricity transmitted by the charged touch of Olga Alexandrovna and Vera Andreyevna, leapt across the great divide between the guards and the guarded" (216). The women break out of the panopticon to found a female utopia and leave the Countess locked in her observation tower. The power dynamic that the panopticon enacts is one in which the watcher, or jailer, is as much a prisoner as the prisoners themselves, and it cannot be sustained. Carter thus rewrites Foucault's model of surveillance power in a way that produces an alternative possibility that uses desire to resist dominance.

There is still another important way of understanding time in this novel—a Siberian Shaman's viewpoint. The narrator explains, "The Shaman's cosmogony, for all its complexity of forms, impulses and states of being perpetually in flux, was finite just because it was a human invention and possessed none of the implausibility of authentic history. And 'history' was a concept with which they were perfectly unfamiliar" (253). After a train wreck, Walser (who has amnesia) is taken in by "forest dwellers" (252) and their Shaman. Predictably, Walser has to learn to live by the rules of the native culture. Those rules, as the passage above explains, are self-containing and absolute. The reader is forced to ask exactly what it would mean to be "perfectly unfamiliar" with the concept of history. For the indigenous peoples of Siberia, the narrator argues, "it could be said that, for all the peoples of this region, there existed no difference between fact and fiction; instead, a sort of magic realism. Strange fate for a journalist, to find himself in a place where no facts, as such, existed!" (260). Of course, Walser does not know that he is a journalist, and he is in no condition to wonder about the distinction between fact and fiction. The "magic realism" of the Shaman's world is all that Walser knows, aside from brief memories that lack coherence for Walser and are interpreted as visionary hallucinations by the Shaman. For all of the people of the Shaman's village, "you could not even say they were exiles from history; rather, they inhabited a temporal dimension which did not take history into account. They were a-historic. Time meant nothing to them" (265). Within the context of a narrative that describes the specific historical moment of the turn of the nineteenth-century, the existence of a village that lives completely outside of history provides both a touch of nostalgia, even if it is satiric in nature, and an ideological counterpoint to the rest of the narrative. The narrator explains that the village will soon be pulled into the flow of history through its contact with outsiders, so the reader is witness to its last moments of a-historicity. In this way, Carter suggests that there are ways of understanding time that are so far beyond our socialization that it is impossible to conceive of them. Walser becomes-other as he lives with the Siberians, specifically in the way he relates to time.

Clearly, the narrative does not provide one specific model of time or of the relationship between history and the present. Instead, *Nights at the Circus* describes multiple possibilities for understanding history at the same time as it provides us with its own form of writing the past. The multiple understandings provided by the text, when placed alongside one another, offer a critique of standard modes of historical knowledge. From Lizzie's Marxist viewpoint to Sleeping Beauty's tormented dreams, the narrative refuses to allow history to take on any crystallized, recognizable form. Instead, it develops its own version of history in the form of the narratives of characters' lives. This is a genealogical undertaking, because of its focus on exactly the kinds of moments and scenes that Foucault describes, a poststructuralist approach to history because of its emphasis on multiplicity, and a revisionist history that embraces the fantastic as well as the realistic. The alternative possibilities suggested by the various models of history — the women who break out of the panopticon to found a female utopia, the Shaman's continuous present, personal history — are part of the novel's insistence on proliferation and potentiality, on an ethics of becoming.

Furthermore, Carter's narrative develops an overall sense of hopefulness through its use of the historical moment of the transition from 1899 to 1900. Early in the narrative, as Fevvers relates the story of her childhood to Walser, she explains her surprise when wings emerge from her back. Magali Cornier Michael argues, "Fevvers asserts authority over her own story-history and evades attempts by Walser to fix an identity upon her" (174).[30] The owner of the whorehouse where Lizzie lives and where Fevvers grows up is a generous woman, in her own way, who is moved by Fevvers' transformation: "'Oh, my little one, I think you must be the pure child of the century that just now is waiting in the wings, the New Age in which no women will be bound down to the ground'" (25). Fevvers represents new possibilities for women in the twentieth-century; she is the New Woman. In order to become herself, to become the New Woman, Fevvers has to embrace her existence as a hybrid of woman and bird. Practically speaking, she has to learn to fly. The moment in which Fevvers contemplates her first leap off of the roof describes both the excitement and the terror of becoming: "Mingled with the simple fear of physical harm, there was a strange terror in my bosom that made me cling, at the last gasp of time, to Lizzie's skirts and beg her to abandon our project — for I suffered the greatest conceivable terror of the irreparable *difference* with which success in the attempt would mark me" (34). Fevvers is afraid to jump, but Lizzie, like any good mother bird, pushes Fevvers off of the roof and into flight. In this way, Fevvers *becomes*. Her difference is also her gift, and when she shares that gift, she provides hope for what others might become in the rapidly approaching new century. Her hybridity is her power to escape the past and create a new future.

Near the end of the novel, as Lizzie and Fevvers search for Walser in Siberia, Lizzie cautions Fevvers about her future with the journalist. Lizzie warns that Fevvers is headed toward a happy ending, which always means marriage, and Fevvers has a moment of indecision and fear. However, Fevvers decides that Walser will have to be the one to give himself to *her*; she will not give herself away to anyone. Fevvers explains to Lizzie that she should see Walser as an opportunity:

> Think of him as the amanuensis of all those whose tales we've yet to tell him, the histories of those women who would otherwise go down nameless and forgotten, erased from history as if they had never been, so that he, too, will put his poor shoulder to the wheel and help to give the world a little turn into the new era that begins tomorrow. And once the old world has turned on its axle so that the new dawn can dawn, then, ah, then! All the women will have wings, the same as I [285].

Fevvers's optimistic words are carried further at the end of the narrative, when Walser begins an altogether different kind of interview with Fevvers.[31] His amnesia from the train wreck has left him open to Fevvers in a way that he could not be at the beginning of the narrative. Walser is, in fact, the New Man who, through his experiences learning Fevvers' story, losing his memory, and living among the Siberians, engages in multiple becomings. In this way, Carter leaves us with a final image of hope that is anchored in a belief that past and future are both open. The multiple possibilities for understanding time and history are left to stand next to one another.

An Ethical Approach to History

Social change requires an understanding of the mechanisms through which history operates, the channels by which it travels. The texts discussed in this chapter are deeply concerned with the operations of historical knowledge. They refuse attempts to make history closed-off or sealed, preferring the messiness of multiplicity to the sterility of monolithic narratives. It is the kind of approach Foucault advocates as a genealogical method, making it particularly well suited to analysis of dominant *and* counter discourses. The approach also bears a strong relationship to the traumatic processes that theorists have developed in relation to history. Traumatic history — both personal and cultural — appears to be inescapable, not because history and trauma are simply one and the same, but because any thorough investigation into the nature of historical knowledge cannot escape the kinds of knowledge that push on the limits of representation. Repetition, reiteration, and revision are all aspects of trauma that are evoked in the work of the writers discussed above. Power and its fluctuations are, of course, likely to be intertwined with traumatic historical events, so that genealogical inquiry and traumatic theory — aside from sharing procedural affinities — can be profitably linked. In practical terms, the texts provide analyses of those aspects of existence that traditional histories tend to ignore, as well as metacritical examinations of their own approaches to history. Butler's characters question their awkward transitions between present and past and back again; Winterson directly addresses issues of history/story/memory; and Carter works through a variety of modes of historical knowledge.

It is through the integration of fantasy and history, however, that Butler, Winterson, and Carter are able to offer alternatives that collectively can be understood to be advocating an ethics of becoming. In relation to *Nights at the Circus*, Michael argues that "fantasy's subversive potential is postmodern in the sense that fantasy continuously questions the reality status of what is being presented, thereby creating a climate of perpetual indeterminacy that threatens the established order" (199). The device of time travel in Butler and Winterson's narrative elisions and character blending allow the writers the freedom to define a mutually constitutive relationship between the past and the present. Grotesque figures like Dog-Woman and Fevvers the swan/woman hybrid enable Winterson and Carter to revise the gendered and sexual power dynamics in their texts. According to Farrell, "Trauma is a 'mind-blowing' experience that destroys a conventional mindset and compels (or makes possible) a new world-view" (19). These texts exploit the "mind-blowing" capacity of trauma by emphasizing time periods of upheaval and change in order to reopen our own sense of what is possible in the present. In addition, explorations of traumatic experiences through fantastic literary lenses — such as Dana's experience of being pulled backward and forward in time or Henri's double existence in the past and present — provide writers with ways of representing the otherwise unrepresentable. It is through the fantastic that the texts discussed in this chapter find ways to create revisions of traditional history even as they perform critical analyses of the production of historical knowledge. In other words, they offer new possibilities through their uses of the fantastic.

Over and over, the novels discussed here demonstrate how the traditional western notion of unified subjectivity is tied to a problematic understanding of history as linear, monolithic, and closed. Characters are thrust into new relationships with time and experience the joy, fear, and possibilities of becoming as they learn to accept a nomadic understanding of their own subjectivities. History, memory, and story intertwine as subjects exist in past, present, and future. Distinctions are not lost, but they are carefully troubled so that the future becomes a site of potential and possibility.

THREE

Working Through the Wreckage in Dystopian Fiction

Revising the Present

Dystopian fiction portrays futures involving the destruction, or at least the deterioration, of the social and political structures of the present. Although the focus in this chapter shifts to speculative texts set in the future, the emphasis on the nature of the production of knowledge — particularly historical knowledge — is as important here as in previous chapters. Indeed, certain dystopian narratives can, and should, be read as revisionist rewriting of the present. The rewritten fairy tales and revised histories in previous chapters rely, in part, on implied absent texts. Revisionist narratives defamiliarize the standard or traditional texts that they rewrite, producing critical distance from those original texts. In the dystopian fictions explored in this chapter, the implied text is the present, lived experience of the reader. When our current reality is defamiliarized in fiction, it becomes much more possible to see both the destructive aspects of how we live in the world now and the potential to live in other ways.

Texts by Margaret Atwood, Octavia E. Butler, and Doris Lessing will be explored below, all of which evaluate power structures and imagine alternative possibilities in the wakes of the failures of those structures. The texts in question here tend to focus on the relationship between an individual protagonist and the larger social structures in which she (sometimes he) lives. These protagonists describe the collapse of social structures familiar to the reader, as well as what happens in the fallout. Their lives take on new pressures and new possibilities when the social structures they recognize dissolve, decay, or explode; they find ways to read, evaluate, and respond to power structures. Dystopian scenarios provide contemporary women writers with opportunities

Three. *Working Through the Wreckage in Dystopian Fiction*

both to produce crucial social criticism of the present and to create narrative spaces of potential in the unknown future after destruction in which protagonists negotiate for their lives and futures. The texts in this chapter offer social visions that require a reorientation to the present. They are *The Memoirs of a Survivor* (1974), *Mara and Dann: An Adventure* (1999), and *The Story of General Dann and Mara's Daughter, Griot, and the Snow Dog* (2006) by Doris Lessing; *The Handmaid's Tale* (1985) and *Oryx and Crake* (2003) by Margaret Atwood; and *Parable of the Sower* (1993) and *Parable of the Talents* (1998) by Octavia E. Butler.

In their analyses of social structures, these dystopian narratives engage in critical examinations of power that parallel those found in the texts discussed in previous chapters. The emphasis thus far has been on how rewriting can function to demystify the power dynamics in narratives and to enact genealogical inquiry based in the explorations of the production of historical knowledge. Critical demystification of fairy tales or historical knowledge leads to new space for possibilities that the writers use to develop alternatives. Fantastic revisions allow contemporary women writers to appropriate and redirect literary forms. Further, such work can be read in relation to the development of an ethic of becoming that resists closure and emphasizes nomadic subjectivity. In the critical dystopian narratives that are the focus here, there is a particularly self-conscious emphasis on the possibility of such an ethic. The difference between morality and ethics that Gilles Deleuze describes is a notable theme in all of the narratives discussed below. In the shifting power structures of critical dystopias, there is also space for new power formations that support alternative social structures and nomadic subjects.

Rosi Braidotti explains the connection between the social and the individual in terms that are particularly relevant to the texts discussed below: "It is the changing historical scenario that engenders the urge for — if not the conditions of possibility for — a radical restructuring of the subject as a desiring entity. In other words, the move from negative to positive schemes of desire has to do with the necessity to shift political paradigms in changing historical conditions" (*Metamorphoses* 101). In these narratives of grand-scale destruction and disintegration, the possibility of an utterly different kind of relation to subjectivity is considered. What is to be gained? Braidotti's hopeful account is that "by entering into relations, nomadic becomings engender possible futures, they construct the world by making possible a web of sustainable interconnections. This is the point of becoming: a collective assemblage of forces that coalesce around commonly shared elements and empower them to grow and to last" (*Metamorphoses* 135). The readings of critical dystopian narratives below will focus on what would have been — in traditional dystopias —

end points, but are instead moments of nomadic becomings engendering possible futures.

Hopeful Horizons

Within the tradition of generic dystopian fiction, Atwood's, Butler's, and Lessing's texts are all examples of critical dystopias that trace how power dissolves and reforms, and examine the past and present in relation to potential futures. Tom Moylan uses the term "critical dystopia," which he credits to Lyman Tower Sargent, to describe "a textual mutation that self-reflexively takes on the present system and offers not only astute critiques of the order of things but also explorations of the oppositional spaces and possibilities from which the next round of political activism can derive imaginative sustenance and inspiration" (xv). The dual process that revisionist rewriting enables — demystification through close attention to the production of discourses coupled with the opening out of traditional narrative or history into alternative possibilities — is echoed in Moylan's description of how critical dystopian fiction both "critiques the order of things" and explores "oppositional spaces and possibilities." It is the particular focus on "the order of things," however, that distinguishes critical dystopian texts. In order to create speculative futures, critical dystopian narratives begin by focusing on the conditions of the present. Extrapolating from current conditions, which constitute the subject matter of their critiques, critical dystopias trace potential shifts in power. In some cases dominant discourses become less and less defined, as in Lessing's depiction of London in *Memoirs*. Other critical dystopian visions bear a stronger resemblance to traditional dystopias and trace the way power can become increasingly rigid and solidified into domination; that is the case in Atwood's *The Handmaid's Tale*.[1] Crucially, critical dystopias — regardless of the paths of their speculations — do not close down all avenues of hope. Raffaella Baccolini also uses the term critical dystopia, stating that "critical or open-ended dystopias are texts that maintain a utopian core at their center, a locus of hope that contributes to deconstructing tradition and reconstructing alternatives" ("Gender" 13). The "open-ended" nature of critical dystopias means that they contain a horizon of hope that is, at least in part, due to the essential understanding that critical analysis can open space for new possibilities.

There is an important distinction between traditional dystopian fiction and the kind of work that can be classified as a critical dystopia. Moylan offers an interesting analysis of the distinction:

Three. *Working Through the Wreckage in Dystopian Fiction* 107

Although all dystopian texts offer a detailed and pessimistic presentation of the very worst of social alternatives, some affiliate with a utopian tendency as they maintain a horizon of hope (or at least invite readings that do), while others only appear to be dystopian allies of Utopia as they retain an anti-utopian disposition that forecloses all transformative possibilities, and yet others negotiate a more strategically ambiguous position [147].

While it may be possible to read most dystopian fiction as maintaining an interest in the operations of power, it is not always the case that such an interest leads to the possibility of reversing, reconceiving, or reinventing power structures. Further, even if there are potential alternative structures suggested by a dystopian text, those alternatives may be — and frequently are — effectively closed down within the narrative.[2] There are, however, some lines of affinity between classic dystopias and the more critical variants. Moylan points out that "the typical narrative structure of the dystopia (with its presentation of an alienated character's refusal of the dominant society) facilitates [a] politically and formally flexible stance" (147). The protagonists in the dystopias by Atwood, Butler, and Lessing develop critical stances toward the power structures of their respective fictional worlds.

In her particular focus on *feminist* critical dystopias, Baccolini raises a point that is relevant here: "It is precisely the use, re-vision, and appropriation of generic fiction that constitute an oppositional writing practice and an opening for utopian elements in the dystopian science fiction" ("Gender" 13). One of the methods whereby writers can create the kinds of openings that mark the shift from dystopia to critical dystopia is through a reevaluation of generic codes. The rewriting of dystopia as feminist critical dystopia is another revisionist procedure that involves addressing an original text in order to create an alternative. These revisionist dystopias incorporate a variety of generic elements. The revisionist mingling of genres in critical dystopian work is something that Baccolini emphasizes in her readings of Atwood and Butler:

> By creating texts that resist easy classification, [...] Atwood, and Butler [...] deconstruct the confines between official history and personal stories and question the supremacy of the former over the latter. From this revisionist strategy emerges the realization that our present — and our future — depend on our past. Furthermore, our gendered, racial identities are grounded in history ["Gender" 30].

The use of multiple genres can be read as a direct confrontation with totalizing discourse, or normalizing power. In some respects, this is an important and valid claim. As Chapters One and Two illustrate, the use of the fantastic in contemporary literature can transgress genre boundaries in ways that suggest that those categorizations are both faulty and unnecessary. The specific use of dystopia in relation to genre categories that might be more typically coded as "female," such as personal diary, involves a choice to appropriate and redefine the limits of literary forms. Blurring the line between official and personal history is a central activity for all of the texts discussed so far. Such work reexamines the relationship between past, present, and future, and emphasizes the subject's particular historical situation. To Baccolini's description of genre blurring, this chapter adds an emphasis on the important uses of the fantastic to undermine the binary logic between fiction and reality, and to ask for a reevaluation of the very systems upon which the subject is founded.

Considering the range of genre possibilities taken on by the texts in this chapter, it is not surprising that they also manage to fall under Ronald Granofsky's definition of the "trauma novel." In his study of *The Trauma Novel*, Granofsky includes a reference to Atwood's *The Handmaid's Tale* and a detailed analysis of Lessing's *Memoirs of a Survivor*. He explains that one of the main features of such work "is a self-conscious attitude to the witnessing of historical events in the collective disasters which are the subjects of trauma novels" (13). The traumatic resurgence of significant cultural moments is, then, something that the critical dystopian narratives discussed here have in common with the revised historical novels in Chapter Two. Granofsky emphasizes the "self-conscious" attitude of the texts, which is another way of thinking about their preoccupation with the production of historical knowledge. While the texts discussed below do not explore history in terms of revisiting the past, they do maintain an interrogative stance toward historical processes. Another marker of the trauma novel that Granofsky identifies is "the theme of survival. If history is written by the victors, trauma novels are often presented as the narratives of survivors" (13). He offers *The Handmaid's Tale* as an example, but all of the novels in this chapter are evidence of his claim. The protagonists tend to be the story-tellers, although Butler's second *Parable* novel and Lessing's *Dann* novels complicate things by including multiple narrative perspectives. As in classic dystopias, the position of an individual in relation to larger social structures is central to the development of the trauma novel. Granofsky's emphasis on survival, however, links the trauma novel more specifically to the utopian potential produced by critical dystopian narratives.

Survival and the possibility of something better are what mark the utopian horizon in critical dystopian fiction, yet the readings below differ from Granofsky's, as well as from Moylan's and Baccolini's. In a joint statement on the subject of hope in critical dystopias, Baccolini and Moylan write,

> The new critical dystopias allow both readers and protagonists to hope by resisting closure: the ambiguous, open endings of these novels maintain the utopian impulse *within* the work. In fact, by rejecting the traditional subjugation of the

individual at the end of the novel, the critical dystopia opens a space of contestation and opposition for those collective "ex-centric" subjects whose class, gender, race, sexuality, and other positions are not empowered by hegemonic rule [*Dark Horizons* 7].

The protagonists of the works discussed here certainly benefit from the lack of closure in their respective texts. In each case, the creation of an open ending happens in a different way so that it is difficult to generalize about the role of individual agency. Nevertheless, what is particularly interesting about Baccolini and Moylan's statement is their conflation of the protagonist with the reader. They locate the reader's hope within the narratives' treatments of the protagonists, rather than in the critical attention to production of knowledge or specific alternative possibilities presented within individual texts. While the readings here agree with the premise that dystopian texts provide hopeful possibilities, they emphasize a different way of thinking about the construction of those possibilities. Furthermore, Baccolini and Moylan's statement does not account for the particular emphasis on nomadic subjectivity that is the outgrowth of the kind of systemic critiques of normalizing power found in the novels discussed here.

Still, the concept of a critical dystopia is a useful one, and the texts discussed here are particular examples that develop an ethical approach that goes beyond the critique many critics have described in dystopian narratives. In the shifting power formations that mark critical dystopias, there is room for analysis of the ways in which historical and social knowledge are produced. At times, such analysis can lead to a specific focus on the shift from morality to ethics — and to an ethics of becoming.

Fantastic Alternatives: The Memoirs of a Survivor, *Doris Lessing*

In *The Memoirs of a Survivor*, Doris Lessing's narrator, a middle-aged woman known to the reader only as the Survivor, does not explain why social structures in her world are breaking down. All she seems to know, and all the reader knows, is that London's power structures are disintegrating and leaving hunger, violence, and fear in their wake.[3] The Survivor watches from her apartment window as wave after wave of refugees flees the city, and she must find ways to live with less and less available to her. The novel suggests that humanity has been on a course leading to its own inevitable destruction for a long time. In the name of progress, human beings have managed to destroy the very world in which they must live. The past in *Memoirs* is our present, allowing for the kind of genealogical inquiry and defamiliarization that can be produced by critical dystopian narratives.[4] The past of the novel — the reader's present — is described as a time of carelessness on a grand scale. However, Lessing's critique is not limited to the larger structures and ideologies that govern society and enable carelessness. Power relations that exist at the level of the nuclear family are also targets of damaging critique in the novel.

Even more interesting than the Survivor's experience of power and its collapse, however, is the fact that she begins to see and participate in scenes beyond her apartment wall. There is no explanation for these scenes/experiences and the Survivor herself is at times afraid that she is going mad. Each visit behind her wall is a fantastic interruption into the dystopian narrative, as well as a location for the possibility of some hope. In addition to her sojourns behind the wall, the Survivor also finds herself charged with caring for a girl named Emily, who is unceremoniously given to her by an apparent agent of the unknown and rapidly disappearing power structures of the Survivor's world. In some of her visits behind the wall the Survivor encounters what she terms "personal" scenes, which seem to be from Emily's childhood and reveal the dysfunction, pain, and repression created in a traditional, nuclear, patriarchal family environment. Lessing's analysis of power thus works on both micro and macro levels. The Survivor also experiences "impersonal" scenes behind her wall that offer both the Survivor and the otherwise closed dystopian narrative with an alternative. The particular alternative that is developed through the "impersonal" scenes can be productively read in relation to an ethics of becoming; it embraces shared work, community, and the basic premise that positive change is possible through such efforts.

Beginning with the novel's treatment of power at the macro-level, the main point that comes up over and over in different ways is a *lack* of knowledge. The Survivor uses the word "it" to describe what is happening in the world around her, implying an inability to articulate what "it" is, and/or a lack of precise information. The Survivor is clearly a marginal figure in her society; she has little wealth or power, but enough to, well, survive. Her lack of access to information is part of an overall breakdown in society, but her marginalized position makes it particularly difficult for her to figure out how to understand what she sees happening all around her. When "it" begins people are bewildered, and understandably slow to acknowledge the changes happening around them. The Survivor does her best to read the situation:

> Attitudes towards Authority, towards Them and They, were increasingly contradictory, and we all believed that we were living in a peculiarly anarchistic community. Of course not. Everywhere was the same. But perhaps it would be better to develop this later, stopping only to remark that the use of the word "it" is

always a sign of crisis, of public anxiety. There is a gulf between "Why the hell do they have to be so incompetent!" and "God, things are awful!" just as "Things are awful" is a different matter again from "It is starting here, too," or "Have you heard any more about it?" [*Memoirs* 5].

There is no one in particular to hold accountable, and thus no single entity one can fight against. "It" is amorphous and happens *to* people; the best they can do is talk to one another and gather as much information about "it" as possible.[5] These are only pieces of information, and they do not provide any notion of a single force or entity that one might be able to oppose. It is possible to prepare for an earthquake or argue with religious doctrine, but what action can one take against an "it" with no other name? "It" is multiple, changing, and without definition. Here, Lessing presents a model of power that is disturbingly unavailable for critique. The Survivor has found herself within a field of shifting power relations, and her marginalized position within that field makes it impossible for her to see the field itself.

Much later in the narrative, the Survivor offers a more concrete example of how "it" operates for her after Emily comments that the "air outside has become impossible to breathe" (188). The Survivor thinks,

> And I understood it was true: this was a moment when someone said something which crystallised into fact intimations only partly grasped that had been pointing towards an obvious conclusion ... in this case, it was that the air we breathed had indeed become hard on our lungs, had been getting fouler and thicker for a long time. We had become used to it, were adapting: I, like everyone else, had been taking short reluctant breaths, as if rationing what we took into our lungs, our systems, could also ration the poisons—what poisons? But who could know, or say! This was "it" again, in a new form—"it," perhaps, in its original form? [188, ellipses in original].

Lack of attention and denial have contributed to the Survivor's inability to see the world around her as it is, rather than as she assumes it should be. Her young companion, Emily, consistently awakens the Survivor to realities that she has not seen for herself.[6] In this situation, the Survivor's realization that the air has become poisoned brings her back to the problem of "it," the problem of putting a name to what is happening. Granofsky reads "it" as the label the Survivor gives to "trauma itself, an experience so severe that it permanently alters one's world view" (35). Trauma may indeed account for the Survivor's reluctance to see the truth of her situation, but "it" seems to function more particularly here as a linguistic space-holder for the things that the Survivor cannot have knowledge of or access to. There is no single person or entity that the Survivor can blame for poisoning the air, or even for keeping her unaware of that poisoning. Instead, it is a situation in which power operates as an omnipresent field of relations that leads to unbreathable air. The lack of a "Them" or "They," brought about by disintegrating social structures, foregrounds the reality that power is a complicated network beyond the influence — and, in this case, understanding — of the individual. The Survivor's denial of reality is the result of this network, this field, of power, of which she is a part. Finding a way to respond to this Foucauldian power field is the central challenge of the novel.

The Survivor has more to critique before she can begin to find alternatives, however. The dissolution that marks social structures at the macro-level in *Memoirs* is also present in more local concerns about power and control. Lessing's Survivor is faced with the challenge of historical trauma located within the personal space of the family unit. Behind the wall of her apartment, the Survivor begins to see unkempt rooms and, eventually, scenes from what appear to be Emily's childhood, which the Survivor calls "personal," and they are stifling — if not terrifying — images of stunted growth and potential. Many critics have taken up the problem of how to read the existence of a second reality in Lessing's text. Not all of them would agree with the claim that the scenes behind the wall produce moments of highly charged inquiry into power relations. For example, Betsy Draine argues that "In moving from the world of material reality to the world of imagination and vision, Lessing has moved from Marx to Jung" (136). Similarly, Mona Knapp claims that "the dissolving walls indicate the shifting borderline between the 'real' and the subconscious" (123). By reading the episodes behind the wall as purely within the Survivor's closed personal reality, not only do Knapp and Draine ignore the provocative ending, they divest those moments of their fantastic disruptive potential.[7] Katherine Fishburn provides an alternative reading, arguing, "what Lessing establishes as the problem ... is whether or not we can accept the world behind the wall. In setting up this problem ... she confronts us with extensive defamiliarization that disturbs our view of reality itself" (38). For Fishburn, the Survivor's experiences behind the wall are meant to challenge the reader's sense of a stable reality. To that important point must be added an emphasis on the way the fantastic moments in the text defamiliarize the reader from his/her own reality. Finally, Gayle Greene states that "this intermingling of the extraordinary and the ordinary makes the point that the world we think of as real is actually quite fabulous" (143). Greene's reading is not quite as interesting as Fishburn's in that it turns the moments behind the Survivor's wall into allegory or metaphor, but she does not read them out of the narrative by presuming that it was all in the Survivor's mind. In order to see the potential for an ethics of becoming in the novel, the scenes behind the wall have to be accorded the status of fantastic literary moments.

That the existence of the scenes behind the Survivor's wall forces the

Three. *Working Through the Wreckage in Dystopian Fiction*

reader to reconsider the nature of reality is an important point that emphasizes the novel's investment in opening up alternative possibilities, or realities. The distinction between morality and ethics, discussed in the introduction, resonates with the texts explored throughout this project, but Lessing's *Memoirs* is particularly explicit in its emphasis on distinguishing between the two. In the analysis familial life, the text critiques morality as clearly delineated boundaries for good and evil, as opposed to the kind of ethical becoming that is possible in the impersonal scenes. The small, local, and direct applications of power follow a distinctly top-down model of patriarchal control, yet they are part of a larger field of power that remains unidentifiable to the participants. The Survivor is understandably reluctant to view these personal scenes: "I had approached a door, apprehensive but also curious to see if I would open it on the poltergeist's work, but instead it was a scene of clean tidiness, a room that oppressed and discouraged because of its statement that here everything had its place and its time, that nothing could change or move out of its order" (66). The world of the personal scenes is stifling, but it is interesting that the Survivor characterizes that world as stagnant. So much of what the Survivor says about the real world emphasizes the negative changes there; her distaste for constancy in the personal scenes comes as a surprise. Through the personal scenes, the Survivor realizes that the ability to imagine and create change is necessary for any alternative conception of power and social structures. Going back to the way things were, or trying to prevent the process of becoming, are equally unappealing options.

As the personal scene continues, the Survivor notices a fashionably dressed woman talking to a visitor about the trials of being a mother. The woman's husband is in the room, as are her children, including a little girl named Emily: "From this child emanated strong waves of painful emotion. It was guilt. She was condemned. And as I recognised this emotion and the group of people there in the heavy comfortable room, the scene formalised itself like a Victorian problem picture or a photograph from an old-fashioned play. Over it was written in emphatic script: '*GUILT*'" (67). The scene is about a woman who is frustrated by the role of wife and mother, but who has never considered or been offered any other roles in life, and the way that her frustration and guilt infect her children and husband. The Survivor explains,

> She was trapped, but did not know why she felt this, for her marriage and her children were what she personally had wanted and had aimed for — what society had chosen for her. Nothing in her education or experience had prepared her for what she did in fact feel, and she was isolated in her distress and her bafflement, sometimes even believing that she might perhaps be ill in some way [69].

Clearly, when the social structures of the Survivor's society were working, they were not producing desirable effects — at least not for some. The woman in the scene is trapped by normalizing forces, and her inability to locate or understand those forces results in guilt and frustration. Lessing's inclusion of the personal scenes, then, allows her to extend the narrative's critique of power beyond the dissolving structures of the Survivor's reality to the nature of the structures themselves. The dissolution of familiar power structures is indeed frightening for the Survivor, but the personal scenes serve to remind both the Survivor and the reader of the dangers of the old structures.

Memoirs offers another critique of the kind of authoritative power that shows up in the personal scenes later in the text when Emily is engaged in an effort to organize and help parentless children. The Survivor explains, "I understood now what I had half noticed before — the way the children reacted when they saw Emily. This was how people respond to Authority" (129). As she does throughout the narrative, the Survivor reads the situation around her; much of what the Survivor reads has to do with power and how power functions. The Survivor understands that for Emily, authority is something to be avoided and feared: "Only a few days before, Emily had come in late from this household, and had said to me, 'It is impossible not to have a pecking order. No matter how hard you try not to.' And she had been not far off tears — and a little girl's tears, at that" (129). Emily is striving for a community of equality rather than hierarchy, but the children require her to take a position of authority. She is frustrated by the need to take a position of power over others, yet she cannot accomplish her goals of helping and providing for the children without doing so. Here, the narrative affirms the Foucauldian notion that power relations are inescapable. The lesson Emily learns is one that each of the protagonists in the narratives discussed in this chapter must confront. Emily cannot avoid power; she can only attempt to use it productively rather than destructively. The narrative emphasizes that power is not something that can be eradicated, but rather something that can be molded and directed in new, more constructive ways.

In contrast to the community that Emily attempts to build, *Memoirs* also offers a depiction of parentless children who have no one to look to for authority or power. The Survivor, like the other adults who see gangs of children forming and functioning, has no idea how to respond to children who are entirely outside the bounds of family and community. She explains,

> The oldest were nine, ten. They seemed never to have had parents, never to have known the softening of the family. Some had been born in the Underground and abandoned. How had they survived? No one knew. But this is what these children knew how to do. They stole what they needed to live on, which was very

little indeed. They wore clothes — just enough. They were ... no, they were *not* like animals who have been licked and purred over, and, like people, have found their way to good behavior by watching exemplars. They were not a pack, either, but an assortment of individuals together only for the sake of the protection in numbers [172, ellipses in original].

These children operate solely through an instinctual drive for self-preservation, which is terrifying to the Survivor. In contrast to her reactions to the stifling scenes from Emily's childhood, the Survivor here laments the loss of familial structures. Outside of family and community humans cease to be human in the way that the Survivor — and the reader — define them. This seeming contradiction about the nature and purpose of the family is an important reminder of what has been lost in the disintegration of social structures. Emily's faltering attempts to build a community, the Survivor's fearful glances out the window, and a world behind a wall are all that really hold this narrative together. Children who have no community, no structure, are horrifying; clearly, anarchy is not one of Lessing's positive alternatives. The Survivor can only compare the children's desperation to the alternative of the authoritative family structure, but the narrative itself suggests that there may be other alternatives through the "impersonal" scenes behind the wall.

The young Emily the Survivor sees in the personal scenes behind her wall is the victim of social arrangements over which she has no control; the Emily that is left with the Survivor by the powers that be in the real world is also a victim of the social conditions that surround her. However, the Emily of the Survivor's world refuses to be a passive observer. People are leaving London, and as they come through her neighborhood, the Survivor watches. Emily joins them. As the Survivor explains, "It happened that during the early autumn, day after day, fresh gangs came through. And, day after day, Emily was with them. She did not ask if she could. And I wasn't going to forbid her, for I knew she would not obey me. I had no authority" (39). The Survivor maintains the role of passive observer of Emily's life, both behind the wall and in the real world. In this role the Survivor witnesses events around her, does her best to interpret those events, and offers us her record of them. She is the reader within the text who demonstrates the work it takes to decipher how power works. Only in the other scenes behind the wall — the impersonal scenes — does the Survivor take an active role.

The "impersonal" scenes offer the Survivor a sense of freedom and escape, as well as a location for an ethics of becoming to take shape: "It was always a liberation to step away from my 'real' life into this other place, so full of possibilities, of alternatives" (64). While the real world and the world of the "personal" scenes are closed systems of power in which the Survivor exists simply *to* survive, the "impersonal" scenes offer opportunities for action with productive consequences. For example, there are rooms that need cleaning, gardens that require tending, and a seemingly endless patchwork rug to which each person must contribute: "Behind the wall I found a room that was tall, not very large, and I think six-sided. There was no furniture in it, only a rough trestle around two of the sides. On the floor was spread a carpet, but it was a carpet without its life: it had a design, an intricate one, but the colours had an imminent existence, a potential, no more" (78).[8] The language of this passage is suggestive of a particular kind of alternative that is based on "imminent existence" and "potential," of an ethic that embraces becoming. In order for the carpet to come to life and to realize the potential the Survivor senses in it, work and collaboration are required. The Survivor continues, "It was like a child's game, giant-sized; only it was not a game; it was serious, important not only to the people actually engaged in this work, but to everyone. Then another person bent with a piece chosen from the multicoloured heap on the trestles, bent, matched, and straightened again to gaze down" (78). Finally, the Survivor looks away and "The room disappeared. I could not find it when I turned my head to see it again, so as to mark where it was. But I knew it was there waiting; I knew it had not disappeared, and the work in it continued, must continue, would go on always" (79). In contrast to the futility and stagnation that mark the Survivor's powerlessness in the "real" world and in the "personal" scenes, this is tangible work that yields results and invites the opportunity for change. Throughout the text, the impersonal scenes create the possibility of an alternative structure that remains only loosely described, but that is clearly predicated upon cooperation and productive creation.

At the end of the narrative, the Survivor and her companions have nothing left in London. Emily has pulled together a small community of children and adolescents, which she brings to the Survivor, and, in turn, the Survivor brings them all behind the wall. The Survivor explains,

> We were in that place which might present us with anything—rooms furnished this way or that and spanning the tastes and customs of millennia; walls broken, falling, growing again; a house roof like a forest floor sprouting grasses and birds' nests; rooms smashed, littered, robbed; a bright green lawn under thunderous and glaring clouds [212].

The Survivor and the other characters that cross into the world behind the wall are empowered there because they can change their surroundings and they can have a direct effect on their own futures. There is no mysterious "it" with which to contend, just as there are no strict structures of family (or familial hierarchies) to impose upon their decisions. They are in a place of endless potential, encompassing millennia but reclaimed by the natural world.

Lessing continues, "And on the lawn a giant black egg of pockmarked iron but polished and glossy," out of which comes first a vision of the carpet pieced together, and then the One — a woman who leads Emily and the others into the new world. The novel ends with the words "the last walls dissolved" (213). Ultimately, the fantastic alternative is the only one worth pursuing, and the Survivor leads a small new community into its possibilities.

The ending of *Memoirs* has been read as both a careful narrative decision designed to lead the reader into moving beyond "conventional thinking" (Fishburn 51) and, in contrast, as a failed attempt to combine allegory and fantasy that leads the reader to reject the text (Draine 139). Within the context of an ethics of becoming, the movement to the space behind the wall is a positive gesture toward the possibility of an alternative conception of social structures. The clear emphasis on potential, proliferation, productivity, endless possibilities, and the opportunity to become-other are particularly significant in a text written at such an early moment. Lessing wrote *Memoirs* well before the time Moylan marks out for critical dystopias in the 1990s, yet the dual function of critical analysis of power structures *and* the creation of alternative space is clearly in evidence.

Debrah Raschke states that "the unsatisfactoriness of the ending is precisely the point, in that it functions less as an ending than it does as catalyst to further speculation" (51). Indeed, recoding such an ending as satisfying may be a way to embrace an ethics of becoming. Reading through the lens of an ethics of becoming requires accepting endings that do not "satisfy," since the traditional narrative closure that would ostensibly be satisfying would also mean the text is sealed against further possibilities. The fairy tales discussed in Chapter One are always open because they are cultural texts that we revise and rework. The historical narratives in Chapter Two develop ways to read history as open. The narratives in this chapter similarly offer the chance to read potential and hope into even the direst of dystopian situations. In fact, the "unsatisfying" ending will come up over and over in this chapter.

Speculative Possibilities: Mara and Dann *and* The Story of General Dann, *Doris Lessing*

With *Mara and Dann: An Adventure* (1999), Lessing weaves together the generic and thematic threads that were dispersed among her earlier speculative works, especially *The Memoirs of a Survivor* (1974) and the five texts of the *Canopus in Argos: Archives* series (1979–83), which are addressed in Chapter Four. Ecological devastation, social deterioration, survivalism, mythological allusions, and — most importantly — the inevitability of change and loss, are all in evidence in all of Lessing's speculative texts. The sequel to *Mara and Dann*, somewhat awkwardly titled *The Story of General Dann and Mara's Daughter, Griot, and the Snow Dog* (2006), adds to the complexity of the new work by further developing those and other strands from Lessing's earlier narratives dealing with the struggle to find meaning and the relationships between humans and animals. The reading that follows will focus on Lessing's uses of the fantastic in the *Dann* novels as a mode of critical social analysis of the present, and as a device for creating unromanticized alternatives.

The fantastic celebrates our ability to construct and to create; disrupting "reality" is a way of requiring readers to rethink the very truths that they accept on a regular basis. *Mara and Dann* describes a bleak, dystopian future in which a brother and sister travel northward across the African continent, known as "Ifrik," in order to escape drought, famine, and war. The story takes place after the next ice age, when ice that has covered the northern continents is receding and desert conditions are returning to Africa. A passage early in the first novel describes the conditions in a town where Mara has been living: "There were fewer people.... The old people had died, and three new babies. There was not one baby or small child in the village. Up north, so it was believed, things were better, even normal, and so many families had left or were leaving" (61). Mara watches as people leave and cares for the elderly woman who once took her and her brother in. There are distinct echoes of Emily and the Survivor from *Memoirs* here, although the perspective has shifted as the reader now sees things through the young woman's eyes. Also, the "It" that the Survivor describes in *Memoirs* as an unknown force of change is much more obvious and pronounced here; as the climate warms people must respond by leaving or suffer the consequences.

The dystopian conditions of the *Dann* novels are, not, however, the entire story. Extrapolating from current conditions, which constitute the subject matter of their critiques, critical dystopias trace potential shifts in power. In some cases, dominant discourses become less and less defined, as in Lessing's depiction of London in *Memoirs*. The crucial aspect of critical dystopias is that they do not close down all avenues of hope. While the *Dann* novels never suggest a utopian solution, they do provide us with productive and hopeful models that counter the critiques which are so central to both texts. An ethics of becoming arises as an alternative in the novels, and particularly through story-telling or myth making and community building as concrete expressions of that ethics.

Reviews of Lessing's more recent "genre" fiction have not always been favorable, as Susan Watkins has pointed out. She describes reviewers' responses to *Mara and Dann* as concluding that "the novel is a failure as science fiction" largely because "Lessing never quite manages to jettison her realist roots" (6–7). This is precisely where so much of the discomfort with Lessing's recent work lies. She writes speculative fiction, but not genre fiction. The lack of an adequate category for much of Lessing's work occasionally leaves readers unhappy and even unsatisfied. However, if the concept of a critical dystopia is adopted in relation to the *Dann* novels, Baccolini's claim for revisions of genre categories in critical dystopias (discussed at the beginning of this chapter) allows for a new reading of Lessing's uses of generic fiction. It is, indeed, the lack of a clearly defined generic structure — even the revision and appropriation of certain tropes and characteristics of genre fiction — that help Lessing to accomplish new things. Further, the frustration that leads readers and reviewers to code the *Dann* novels as "unsatisfactory" is very much like reading the ending of *Memoirs* as a failure. In order for literature to express, even embody, an ethics of becoming, it will necessarily fail to conform to readerly expectations of closure and containment.

In *Memoirs* Lessing balances critiques of power at both macro and micro levels. A similar balance is struck in the *Dann* novels, this time between a long-term view and the lives of specific characters. Much time is spent on revealing elements of the mysterious past — our present — in which people flew in airplanes and used machines to do amazing calculations. While the *Dann* novels take place in a future far removed from our own, they still embed a critique of the present. One of the science fictional techniques Lessing borrows is that of estrangement (Darko Suvin's term) or defamiliarization. In fact, Virginia Tiger noted the presence of defamiliarizing techniques throughout *Mara and Dann* soon after its publication (cited in Carter, "Temporal Temptations"). An early example of defamiliarization in the first novel occurs when Mara encounters elephant bones: "Mara saw tusks so long and thick they were like trees; she saw enormous white bones; she saw cages made of bones, but she knew they were ribs. She had never imagined anything could be this big" (18). The man traveling with Mara and her brother Dann explains that the bones come from an extinct animal that died out hundreds of years ago due to a drought that killed all large animals. Lessing defamiliarizes our own reality so that the reader is made to rethink both what a privilege it is to have elephants in the world and how tenuous their existence really is. In typical science fictional fashion, as our world is defamiliarized it is also decentered in order to make room for the alternative reality of the novel.

Watkins argues that Lessing's recent speculative works can be understood in terms of what Deleuze and Guattari describe as "minor literature," and in particular that the concept of "becoming-animal" is relevant to Lessing's narratives. In the *Dann* novels, there are a number of ways in which these concepts are important. Ruff, the snow dog who is Dann's companion, is a fully developed character. He is as much a victim of the changing world as his human companions, and he is also an agent who helps to make their existences bearable. While it is not clear that any of the characters "become-animal" in the way that Deleuze and Guattari describe, Lessing's incorporation of such a character is an invitation to the reader to reconceive the relationship between human and animal. Ruff is the soul of this narrative and thus, as Watkins puts it, an "attempt to block the impulse to read the human/animal metaphorically" (6).

Another, perhaps even more obvious, way in which the concept of becoming is evident in the novels is through their insistence upon living in the present moment — something that Theresa Carter emphasizes in her reading of *Mara and Dann*. Between coping with traumatic events and understanding the nature of historical time, the *Dann* novels, like Lessing's other speculative works, emphasize that change is constant. Coping with change is, therefore, central to the texts. Many of the characters peppered throughout both novels are plagued by denial; they do not see the reality of the changing conditions surrounding them. In one city called Chelops in *Mara and Dann*, Mara exists as one of a number of slaves who live relatively comfortable lives and do not wish to accept that their city is doomed; Mara attempts to tell her fellow slaves that people are leaving and that they will eventually be overthrown along with the rulers, but they will not accept what she has to say (144–45). An example from the second novel occurs when Dann journeys to island communities that will soon be destroyed due to the melting ice:

> Dann saw they had no conception that their way of life would soon change, and on some islands, the lower ones, end. Yet "up there" everyone knew it. The inhabitants of the lower islands would move to the higher ones, and then to the higher ones still — did they know that under the waves that surrounded them were the ruins of great cities? No, they laughed when he mentioned this and said there were all kinds of old stories about that time. These people did not want to know [*General Dann* 48].

The inability or unwillingness to see and accept change is a frailty against which Lessing's novels consistently work. The texts maintain that in order to live in the world in a meaningful way one must see and accept change. Embracing an ethics of becoming is a meaningful way to respond to change.

One of the tonics to the denial that plagues so many in the novels is story-telling. Denial is linked to a lack of imagination in the second novel. Dann travels the island communities as a story-teller who recites a somewhat tamed version of his travels with his sister: "But there was always a point in his recitals when his audience was not with him. They did not believe him. Their imaginations had gone fat and soft with the comfort of their lives" (54). This is, then, one of the objectives of the novels themselves: to prevent our imaginations from going "fat and soft." Near the end of the first novel, Mara and Dann hear of "Yerrup" and our time, which, according to the lesson, lasted for a period of twelve thousand years. They are told "that people always have a tendency to believe that what they have is going to continue for ever" (373). Quite clearly, that is not the case and Lessing wishes to remind us that change is inevitable. There are lessons from the past, but there is also a need to be aware of the present, to constantly become anew and to be prepared for the future. As Tiger reminds us, the second novel's incredibly long title begins with the words *The Story* for a reason; Lessing's stories help the reader to imagine other possibilities so that we of the present do not fall into complacency and forget the realities of the world around us.

Even more, however, the *Dann* novels offer hope — the hopefulness that is characteristic of a critical dystopia. They do so through their emphasis on what is possible when change is met openly and with willingness rather than with denial and resistance. *Mara and Dann* ends with the creation of a small community on a farm. Specifically, the novel ends with the members of that community gathered around the kitchen table discussing what work they can do to contribute (398); Carter connects the image of the community table to other important works in Lessing's canon including *The Good Terrorist, The Fifth Child,* and even *The Golden Notebook* and *The Four-Gated City* (19–20). Creating a community is one way of coping with the tumultuous time of change and uncertainty that the dystopian novel presents; it is a common way for critical dystopias to offer hope.

The second novel, *General Dann*, carries the concept of community much further; Griot,[9] Dann's protégé from a time when he was General Dann in the first novel, establishes a community of soldiers for Dann to command. Lessing describes the soldiers as being "of every kind and colour" (125). They are refugees from war and famine, male and female, and even some with children. Later it reads: "There were assemblages of clothes so various that this diversity itself united them; never had there been such a multi-hued and many-shaped mass of people" (140). Griot establishes an army that is less about making war than it is about creating a community of disparate and frightened people who need a common ground and common purpose. Because Dann is so reluctant to fight, the army that Griot has put together for him turns into a traveling camp that is welcomed upon its arrival in the neighboring, and languishing, country. In fact, this new society of soldiers has also become a community of pooled knowledge due to Griot's insight and Dann's demand that new members be questioned as to what they know and are capable of. In that way, what is known will carry on and be used rather than lost. As the second novel ends, Griot wonders if the new stable country they have established will be invaded, calling such an act "stupid"; Dann agrees with Griot's assessment but is not as quick to dismiss the possibility since stupidity does not seem to have prevented such acts in the past. The essential point here, however, is that the two novels culminate in the creation of a new society that embraces knowledge, change, and difference. Community building is one of the central tropes of all of the dystopian narratives in this chapter although Lessing and Butler emphasize it much more than Atwood. It seems essential to pause here to consider how the model of nomadic subjectivity employed in previous chapters can translate to new ways of conceiving of and building communities. An ethics of becoming is not meant to be the pursuit of an individual, but rather the substance of a collective effort.

Resistant Subjectivity: The Handmaid's Tale, Margaret Atwood

Power in Margaret Atwood's *The Handmaid's Tale* is much more easily traced than in the novels by Lessing discussed above, yet the possibility for resistance remains located in practices that align with an ethics of becoming. Atwood's narrative depicts a specific type of totalitarian formation that has arisen out of the kind of societal breakdown that gets more attention from Lessing and Butler. Lessing's *Memoirs* is sometimes read as a Marxist critique of capitalism's inevitable decline, but even if it is not read through a strictly Marxist lens, it is certainly a response to poverty, urban decay, and disenfranchisement. In contrast, Atwood's novel about Cambridge, Massachusetts, was published in the mid–1980s and is generally read as a response to the coalescing conservative right in the United States during the Reagan years.[10] Evaluating how that particular historical moment might develop into a rigidly patriarchal dystopia, Atwood offers a "tale" about the horrors of dominating power that takes the form of official, state-sanctioned control. Generically, this narrative is particularly interesting in that it, as Baccolini and Moylan claim, makes use of "the conventions of the diary and the epistolary novel" (*Dark* 8), so that there is a first-person account of events as in Lessing's *Memoirs*. However, the memoir form employed by Lessing uses the past tense, whereas *The Handmaid's Tale* is written in the present tense; the particular difficulty with this is that the protagonist is not given access to any materials with which she could record her story during the course of the actual narrative.[11] Further,

Atwood's use of the word "*Tale*" in the title suggests another genre category that conflicts with the realistic nature of the narrative, despite the lack of explicitly fantastic interruptions to provide relief from the horrors of daily life in Gilead. The instability of genre in the narrative is both in keeping with critical dystopian narratives and productive of a much needed critical space in this devastating text.[12] Leaving the location of the narrator's utterance undefined is a gesture that allows space for possibility at the end of the text, and calling it a "tale" keeps the narrative wavering in a space between realism and the fantastic. The multiplicity of genres and indeterminacy of the narrative are part of what aligns it with an ethics of becoming.

Atwood's protagonist, named "Offred" by the newly established official powers of her world, finds herself torn out of a life of relative complacency when ultra-conservative structures take over her corner of the world. Her existence as a working wife and mother is shattered when a right-wing Christian organization seizes power. At first, she loses control of her money and must rely on her husband for financial support. As things progress, she and her husband realize that they must leave or become subjects of this new regime. However, when they attempt to escape, they are captured and separated from each other as well as from their daughter. Offred finds herself undergoing a process of reeducation with other potentially fertile women who will serve as "handmaids" to important men whose wives cannot bear children. Once her training is complete, Offred is placed in a home and charged with the task of bearing children. She repeatedly says that she does not want to be telling her story, and the reader cannot help but share her reluctance. Offred's story, her tale, is an assault; it is dystopian fiction at its most jarring. While the characters in Lessing's dystopias struggle with amorphous and undelineated change, the handmaid finds herself in a society founded on complete control, especially over women. Offred's official function is to bear children for an important man in the new regime, the Commander. Her reproductive potential is all that is important in this new order, since she is neither "pure" enough, nor important enough, to be a wife. She is hated by the Commander's wife, avoided by other wives who bear resentment toward any handmaid, completely secluded from others through constant surveillance, and generally forced to suffer continuous humiliation. Power is not subtle, nor is it easy to come by for any woman in this text. Offred's production of her own story is her opportunity to take the only action that is available to her.

Even though the form power takes on the macro-level in Atwood's narrative is far more structured and coherent than the power in Lessing's texts, Offred feels the same desire for information that the Survivor expresses when she describes the unknown "it" that surrounds her. Offred explains, "I'm ravenous for news, any kind of news; even if it's false news, it must mean something" (20). Offred is denied access to most of what is happening around her and is constantly looking for things to read, things that might offer some way of understanding what is happening. The stifling atmosphere Atwood creates for Offred is another link to Lessing's characters who are similarly hemmed in. There is little for Offred to examine other than the small, local examples of power that she encounters in her daily life. Early on, as she passes young male guards who are clearly frustrated by the rules — the highly moralized rules — that require them to stay away from women who do not belong to them, Offred feels a sense of power: "I enjoy the power; power of a dog bone, passive but there" (22). Her status as an object of desire is all that gives her power in this world. By calling attention to this small moment, Offred makes it clear that she is painfully aware of her overall *lack* of power in every other situation.

Those who run Gilead, which is the name given to the new order, are alert to the nature of the power they wield, and work to make sure that even small, local, or micro-level incidents do not interfere with their total control. They use familiar scare tactics, such as displaying the hanged bodies of those who violate the beliefs sanctioned by the state, and take measures to repress women by preventing their educations and even their access to basic literacy. Offred observes these strategies and recognizes the logic that motivates them. She explains, "The Bible is kept locked up, the way people once kept tea locked up, so the servants wouldn't steal it. It is an incendiary device: who knows what we'd make of it, if we ever got our hands on it?" (87). Atwood's indictment of moralistic thinking as opposed to a more open, ethical stance is obvious. More interesting is that Offred realizes power resides in the ability to use language to make meaning, and that the Bible cannot be freely available in Gilead because access to it would leave open channels of access to power to those whom the officials wish to keep powerless.[13]

The Gileadean regime's anxiety over access to the Bible is an important illustration not only of Offred's ability to analyze the workings of power around her, but of the thinking of those in charge of the regime. The commanders, who appear to wield the most power in Gilead, realize that meaning is made through language and that those in power can dictate meaning. In a discussion about the concept of love, Offred's Commander tells her, "I've read the magazines, that's what they were pushing, wasn't it? But look at the stats, my dear. Was it really worth it, *falling in love?* Arranged marriages have always worked better" (220, italics in original). The new regime is "pushing" the view of marriage that they find most useful for their purposes, and thus calling attention to what they see as an artificial concept of romantic love.

Offred is not convinced that love can be dismissed as a construct, but the Commander is clear that he believes what he and the other commanders are doing is right: "Those years were just an anomaly, historically speaking, the Commander said. Just a fluke. All we've done is return things to Nature's norm" (220). The Commander's beliefs, and Gilead's social structure, are rooted in restrictive moral terms that require the binary logic of good versus evil, and natural versus unnatural. Further, the Commander's comments illustrate that any concept can be naturalized through discourses of power. Offred, however, refuses to be taken in by moralizing claims about what is "natural" or "right."

One of the ways Offred is able to maintain her resistance to the discourses of Gilead is through her memories of her life before the commanders rose to power. Baccolini points out, "Offred's reflections on the past, her family, and her lack of future prospects constitute a site of resistance and struggle against the obliteration of individuality the regime enforces" ("Gender" 22). Offred has no alternative world to enter as the Survivor does, but she uses her own memories and imagination to create an alternative space for herself. In fact, in weaving her own tale, Offred embraces the possibility of power in storytelling that Lessing's *Mara and Dann* novels support. As she tells her story, Offred intertwines memories of her life before Gilead with her experiences as a handmaid. Atwood creates an ongoing sense of narrative instability through the interruptions of memory into the text, which Elisabeth Mahoney refers to as "non-linearity" that is "emphasised by the surfacing of memory" (36). Mahoney further develops her point to argue that Atwood is engaging in "genre subversion" (37) whereby, like the inclusion of Offred's memories into the main narrative, Atwood is inserting (or even "transforming," in Mahoney's terms) the dystopia into a space for "new textual identities [...] which allow women to move towards self-representation" (37). As Mahoney suggests, the revisionist and critical nature of Atwood's dystopia is, in part, related to the use of personal history.

Magali Cornier Michael takes up the same point, stating:

> Offred's story both challenges Gilead's official history and constructs new histories by filling in the gaps that separate official existence from daily life as individuals experience it. The novel's focus on that which exists in the margins or gaps of the official Gileadean regime enables it to demonstrate that possibilities for change always exist, since there are gaps in all systems [146].

The use of memory, then, is both a way for Offred to create space in her existence in Gilead for alternative narratives to those that are forced upon her daily, *and* a narrative technique that enables Atwood to maintain narrative instability while emphasizing a marginalized historical perspective. Within her own telling of her own story, Offred is a nomadic subject moving among places and times as she sees fit. She constructs her own subjectivity well beyond the confines of her existence in Gilead. Story-telling becomes Offred's method for self-construction in a manner that eludes — even actively resists — the control of Gilead's morality.

Foremost among Offred's memories are those that give her access to the feelings of freedom she experienced before Gilead, and the seemingly unlimited possibilities of her old life in contrast to the strictly enforced constraints of her existence in Gilead: "If you don't like it, change it, we said, to each other and to ourselves. And so we would change the man, for another one. Change, we were sure, was for the better always. We were revisionists; what we revised was ourselves" (227). The ability to construct, and reconstruct, the self were taken for granted in the past, but the memory of the power she once held helps Offred to maintain a critical distance from the present. She knows there are other ways of being and thinking. However, there is a certain disapproval in Offred's tone here, indicating that her memories are not entirely comforting. The frivolous choices she describes are a waste of the power and freedom she had. The gradual rise to power of those who founded Gilead plays a large role in Offred's memories. Her experiences in Gilead lead her to reassess her past, and to reexamine how she lost her power and agency. Barbara Hill Rigney argues that Offred's memories suggest that the rise of Gilead and the accompanying loss of freedom is the result of a lack of political awareness and involvement: "Not paying attention, in fact, is the great fault of Offred's entire society, and the price exacted is the loss of freedom" (113). The basic cautionary function of dystopian narratives is crucial in critical dystopias; Atwood does indeed point out that it is foolish to give away one's power. Offred's struggle to come to terms with her past is an example of how Atwood's text engages in a revision of the present, as well as part of Offred's construction of her own nomadic subjectivity.

One particular memory that further exemplifies the way the novel asks the reader to rethink the present involves the loss of Offred's job, which she equates with the loss of independence from her husband. The power relation between herself and her husband — that she had assumed to be equal — is revealed to be more precarious than she realizes when she sees that her husband willingly accepts the dominating role of protector and provider: "Something had shifted, some balance. I felt shrunken, so that when he put his arms around me, gathering me up, I was small as a doll. I felt love going forward without me" (182). Individual relationships exist within larger social structures of power, and when Offred loses her job and her ability to hold property because she is a woman, she also loses equality with her husband; this is an example of the direct link between macro- and micro-level power in Atwood's text.[14] The Commander's disdain for the concept of love, discussed above, makes sense given that Gilead is created specifically in order to prevent equal relationships between men and women; Offred senses that love cannot exist once she is subordinate to her husband. Offred's memories, then, serve as reminders of what she has lost as well as opportunities for her to analyze how things went wrong.

Offred struggles to come to terms with both the past and present, while she looks for a way to create hope for the future. She constantly analyzes her own sense of self and her position within the larger power flows that surround her. Early in the narrative, when she first arrives at the Commander's house, Offred observes: "But a chair, sunlight, flowers: these are not to be dismissed. I am alive, I live, I breathe, I put my hand out, unfolded, into the sunlight. Where I am is not a prison but a privilege, as Aunt Lydia said, who was in love with either/or" (8). At this point, her life is beyond her control, but she looks to small moments, such as feeling the sunlight, in order to maintain a sense of self. Aunt Lydia, one of the women who was in charge of reeducating Offred in the ways of Gilead, is also beyond Offred's reach; Offred cannot contradict Aunt Lydia in reality, but she can think contrary to the Aunt's moralizing teachings. Her antagonism toward Aunt Lydia finds an outlet in her narrative, and so it is through the story she tells about herself that Offred is able to maintain independence of thought and a critical distance from the discourses and ideologies of Gilead.

Later, Offred comments more directly upon her status within Gilead: "I wait. I compose myself. My self is a thing I must now compose, as one composes a speech. What I must present is a made thing, not something born" (66). In order to survive in Gilead, Offred must "compose" herself in a way that is suitable to her role as a handmaid, and acceptable to those who hold power over her. Michael sees Offred's narrative as a construction of subjectivity, arguing that "she literally tells herself into existence, into subjecthood" (161), and Louis Feuer states "Offred's reconstruction of herself can be seen as a rebirth" (91). The narration of her story allows Offred to analyze her own responses to power, and to preserve a sense of self outside the control of those who objectify her. Through telling her story, Offred seems to create a space for her own becoming-other that, unlike a "rebirth" or even a telling "into subjecthood," maintains an instability of subjectivity which Offred wishes to embrace and the narrative appears to endorse. In other words, Offred is not "reborn" as a new and stable person, but rather, as Michael puts it, "tells herself into existence," or becomes, in a manner that necessarily embraces the indeterminacy of language and the process of storytelling.

Offred uses her narrative voice as a means of actively engaging with power structures that are otherwise beyond her control. Even in the horrifying details of Offred's account of life in Gilead, there is a sense that women cannot be "gotten rid of," cannot be silenced. Much of the force of Atwood's text comes from the moments of self-conscious narration in which Offred deals with the nature of narrative itself. For example, after a particularly devastating memory, Offred explains,

> I would like to believe this is a story I'm telling. I need to believe it. I must believe it. Those who can believe that such stories are only stories have a better chance. If it's a story I'm telling, then I have control over the ending. Then there will be an ending, to the story, and real life will come after it. I can pick up where I left off. It isn't a story I'm telling. It's also a story I'm telling, in my head, as I go along [39].

Here, Offred makes explicit the tension between narrative and the actual events of her life. The conditions of her existence are so restricted that she is not allowed to write; reading and writing are strictly forbidden for women. Offred cannot physically change her conditions, but she can document her experiences, and, more importantly, she can maintain a position of critical distance and inquiry throughout her narration of events, and thus create a space of potential becoming. This is the only power Offred has to counter the nearly absolute power that keeps her so thoroughly controlled.[15]

Still, there is hope in the cracks of Offred's story, and in her uncertain end. We never know what happens to her after she attempts to escape Gilead, but we do know that her story is preserved. Within her narrative, Offred allows herself to hope; she is unwilling to believe that the power structures of Gilead are as all-encompassing as they seem. She explains, "I believe in the resistance as I believe there can be no light without shadow; or rather, no shadow unless there is also light. There must be a resistance, or where do all the criminals come from, on the television?" (105). As the narrative develops, we learn that Offred is probably correct to hold out hope; the text suggests that there is in fact a resistance and that it comes to her aid. At the end of her narrative, Offred takes a step into the unknown, much as the Survivor does at the end of *Memoirs*. For Offred, the only option is to go with the men who arrive to remove her from the Commander's house, knowing that her refusal to submit to the powers of Gilead, to the discourses that would make her into little more than a baby-making machine, means that she will either be killed or saved. She describes her thoughts as she leaves the Commander's house for an unknown destination: "Whether this is my end or a new beginning I have no way of knowing: I have given myself over into the hands of strangers, because it can't be helped. And so I step up, into the darkness within; or else the light" (295). Like the Survivor, Offred can no longer exist within the world she has inhabited, and must surrender to the hope of another possible world.

Offred's step into the unknown is not, however, the end of Atwood's text. Atwood chooses to provide the reader with some knowledge of what becomes of her protagonist. In the "Historical Notes" at the end of *The Handmaid's Tale*, the reader learns that Offred's narrative has survived, and that Offred herself most likely escaped Gilead. The narrative is taped rather than written, and it is the object of scholarly scrutiny at a conference that takes place two hundred years after Offred's experiences in Gilead. The scholars who discuss Offred's narrative treat it as an inadequate source of information about the "important" figures of Gilead. Professor Pieixoto complains, "Many gaps remain. Some of them could have been filled by our anonymous author [Offred], had she had a different turn of mind. She could have told us much about the workings of the Gileadean empire, had she had the instincts of a reporter or a spy" (310). Clearly, personal narrative and the individual experiences of a woman are of little consequence to the scholars at the conference; they are far more concerned with figuring out which powerful man the Commander was and what happened to him. Arnold E. Davidson reads the closing section of text as a commentary on the nature of knowledge production: "In this projection of past, present, and future, the academic community is shown to have a role, not simply an 'academic' role (passive, accommodating) but an active one in recreating the values of the past — which is, Atwood suggests, the way to create the values of the future" (120). The scholars are interested in those who wielded power, not those who were objects of control. By inserting the "Historical Notes" at the end of Offred's tale, Atwood accomplishes two important tasks: she adds a level of genealogical inquiry into the production of historical knowledge that could not be present within Offred's narration of her own story due to her limited perspective, and she develops a specific critique of the methods whereby the past, present, and future become closed off from one another. The academics who study Offred's narrative fail to recognize the value of history outside of traditional history and they blame her for her lack of access to knowledge and power.[16]

Perhaps Professor Pieixoto's most egregious insult to Offred is when he cautions against "passing moral judgment upon the Gileadeans" (302). He goes on to say, "Our job is not to censure but to understand" (302), and that statement is followed by applause from the other scholars. Atwood's indictment of scholarly detachment and pretensions to objectivity is clear. Moral judgment — as the regime in Gilead demonstrates — is indeed a dangerous approach. However, Atwood requires the reader to consider an alternative to relativism and inaction. A reading of *The Handmaid's Tale* as supporting an ethic of potentiality and becoming, which is vigilant in its attention to power flows and the production of knowledge, is directly supported by the inclusion of the "Historical Notes."

Global Subjects: Oryx and Crake, *Margaret Atwood*

Margaret Atwood's more recent dystopian novel, *Oryx and Crake*, examines power structures and their destruction at the global level. The first line of the narrative invokes the familiar literary device of awakening as the reader is pulled into consciousness with Snowman: "Snowman wakes before dawn" (3). Yet his initial awakening is fraught with a sense of confusion and loss. He and the reader wake up to the reality of a world being reclaimed by nature—a world without the familiar structure of clock time. A post-apocalyptic setting takes shape around Snowman and the reader has a mystery to solve. What happened and why? As the narrative develops, clues surface. Atwood requires the reader to take the journey with Snowman through his memories to uncover the story of how humanity has become nearly extinct. It is only through the process of reading that the strands of the narrative form a woven whole. Once again, the revision of the present is absolutely central to the project of the novel. The narrative moves between Snowman's attempts to survive in the post-apocalyptic world and his memories leading up to the almost complete destruction of humanity, helping the reader see the present in a defamiliarized way. The comparative structure between Snowman's present and past, which is in many ways similar to Offred's tale, creates opportunities for Atwood to link Snowman's despair directly to a world consumed by materialism, greed, and ecological ignorance.

Oryx and Crake, perhaps even more than the other dystopias discussed above, emphasizes the importance of recognizing the power structures that limit our abilities even to see the realities of our world. A careful reading of Atwood's novel illustrates an ethical stance characterized by a transnational sensibility grounded in local realities, as well as an emphasis on embracing becoming over stability. The name "Snowman" is one that the main character adopts after the apocalyptic events, and he remembers himself as a boy and young man named Jimmy. The split between Snowman, the adult survivor, and Jimmy, the child of his memories, is partly a representation of his inability to reconcile with himself after the trauma of what he experiences, but it is also a brilliant narrative device that allows Atwood to tell two stories from the point of view of the same character. Snowman knows what will happen and understands his own complicit involvement in the system; Jimmy is blissfully unaware. The reader cannot help but feel part of the system.

In addition to using a carefully crafted formal structure to explore power relations, Atwood confronts the complicated nature of globalized power through a few important strands of the narrative. Snowman is a privileged white male in North America who lives within the relatively secure structures of what have become corporate towns. Through Snowman's memories, Atwood depicts a near future in which class stratification has become the defining factor of existence; those who have jobs with good corporations live within the walls of those corporations, while those who do not have such protection live with the general population in the poverty ridden Pleeblands. As a child, Snowman's privileged existence includes parental apathy, internet access to the most obscene forms of pornography and torture, and web-based gaming that emphasizes violence and competition. One of the more jarring and significant episodes in the chapters of memory occurs when the narrative demonstrates how Snowman's affluence is related to the brutality experienced by a little girl sold into sexual slavery on the other side of the world by carefully constructing a set of encounters for the reader. First, Snowman remembers seeing one specific girl—one among many—while perusing a pornographic website when he was only a young adolescent and still called by his real name, Jimmy: "She smiled a hard little smile that made her appear much older, and wiped the whipped cream from her mouth. Then she looked over her shoulder right into the eyes of the viewer—right into Jimmy's eyes, into the secret person inside him. *I see you*, that look said" (91). The little girl turns Jimmy's gaze back on him in a way that he remembers all of his life; she requires him to see his guilt, his role in the system that controls her life. Later, he falls in love with a woman who may or may not be the same person as the little girl—Oryx.

It is useful to consider the juxtaposition between Snowman and Jimmy in light of another complex juxtaposition in the novel between utopia and dystopia. The corporate compounds in which Jimmy grows up are contrasted with the "Pleeblands." Jayne Glover points out that "reading compound life as utopian and pleebland life as dystopian is a false dichotomy. Compound life is completely controlled and becomes a prison for Jimmy's mother [...] In contrast, [...] the pleeblands, despite their problems, are 'mysterious and exciting' (231), 'so boundless, so porous, so penetrable, so wide open' (231)" (54). Glover goes on to say that the novel "highlights the darker side of utopia and the ambiguous nature of dystopia" (54). Therefore, there is no ideal, no alternative, no outside in this novel. It is a Foucauldian representation of power that functions on multiple levels and in a variety of ways. For Glover, the pleeblands are a site of potential. In the pleeblands, regulations lack the systemic, surveillant, control society structure they have in the corporate compounds. Of course, the lack of economic means and other, repressive, power structures exist there in ways they do not in the compounds, but there is possibility there that is missing from the contained corporate world.

Oryx and Crake further develops a defamiliarizing lens through which to see our present in its analysis of the mechanisms that enable societies to perpetuate hierarchical thinking, inequity, and oppression. Atwood relies on a bit of the fantastic in order to emphasize the need to address entire systems of domination. In the present of the novel, after the near destruction of all humanity, Snowman lives alongside a genetically engineered race of beings who are meant to be as benign to the environment as humans were destructive. Snowman's best friend, Crake, designed the new species to replace humanity, believing that humanity's flaws were genetic and irreversible. Unfortunately, in order to be benign, they also have to be very far from human: they are no longer hierarchical or omnivorous, but they are also no longer artistic or sexual (Atwood 305). They would be a utopian alternative, but they lack so much of what is important to us as humans: art, sexuality, and religion (305)—although at the novel's end it is not at all clear that the Crakers aren't developing art and religion. Utopia is not part of this novel's project, not in any real sense; this is Snowman's story, and therefore it is still humanity's story; an alternative species is not the solution. There is still hope in Atwood's novel, however. The hope lies in listening to the story being told and finding an alternative. Jimmy's childhood is so nearly our future; Atwood reminds us that all lives are interconnected, and therefore there are no excuses for apathy.

Oryx and Crake is, in other words, intently focused on the notion that one boy's existence cannot be separated from the world around him; the disaster that befalls almost all of humanity becomes, in a way, Snowman's responsibility. Much like *The Handmaid's Tale*, *Oryx and Crake* invests in the power of stories. At least, that is the case if you read the end of the novel with the belief that Snowman will go to the discovered survivors in peace. Danette DiMarco offers a convincing case for optimism, stating that "Snowman serves as a potential site for change" (170). In the end, Snowman has to choose how to act when faced with other survivors: "They could listen to him, they could hear his tale, he could hear theirs" (374). Alternatively, "Should he kill them in cold blood?" (374). How will he act? Atwood doesn't say. The ethics of the narrative clearly embrace becoming and indeterminacy over static control at the social level, but Snowman's subjectivity remains troubling. Throughout the novel, Jimmy is the artistic, language-oriented thinker — qualities which are devalued in an increasingly scientific, technological world of corporate competition. Nevertheless, he has failed to read the people closest to him well enough to stop the destruction. Will he fail again? Or will he embody a subject in becoming that can shift to a different way of living in the world?

The Power of Becoming: Parable of the Sower *and* Parable of the Talents, *Octavia E. Butler*

Octavia E. Butler's two critical dystopian narratives, *Parable of the Sower* and *Parable of the Talents*, offer a very different kind of narrator/protagonist. She is certainly a product and victim of the social structures of her time and place, but she is also an active agent who creates the conditions for an ethics of becoming. She is a protagonist who — in the context of a dangerous post-apocalyptic society — refuses to be controlled for long. Butler's two texts incorporate both the sense of dissolution and fragmentation that characterizes Lessing's novels, and the tyranny of domination found in Atwood's works. As all of the texts examined thus far have made clear in one way or another, power is inescapable and must be embraced and used rather than evaded. Butler's *Parable* novels embrace that knowledge and extrapolate from it. In order to work with power rather than be controlled by it, Butler's protagonist — Lauren Olamina — engages in a constant process of adaptation and becoming. For Olamina (she comes to be called by her surname by most of the other characters in the two novels), gaining power means first coming to terms with forces that are in her way. She has to learn to read and to understand the Foucauldian power fields that surround her before she can begin to respond to them in productive ways. Once she has begun to understand how power operates, she finds ways to respond to it that include demystifying dominant discourses, answering to those dominant discourses with subjugated knowledges, revising aspects of the prevailing structures and myths that do not suit them, building communities that can offer alternative models to traditional hierarchies, and embracing becoming over stagnation.

Parable of the Sower begins in 2024 in a small, multiracial, walled-in community north of Los Angeles and consists of journal entries and verses authored by the protagonist. Once again, genre blending is a fundamental strategy at work in the text, which "combines survivalist [science fiction] with the diary and the slave narrative" (Baccolini and Moylan, *Dark* 8). The verses authored by the narrator add yet another layer to the text, and the second novel complicates the narrative structure further by including entries and letters authored by other characters. Thus, like Lessing and Atwood, Butler creates instability at the level of the narrative, which generally proceeds in linear chronological order. Olamina is a teenager at the start of the journal, and has more in common with Emily — the young girl in the Survivor's care in *Memoirs*— and Mara and Dann than with the Survivor, Offred, or Snowman. Like Emily, Mara, and Dann, Olamina cannot remember a time when things were better. She suffers from "hyperempathy syndrome," which causes her to feel the pain and/or pleasure that she sees others experiencing; the syndrome is the result of her mother's use of a drug known as "the smart pill" during her pregnancy (11). While her "hyperempathy" makes her more vulnerable than most, it is Olamina's strength that becomes central to the plot of the narrative — her strength of mind, body, character, and, eventually, of purpose. She leaves her family's community when it is destroyed by arsonists and travels the highways on foot with two other survivors. Olamina had been prepared to leave because she knew that her community was no longer safe within its walls, and she and her companions are able to survive largely because of the escape pack she had prepared and the supplies she was able to gather from the ashes of her community. As they travel, Olamina selects other travelers to become allies and carefully makes them a part of their group; she creates a growing community of travelers that struggles to survive fires, dog packs, murderers, slavers, and cannibals.

Near the end of the novel Olamina leads them to a new home in Northern California on land belonging to a man she eventually marries, and they establish a cooperative community called Acorn that is dedicated to the teachings of a new religion that Olamina has created: Earthseed. The basic premise of Earthseed is that "God is Change," and the goal Olamina sets out for her followers is to travel into outer space and set up new colonies so that humanity can survive and evolve. *Parable of the Talents* continues where *Sower* ends, with the addition of the retrospective voice of Olamina's adult daughter and a few brief passages by Olamina's husband and a brother who turns out to have survived the fire that destroyed Olamina's childhood community. Acorn is thriving at the opening of the novel, but it is soon invaded by right-wing Christian vigilantes who enslave the members of the community, including Olamina, and who abduct all of the children and place them in adoptive homes. That is how Olamina loses her baby daughter who only finds her mother as an adult. Once again, Olamina finds a way to lead those around her, this time to freedom from slavery. The rest of the novel traces her unsuccessful attempts to find her daughter and her much more successful efforts to establish Earthseed as a nationally-recognized religion.

The combined trajectory of the two narratives makes it clear that one of

Butler's emphases is how her protagonist increases her power. Olamina constructs an alternative community and religion — Earthseed — based on the principle that God *is* change. The texts demonstrate that coping with power requires adaptability, strength, and the willingness to take power for oneself. As it is for Dann, Offred, and Snowman in Lessing's and Atwood's narratives, creating her own story is a way for Olamina to construct herself and to create space for new possibilities. At one point, she explains the importance of her journal: "Sometimes I write to keep from going crazy. There's a world of things I don't feel free to talk to anyone about" (46). Baccolini argues her "critical awareness and empowerment originate in her writing" ("Gender" 25), suggesting that the process of writing is what enables Olamina to undertake the kind of critical analysis of power that is required of her. One distinct difference from the narratives discussed above is that Olamina's journal focuses at least as much on the future as on the past and present. Olamina observes the signs that her world is about to change even as a teenager, and prepares for the future in both thought and practice: "There has to be more that we can do, a better destiny that we can shape. Another place. Another way. Something!" (67). Her determination and planning lead Olamina to claim power of her own and to create alternative systems to those that she sees crumbling around her.

Like Lessing and Atwood, Butler utilizes defamiliarization in order to work against the prevailing discourses that numb readers to the realities of the contemporary world. This is, like all of the narratives discussed in this chapter, an example of revisionist rewriting of the present. Teri Ann Doerksen reads *Sower* as a literary parable, focusing on the text's cautionary function. She argues that "it tells a story that very clearly has a second set of meanings, and that has the potential to change the way the reader/listener acts or believes" (23–24). As a genealogical analysis of the present, the novel calls attention to aspects of the current global situation through defamiliarization. It refuses to allow readers to ignore the conditions of poverty and the warming global climate that create the world Olamina inhabits. Olamina, when still a teenager, is frustrated by the denial she sees in her father and in the other adult members of her community: "They [the adults] never miss a chance to relive the good old days or to tell kids how great it's going to be when the country gets back on its feet and good times come back" (*Sower* 7). Much of Olamina's drive to create Earthseed seems to come from a need to confront reality, and the future that *Sower* offers is designed to force the reader to undertake a similar reevaluation of and confrontation with the contemporary world. In *Talents* the critique focuses explicitly on conservative extremism, so that it becomes obvious that the narrative is warning the reader about what can happen when power is given away. Olamina sees that even some of the members of her own community are supporting the candidate who stands for intolerance simply because they are looking for a strong leader: "they're afraid and ashamed of their fear, ashamed of their powerlessness. And they're tired. There are millions of people like them — people who are frightened and just plain tired of all the chaos. They want someone to do something. Fix things. Now!" (*Talents* 26). The consequence of such a position is the acceptance of tyranny and, for Olamina's community, literal slavery. Power's omnipresence, which is so clearly stressed in all of the novels discussed here, is a central and repeated point in Butler's critical dystopias. Like Lessing and Atwood, Butler cautions against complacence and fear which might lead to giving one's power away.

While there is unwavering attention to the flows, reversals, and fields of power in Butler's novels, the emphasis is on productive responses to power. *Sower* contains verses that Olamina uses to define her beliefs, which collectively become the basis for Earthseed. The first verse that Olamina finds to be accurate enough to commit to her collection articulates a vision of power as both all-encompassing and controllable:

> God is Power —
> Infinite,
> Irresistible,
> Inexorable,
> Indifferent.
> And yet, God is Pliable —
> Trickster,
> Teacher,
> Chaos,
> Clay.
> God exists to be shaped.
> God is Change [22].

"God is Power," and "God is Change." For Olamina, power is about change. Coping with power's omnipresence, in the terms Olamina lays out above, means "shaping" it, directing it, and allowing change to be constant. The inevitable containment of resistance may not be avoidable, but embracing change as she does, Olamina is able to create her own way of coping with power. However, in *Talents*, Butler demonstrates just how insidious and frustrating containment can be when she portrays Olamina's rise to power with Earthseed alongside her daughter's commentary of it. To Olamina's daughter, Asha, her mother is a power hungry cult leader who cares little for the suffering on Earth and who has wasted vast amounts of resources on a pipe dream of space travel. *Talents* begins with Asha's harsh reading of her mother's life's work:

> They'll make a god of her.
> I think that would please her, if she could know about it. In spite of all her protests and denials, she's always needed devoted, obedient followers — disciples — who would listen to her and believe everything she told them. And she needed large events to manipulate. All gods seem to need these things [1].

The subversive potential of Olamina's vision is reduced by her daughter to little more than the externalized desires of one egotistical woman. It is, of course, the very fact that Olamina seeks power that Asha finds disturbing. Those who would "make a god of her" would also be betraying the spirit of Olamina's conception of Earthseed; she cannot maintain control over the concepts she releases into circulation. This narrative is fully aware of power's complex operations.[17] Getting outside of power is never a true option. Yet, through her adherence to the principle that power can be shaped, Olamina achieves — for a time at least — the creation of a significant alternative to the dominant discourses. In fact, Earthseed even sends ships into space to establish new colonies. Containment is not the end of change and possibility in Butler's novels; stagnation is far more dangerous.

One of Foucault's strategies for coping with power is what he refers to as the "insurrection of subjugated knowledges" ("Two Lectures" 81). Foucault explains that subjugated knowledges are both "those blocs of historical knowledge which were present but disguised within the body of functionalist and systematising theory" and those "that have been disqualified as inadequate to their task or insufficiently elaborated" ("Two Lectures" 82). In *Sower*, necessity drives Olamina to seek knowledge about how to make use of the plants available to her for food and medicine; she is surprised when her father tells her that he only learned how to make acorn bread — a staple in Olamina's diet from her early childhood on — from a book about Native American history. *Talents* focuses more explicitly on how knowledges can become subjugated. When extremist Christian Crusaders take over Acorn, they kidnap all of the children in order to make sure that they can be given to "good Christian homes" (208). Earthseed is disqualified as knowledge. As the Crusaders continue to enslave and torture the members of the Olamina's community, they attempt to erase the history of Acorn and of Earthseed: "They've burned our books and our papers. They've burned all that they could find of our past" (*Talents* 212). The Crusaders' acts are demonstrations of power at work; Butler incorporates an illustration of the processes whereby discourses and knowledges can be deliberately silenced. Of course, the Crusaders are unsuccessful in their attempt to obliterate the traces of Earthseed. Olamina and others escape, survive, and tell their stories. Their knowledge is not, ultimately, silenced.

While it is clear that Olamina creates her own concept of god in the *Parable* novels, Butler includes references to Christianity that result in an overall sense that there is a process of revision, or at least conversation, taking place. The titles of the novels—*Parable of the Sower* and *Parable of the Talents*—clearly refer to biblical texts. In fact, each novel ends with the King James version of the appropriate parable. Olamina's father is a Christian minister, and while his religion does not suit her, her beliefs grow out of what she learns from him. At the end of *Sower*, when Olamina has established her new community and they are remembering their dead, she writes: "So today we remembered the friends and the family members we've lost. We spoke our individual memories and quoted Bible passages, Earthseed verses, and bits of songs and poems that were favorites of the living or the dead" (295). A community is born that is based on taking what is useful from past traditions and creating anew what is needed. All of Olamina's revisionings are about responding to what is wrong with the dominant discourses, changing what needs to be changed, and reclaiming what is useful.

The alternative and revised discourses that Butler emphasizes find concrete expression in the communities that Olamina builds throughout the novels.[18] When Olamina loses her childhood community, it does not take her long to begin to choose people to accompany her on her journey; she looks for those who are in mixed racial groups (as she and her companions are) and those who can benefit from her help. *Sower* culminates in the creation of Acorn, a community of refugees that Olamina has brought together during her travels that lives according to the ideas of Earthseed. Acorn continues to grow at the beginning of *Talents*, and Olamina's vision for how the community should function is expressed in its weekly gatherings, cooperative efforts to educate its children, and daily work that is both necessary and purposeful. Patricia Melzer argues, "The construction of utopian societies is primarily a re-articulation of power relations" (par. 4), and she sees this kind of re-articulation at work in Acorn. Olamina maintains a position of power within the community as its founder and as a kind of leader, but even as she attempts to direct the future of Acorn, she does not exert authority over it in any direct way. At the weekly gatherings, all members of the community are invited to speak and to question, and major decisions are decided by vote. Olamina and the residents of Acorn reimagine what it means to coexist in ways that do not require domination or control, and in so doing they create true alternatives to existing power structure even as they take power for themselves.

The ultimate successes of Olamina's responses to power are the direct result of her ability to adapt to the multiplicity of forces surrounding her. For Deleuze and Guattari, the subject is itself multiple; embracing that multiplicity through becoming is their prescription for coping with power. Olamina's "hyperempathy syndrome" leads her to share in what she perceives others are feeling: "I feel what I see others feeling or what I believe they feel" (*Sower* 10). At the moment when Olamina encounters a person in pain, the boundaries between self and other dissolve. Thus, Olamina constantly experiences the process of becoming-other. She is always aware of the possibility of the loss of self. One of the verses from Earthseed that appears in *Talents* illustrates how Olamina perceives the self:

> Self is.
> Self is body and bodily
> perception. Self is thought, memory,
> belief. Self creates. Self destroys. Self
> learns, discovers, becomes. Self
> shapes. Self adapts. Self invents its
> own reasons for being. To shape
> God, shape Self [235].

As a "hyperempath," Olamina sees the self much as Deleuze and Guattari do: an assemblage that is merely one possible version amongst multiple possibilities. According to Deleuze and Guattari, "the self is only a threshold, a door, a becoming between two multiplicities" (249). The nomadic subject knowingly embraces self as open, changing, and becoming.

Olamina's understanding of the self's heterogeneous potential translates directly into what she believes and does. Early in *Sower*, as she is sorting out the ideas that will become the basis for Earthseed, Olamina contemplates the problem of perpetual change:

> Everyone knows that change is inevitable. From the second law of thermodynamics to Darwinian evolution, from Buddhism's insistence that nothing is permanent and all suffering results from our delusions of permanence to the third chapter of Ecclesiastes [...], change is part of life, of existence, of the common wisdom. But I don't believe we're dealing with all that that means. We haven't even begun to deal with it [23].

Coming to terms with change is, for Olamina, the core of Earthseed. God is change because change is *the* constant. Beginning with the boundaries of the self and extending to her perceptions of the world around her, Olamina develops a belief system that enables her to cope with power by remaining continually aware of change and open to becoming. The culmination of her meditations on how to contend with a god that is change is the goal she creates for Earthseed: "to take root among the stars" (*Sower* 68). In *Talents*, she explains the reasoning behind that goal: "'I wanted us to understand what we could be, what we could do. I wanted to give us a focus, a goal, something big enough, complex enough, difficult enough, and in the end, radical enough to make us become more than we ever have been'" (358). Becoming emerges as the principle upon which the goal of Earthseed is founded. Olamina, whose "hyperempathy" makes her uniquely positioned to understand becoming, creates an alternative discourse that answers to dominant power structures and that works from the concept of becoming.

The *Parable* novels warn of a future that may still be preventable, but — more importantly — they also examine what it would mean to approach power from a position of acceptance and awareness. Olamina embraces the idea that power is fundamental to everything, and in so doing she finds a way to mold power to create viable alternatives to the dominant hierarchical structure. The fact that Olamina's actions are questioned by her daughter in the second novel is evidence of Butler's awareness of the difficulty of taking and using power; there are no easy answers to be found in these texts, only complex examinations of the possibilities that are available when power is understood and confronted.

Powerful Possibilities

The critical dystopian narratives discussed above demonstrate an investment in a particular kind of approach to the future that encourages an ethics of potential and becoming that is both deeply aware of power and capable of creating new relations to and with power. Through their uses of genre blending and narrative defamiliarization, Lessing, Atwood, and Butler create texts that perform genealogical explorations of power in the present in order to generate new possibilities for the future. In the process, all three writers foreground the need to replace closed systems of morality with more open structures of ethics. Lessing's Survivor's use of the word "It" hones in on the late twentieth-century sense of the inaccessibility of large power structures, while the personal scenes behind the wall critique the moral discourses surrounding the strictly coded norms of gender and sexuality associated with the nuclear family. The *Mara and Dann* novels emphasize community-building and story-telling as methods of becoming that can counter complex networks of power. Atwood's inclusion of Offred's memories allows for a critique of the complacency that could lead to the rise of a regime like Gilead, which includes the acceptance of increasing levels of moralizing in public discourse. The "Historical Notes" offer an additional comment upon the production of historical knowledge and a further level of defamiliarization; Offred's account is, after all, not entirely without foundation in the historical realities of our world. In

Oryx and Crake, Atwood furthers her analysis of power to encompass contemporary models of globalization. Finally, Butler's *Parable* novels engage with the omnipresence of power by embracing it. In the midst of the collapse of California's social structure, Olamina asserts that the most fundamental aspect of life is change and that change must be shaped.

The protagonists of these critical dystopias are important examples of individuals responding to power. In a discussion of Deleuze's concerns, Braidotti states, "the philosophy and the politics of difference must take into account not only the negative aspects of power, that is to say the experiences of oppression, exclusion and marginality, but also the need to redefine the positive structures of the subject" (*Metamorphoses* 125). The subject in and of power: that is precisely what is at stake in the critical dystopian narratives by Lessing, Atwood, and Butler. Their protagonists are shaped through the "negative aspects of power," clearly, but it is in the texts' redefinitions of the "positive structures of the subject" that hope is to be found. For the Survivor, crumbling power structures leave a vacuum into which Lessing inserts the alternative, fantastic world behind that wall that offers an ethics based in shared work, community, and self construction. Her final exit behind the wall signals a choice to follow her desires, to construct herself, to become. Both Dann and Offred are able to construct possibilities for becoming through the production of their own narratives, and any hope for the future of Snowman's world must reside in the hearing and understanding of his story. Olamina's world is characterized by the dissolution of power structures in *Parable of the Sower* and by dominating power in *Parable of the Talents*. In both cases, her reaction is to take power for herself and to use it to construct an alternative that embraces a theology/philosophy of constant change and becoming.

Four

Becoming-Alien in Feminist Space Fiction

The Possibilities of Space Fiction

Speculative fictions that extrapolate from the present in ways that are both critical of contemporary conditions and productive of new possibilities are not always dystopian. The space fiction narratives discussed here, like the dystopias in Chapter Three, emphasize the need for attention to large structures of power and the potential for new configurations. Doris Lessing who uses the term "space fiction" in her introductory remarks to *Shikasta* (1979); it is appropriate for all of the texts discussed here in that they are mainly concerned with the confrontations between beings from different worlds. Through the use of aliens, as well as inter-galactic travel and instantaneous communications devices, the space narratives discussed below develop crucial criticism of the present on this world, and explore what is at stake in the notion of a post-human becoming. Rosi Braidotti claims that "science fiction enacts a displacement of our world-view away from the human epicenter and that it manages to establish a continuum with the animal, mineral, vegetable, extra-terrestrial and technological worlds. It points to a post-humanist, bio-centred egalitarianism" (*Metamorphoses* 183). The texts discussed below exemplify Braidotti's claims, in part through their development of an ethics of becoming.

Octavia E. Butler's *Xenogenesis* trilogy (now sold and packaged under the title *Lilith's Brood*), Ursula K. Le Guin's *Hainish Cycle* novels, and Doris Lessing's *Canopus in Argos: Archives* series are — like all of the texts examined thus far — deeply concerned with the nature of power and its production. Contrary to readings that characterize space fiction as escapist or apolitical, a specific inquiry into the representations of the fluctuations and flows of power

Four. *Becoming-Alien in Feminist Space Fiction*

in these texts demonstrates that they invite analysis that takes their critiques seriously. The more fantastic elements of the narratives allow the writers to reimagine what is possible. More than any other set of texts examined in this project, the space fiction narratives emphasize alternatives to the contemporary world. These alternatives differ, but they are largely the product of encounters between humans and non-humans, between the "self" of a text and an "other." Making use of the fantastic possibilities of space fiction allows the writers to explore nomadic subjectivity and the becomings those nomadic subjects experience.

In the mid–twentieth century, Kingsley Amis referred to science fiction of his time, arguing, "One is grateful that we have a form of writing which is interested in the future, which is ready [...] to treat as variables what are usually taken to be constants, which is set on tackling those large, general, speculative questions that ordinary fiction so often avoids" (155–56). Within the specific context of contemporary literature, the narratives discussed in this chapter attend to precisely the kinds of questions that Amis found to be central to the canonical science fiction of his time. Feminist space fiction—with its future-oriented thinking and critical/genealogical approach to the present—is particularly suited to the task of representing an ethics characterized by potentiality and indeterminacy. Space fiction itself is one of the more fantastic sub-genres of science fiction, relying on speculation rather than scientifically proven theories. The alien of space fiction is also one of the longest standing figures in science fiction, conjuring images of H.G. Wells's invading Martians. In contemporary feminist writing, the sub-genre takes on new possibilities because, as this project has tried to highlight, some women writers working at the end of the twentieth-century and into the twenty-first are unwilling to retain old forms and formulas. Instead, they rewrite, revise, and—in so doing—recode. Indeed, examples of such processes at work in texts by Butler and Lessing can be found in previous chapters. The focus in what follows will be more on the specific explorations of becoming in the texts than on the revisionist aspects of the works. Nevertheless, the alternatives imagined by Butler, Le Guin, and Lessing develop in part as revisionings of what has come before.[1] Becoming is, of course, a movement from the past/present to the future, and as such it is itself always a process of revisioning.

One way to understand the function of space fiction, and its usefulness for contemporary women writers, is through its revisionist approach to other literary forms. Sarah Lefanu, working against the endless definitions of science fiction as a genre, chooses to describe science fiction by what it does, rather than set limits on what it is. She states,

By borrowing from other literary forms it lets writers defamiliarise the familiar, and make familiar the new and strange. These twin possibilities, apparently contradictory (but SF is full of contradictions), offer enormous scope to women writers who are thus released from the constraints of realism. The social and sexual hierarchies of the contemporary world can be examined through the process of "estrangement," thus challenging normative ideas of gender roles; and visions of different worlds can be created, made familiar to the reader through the process of narrative. SF narrative can be used to break down, or to build up [21–22].

According to Lefanu, science fiction is founded on the ability to borrow from other literary forms. A description of an alien might, therefore, employ strictly realist techniques, it might utilize modernist formal strategies in order to offer a variety of perspectives, or it might even play on gothic conventions. All of those choices have implications for how the alien will be read. The reader will read against conventional realist, modernist, or gothic descriptions, making the science fiction alien a revision of the earlier texts. In *Shikasta* (1979), for example, Lessing works with journal, document, epistolary, and diary forms. As a whole, the collection constitutes an official report that is ostensibly meant to be read by alien agents embarking on inter-stellar colonial careers. Butler's *Dawn* (1987), in contrast, is a linear narrative written in the third person but almost entirely from within the point of view of the main human character. Lessing's text offers a variety of perspectives that vary from the local to the galactic in scale, but there is no complete account. The reader has to settle for partial understanding rather than a totalizing narrative. Butler's novel provides a far more individualized perspective that reflects some of the central themes of the text: isolation, fear, the need for community, and the desire to survive. They are both examples of space fiction, and each works through the specific problem of becoming-alien, but they borrow from different generic traditions. Therefore, they also address and revise different literary models. The revisionist rewriting here is an echo of the kinds of more direct revision discussed in earlier chapters, but it remains directly linked to the ethics of becoming.

The defamiliarizing function of science fiction is covered in some depth in Chapter Three, where the focus is on how speculative fiction set in the future can work to critique the present. In that way, it "defamiliarises the familiar" (Lefanu 21), requiring a reevaluation or demystification of normative discourses. Feminist space fiction can operate in a similar manner; portrayals of other worlds, or of our world in drastically altered contexts, work against the familiar in order to destabilize unexamined power relations. Lefanu's description of an apparent contradiction with the other function she delineates for science fiction is unnecessary. Science (or space) fiction's invention of the "new and strange" is a fantastic literary procedure that can enact both critical, revisionist analysis and the production of alternatives to the system being analyzed. Contemporary women's writing utilizes science fiction — and a variety of other fantastic forms — *both* "to break down" *and* "to build up" (Lefanu 22). In relation to contemporary writing, Marleen S. Barr argues that "speculative fiction in the best cases makes the patriarchal structures which constrain women obvious and perceptible" (*Alien* xx). Like the revisionist rewriting in Chapters One and Two, and the critical dystopias in Chapter Three, the space fiction narratives of Butler, Le Guin, and Lessing render power's machinations in this world more visible. In a different context, Barr makes a second point: "Feminist science fiction presents blueprints for social structures that allow women's words to counter patriarchal myths" (*Lost* 7). While all of the narratives discussed counter dominant discourses with alternative possibilities, it is the space fiction narratives that are best able to offer "blueprints" of an ethics of becoming. That is not to say that they are utopian manuals designed to instruct readers in the production of perfect societies. Rather, the space fiction narratives discussed below are complex investigations of the procedures and promise of becoming that rely upon critical engagement with the present of our world in order to remain grounded, and that emphasize the potential of the future in order to alter perspectives of past, present, and future.

Heterotopia

Despite their clear emphasis on describing alternative configurations of power, the feminist space fiction texts discussed in this chapter are not utopian. In fact, a further point should be made that some of the texts discussed here could be described as dystopian: Butler's *Xenogenesis* trilogy is largely set on a post-apocalyptic version of Earth, all of the texts in Lessing's *Canopus in Argos: Archives* depict at least one form of grand-scale disaster at some point, and Le Guin's *Hainish Cycle* includes a variety of images of galactic warfare, colonial rivalry, and native poverty. The positive alternatives offered in the texts are, then, counterbalanced by equally negative elements. It is useful to return to Michel Foucault's work here, and to his concept of "heterotopia."

In the preface to *The Order of Things*, Foucault describes the origins of his book as arising from a moment of laughter brought on by a passage in Borges. That laughter, according to Foucault, threatened the "age-old distinction between the Same and the Other" (xv). The incongruous, or "the linking together of things that are inappropriate" (xvii) is, ultimately, what Foucault describes as so disturbing in Borges. Even more disturbing, however, is the possibility of complete incoherence, which is what leads Foucault to heterotopia:

> *Utopias* afford consolation: although they have no real locality there is nevertheless a fantastic, untroubled region in which they are able to unfold; they open up cities with vast avenues, superbly planted gardens, countries where life is easy, even though the road to them is chimerical. *Heterotopias* are disturbing, probably because they secretly undermine language, because they make it impossible to name this *and* that, because they shatter or tangle common names, because they destroy "syntax" in advance, and not only the syntax with which we construct sentences but also that less apparent syntax which causes words and things (next to and also opposite one another) to "hold together." This is why utopias permit fables and discourse: they run with the very grain of language and are part of the fundamental dimension of the *fibula*; heterotopias [...] desiccate speech, stop words in their tracks, contest the very possibility of grammar at its source; they dissolve our myths and sterilize the lyricism of our sentences [*Order* xviii].

There is little to inspire celebration in Foucault's initial description of heterotopia. Its "disturbing" qualities include an ability to undermine language and naming, prevent speech, and destroy myths. Yet, there is something freeing in all of those traits. The nature of heterotopia, according to Foucault, is to dissolve stable categories. There may not be space for ideal countries, but is it really necessary to think in terms of ideal countries? Is it not, in fact, far more interesting to consider the possibility of escaping a logocentric model of social construction in favor of one of becoming and potential?

Foucault also uses heterotopia to explain a specific type of social space that is both similar to and antithetical to utopian social spaces. In an article entitled "Of Other Spaces," he describes heterotopias and utopias: "Utopias are sites with no real place [...] They present society itself in a perfected form, or else turned upside down, but in any case these utopias are fundamentally unreal spaces" ("Spaces"). Heterotopias, on the other hand, are "counter-sites, a kind of effectively enacted utopia in which the real sites, all the other real sites that can be found within the culture, are simultaneously represented, contested, and inverted" ("Spaces"). Heterotopias are defined through simultaneity and diversity, unity and difference. They encompass all possibilities, as well as the reversals of those possibilities. It is the notion of heterotopia as "counter-site" that readers of Foucault have found particularly intriguing. The concept of heterotopia has been appropriated by a number of critics who see it as a potentially useful category, or un-category. In *Spaces of Hope*, David Harvey argues that heterotopia "allows us to think of multiple utopian schemes (spatial plays) that have come down to us in materialized forms as not mutually exclusive. It encourages the idea of a simultaneity of spatial plays that highlights choice, diversity, and difference" (184). Harvey emphasizes the simultaneity of heterotopia as a productive possibility, and even as a way of redefining closed utopian models as open through their interplay with one another.

Ralph Pordzik approaches the usefulness of Foucault's concept from a different angle: "Heterotopia represents the site of conflict where a wide range of discourses [...] can be negotiated and tested against the backdrop of the strictly hierarchized closed-system model that usually informs our notion of the static uniformity of utopian or dystopian societies" (5). Utopia and dystopia are, in effect, measuring devices for much speculative fiction, but heterotopia, as Pordzik describes it, offers the possibility of getting outside of this kind of dualistic and potentially hierarchical thinking. In addition, Pordzik's description of heterotopia as a site of negotiated conflict and testing credits it with a kind of dynamic in-process status that aligns it with becoming, as opposed to more static models of utopia or dystopia.[2] Braidotti, it seems, would agree. She explores Teresa de Lauretis's use of Foucault, and comes to the conclusion that "heterotopia" is "the co-existence of mutually undermining meaning systems which point to the dissolution of the unitary notion of the subject" (*Metamorphoses* 183). The instability of the relation between self and other, or "the Same and the Other," as Foucault puts it, is at the heart of heterotopia. It is from within precisely such spaces — literary or otherwise — that the exploration of an ethics of becoming can take shape.

Feminist Genealogy

In an essay discussing Foucault's genealogical project and Gilles Deleuze's emphasis on eternal return in relation to feminist practice, Claire Colebrook argues that it is necessary for feminists to take a strategic approach to the philosophers' concepts. She explains that "[a] feminist genealogy would be both a critical procedure — connecting the subject in general with the forces and techné that have made it possible — and an active becoming, through this encounter affirming the specific value of other techné and other values" (127). Colebrook combines Foucault's focus on subject construction with Deleuze and Félix Guattari's concept of active becoming, which requires the abandonment of the self in order to become-other. The self is tied to being, while the subject is free to become. Thus, Colebrook's formula for a feminist genealogy requires both that the subject be scrutinized as the creation of multiple productive forces, *and* that the potential fluidity of such subject construction be used in order to create active becoming. Butler, Le Guin, and Lessing explore precisely this combination of genealogical analysis and the alternative "techné" and "values" that accompany active becoming in their space fictions.

If read according to the terms laid out above, the feminist space fiction texts discussed in this chapter utilize heterotopian literary spaces to offer an exploration of the relationship between genealogical critique and active becoming, or — in Colebrook's terms — feminist genealogy. The literary depictions of becoming-alien differ so that some are literal, embodied transformations, some are gradual shifts from human to alien perception and understanding, while still others bear more resemblance to the kinds of provisional, momentary becomings described by Deleuze and Guattari. In all cases, the writers stress the terror of the loss of the self. The specific nature of the depiction of becoming-alien in these texts further develops the problematics of the relation between self and other in drastic ways. Becoming-other requires the destabilization of subjectivity; becoming-animal requires a reconceptualization of bodies/rationality/boundaries; becoming-alien is another thing altogether. It is perhaps best thought of in terms of the long history of the monstrous. Braidotti explains,

> We need to learn to think of the anomalous, the monstrously different not as a sign of pejoration but as the unfolding of virtual possibilities that point to positive alternatives for us all. As Deleuze would put it: the pattern of becoming cuts across the experiential field of all that phallogocentrism did *not* programme us to become. In that sense, the fantasmagoric diversity of monstrous beings points the way to the kind of line of becoming which our crisis-afflicted culture badly needs. I tend to think of this as the last-to-date episode in the de-centring of Western thought; the human is now displaced in the direction of a glittering range of post-human variables, however painful this may be to the collective hubris we — including Western feminists — have inherited from centuries of codified Western humanism ["Teratologies" 172].

The monstrous difference of the alien other is the challenge presented to many of the protagonists in the narratives discussed below. To become-alien is to redefine not only the subject, but the desirability of difference. Nomadic subjectivity is a precondition for the possibility of post-human, or monstrous, becomings. I turn now to the "glittering range of post-human variables" offered by Le Guin, Lessing, and Butler.

Provisional Peace Through Nomadic Subjectivities: The Hainish Cycle, *Ursula K. Le Guin*

Ursula K. Le Guin's *Hainish Cycle* is comprised of a loosely connected set of narratives. Considered together, the texts offer diverse possibilities and productive connections. Heterotopian potential pervades the texts at multiple

Four. *Becoming-Alien in Feminist Space Fiction*

levels. Like the critical dystopias in Chapter Three that explore power on micro and macro scales, Le Guin's narratives develop the implications of heterotopia for individual subjects, entire nations, and galactic alliances. Interplanetary solidarity, (mostly) functional anarchy, and "potential sexuality," are just some of the ways Le Guin imagines possibilities for peace in the narratives. In these texts, alien visitors (usually from Terra, our Earth), have to come to terms with the ways of various other worlds and their peoples, just as those peoples have to accept the existence and the ways of the alien visitors. Positioning humans as the aliens in her narratives is the first of many ways that Le Guin defamiliarizes the relation between self and other. The alien human reorients the reader so that otherness is no longer monstrosity, but normality. Narrative after narrative conveys the utter amazement and uncertainty at the heart of any confrontation with the alien other. This is, of course, a common trope in science fiction. However, in Le Guin's narratives characters are placed in situations that require them to reevaluate the boundaries between self and other, and even to become-other. These are heterotopian examinations of vexed and potentially productive confrontations with the alien. Additionally, the *Hainish Cycle* narratives as a whole work toward a larger concept of provisional peace that explores the ethics of becoming on a larger scale. Provisional peace is a way of describing a delicate and temporary state of unity in Le Guin's texts that is always about diversity and openness.

The *Hainish Cycle* narratives, from *Rocannon's World* (1966) to *The Telling* (2000), provide multiple and complex models of confrontation and, often, reconciliation, with the alien other. The Hain are an ancient race who once decided to "seed" worlds with humanity. However, once the Hain had begun their various experiments they either lost contact with or decided to sever ties to the various worlds they had seeded. Le Guin's *Hainish Cycle* narratives take place during a period when the Hain have reestablished contact and formed something called the "League of All Worlds." The various storylines occur over a long period, during which the League is attacked and conquered for a time by the Shing. When the Shing are finally defeated, the new interplanetary organization is called the Ekumen: a much less aggressive and much more open federation. The immense time scale and large — actually, galactic — perspective of the *Hainish Cycle* is interesting given Le Guin's tendency to write about a specific situation within the Hainish universe, and only to return to that situation on rare occasions. There are references to earlier texts in later narratives, but the fabric that holds the *Hainish Cycle* together is thematic rather than character driven. Lessing's space fiction series takes a similar, large-scale view of the universe, but her texts do return to the same characters. Le Guin's Hainish creation is, truly, a heterotopian universe.

Rocannon's World (1966) is one of Le Guin's earliest science fiction works, and it is a useful first example of how Le Guin's *Hainish Cycle* narratives use heterotopia to conceptualize becoming-alien. In this novel, Rocannon (the human who plays the role of alien-other) travels to Fomalhaut II as a representative of the League of All Worlds in order to do an ethnological survey. This story takes place early in the *Hainish Cycle* history, and Fomalhaut II winds up under attack from an enemy that is later identified as the Shing. Rocannon is left on his own on a strange world with no way of contacting his people or getting home, since the Shing have destroyed his ship and killed the rest of his survey team. Le Guin uses variations of this device throughout her work: the alien visitor, for technical/personal/political/scientific reasons is cut off from her/his people and world. There is a lengthy time limit before conditions will permit contact, some obstacle to overcome in order for contact to be made, or even no possibility of contact within the alien visitor's lifetime. In all cases, the alien visitor must acclimate to the world upon which s/he has been stranded. In Rocannon's case, as a representative of the League, he decides that it is up to him to protect this planet from the League's enemy; most of the narrative is about his journey across the planet and his eventual success in defeating the Shing. This journey is later mirrored and expanded in many of the other Hainish narratives.[3]

Perhaps more interesting than the plot of the narrative are the aliens who live on Fomalhaut II.[4] There are multiple sentient species, but the most fascinating are the Clayfolk and the Fiia, who are representatives of darkness/hierarchy/technology and light/equality/simplicity, respectively. These two species were once one, and Rocannon's journey takes him to meet the last living example of that unity: the Ancient One. When he does encounter the Ancient One, Rocannon is disoriented: "It was like the Clayfolk, dwarfish and pale; like the Fiia, frail and clear-eyed; like both, like neither. The hair was white. The voice was no voice, for it sounded within Rocannon's mind while all his ears heard was the faint whistle of the wind; and there were no words" (97). This being is both unity and the promise of diversity, and it prefigures many other forms of unity in Le Guin's later novels. The other sentient species is the Liuar, who are also marked by division. Rocannon's companion on his journey and the woman he marries are both from the Liuar species, which lives in a feudal system divided between the Angyar and the Olgyior, or "midmen."

The world of this novel is sometimes read as being marked by stagnation and conflict.[5] While the species on what will be known as Rocannon's World are divided and seemingly resistant to change, this is not a novel about stagnation. Rocannon's initial decision to survey the planet is brought about by his discomfort with the idea of the League taxing peoples it knows so little about, and those taxes have caused the Angyar to struggle. In addition, the League's interference has brought increased technological knowledge to the Clayfolk, who are certainly not averse to change and technological progress. However, these general observations about Rocannon's World are not as significant as the more specific way in which Rocannon himself is changed by his experience of the world. Through his numerous encounters with various cultures on the planet, and finally his encounter with the Ancient One, Rocannon learns telepathy, or "mindspeak." It is this telepathic ability that ultimately saves the planet, and it is Rocannon's acclimation to the planet that is the ultimate focus of the narrative. Once he has accomplished his task and saved the planet, Rocannon explains, "Who are my people? I am not what I was" (112). Embracing difference, adjusting to alternative ways of being and thinking and, ultimately, becoming-alien are already central themes in this early work. So too, however, are the despair, frustration, and sense of loss that often accompany the process of becoming in these texts. Rocannon is, of course, also still human and will always be so. Becoming-alien is depicted as a risk that involves straddling possibilities. A nomadic subject could also be seen as a homeless one, without specific identity or context. Yet, Rocannon and the characters that follow him in Le Guin's space fictions learn to cultivate nomadic subjectivities in ways that allow them to be both human and alien.

Following closely after *Rocannon's World* is *Planet of Exile* (1966), another narrative about the relationship between the League of All Worlds and an individual planet. In this case a planet called Gamma Draconis III, later named Werel, is home to an entire Terran colony that has lost contact with the League and lives apart from the native peoples. The Tevarens, a native population who live simply and in accordance with the extremely long years of their planet — each year is essentially a lifetime — are in danger of being attacked by another native population, the Gaal. In order to defeat the Gaal, the Tevarens and the Terrans must form an alliance; centuries of distrust and dislike are, however, in the way. The break in this hostility comes slowly and haltingly, but it centers on a love story between a Terran, Jakob Agat, and a Tevaren, Rolery. Like some of Le Guin's later novels, this narrative is structured according to chapters that alternate points of view. Yet, Le Guin does not stray from her use of the third-person to narrate; she simply focuses on the experiences and thoughts of one character or another: Jakob Agat, Rolery, and an elder Tevaran named Wold. Maintaining third-person narration means that Le Guin does not necessarily answer all of the reader's questions about the feelings, motives, and desires of the individual characters. Additionally, it preserves a sense of a larger overall narrative — a heterotopian view, even.

There is no knowing narrative voice to comment upon each of the three characters, but the continuous use of the third-person ties together the various heterogeneous perspectives of the individual characters, who differ greatly in their worldviews, linguistic habits, and approaches to knowledge.

Agat and Rolery create a relationship, despite great differences, that forges the way for a new race that will eventually populate the world. When Agat asks Rolery to return to his Terran city and to marry him, he describes her response: "She bowed her head as if in acceptance; he did not know her gestures well enough to be sure. He wondered a little at her quietness now. The little while he had known her she had always been quick with motion and emotion. But it had been a very little while" (159). As with any intimate relationship, the one between Agat and Rolery requires a process of increasing knowledge and understanding. The added complexity is born of their different modes of relating to the world; each is alien to the other. Indeed, Rolery refers to herself and her people as "human" and to Agat and the Terrans as something else; the Terrans, of course, refer to themselves as human and to Rolery's people as everything from Tevarens to backward natives. Le Guin defamiliarizes through reversal, but by offering more than one perspective she also maintains a heterotopian simultaneity. Not just reversal, but multiplicity, marks the text as a space where an ethics of becoming can develop.

When Rolery does move into the Terran city, she has to adjust to new modes of representing, thinking, and knowing. And, of course, she also brings her own ways to the alien-others of the Terrans:

> The strangest thing in all the strangeness of this house was the painting on the wall of the big room downstairs. When Agat had gone and the rooms were deathly still she stood gazing at this picture till it became the world and she the wall. And the world was a network: a deep network, like interlacing branches in the woods, like inter-running currents in water, silver, gray, black, shot through with green and rose and a yellow like the sun. As one watched the network one saw in it, among it, woven into it and weaving it, little and great patterns and figures, beasts, trees, grasses, men and women and other creatures, some like far-borns and some not; and strange shapes, boxes set on round legs, birds, axes, silver spears and feathers of fire, faces that were not faces, stones with wings and a tree whose leaves were stars [166].

For Rolery, the painting of Terran technology is a pattern of which she can become a part. She sees the world in it, but as a network of heterotopic interlacing possibilities. As is evident from the line "till it became the world and she the wall," Rolery is able to offer Agat and the other Terrans a worldview that, although still wary of difference, is less firmly rooted in the concept of a stable subject. The Tevarens, as a result, become-other with ease. The Terrans themselves have lost most of their technological abilities because, according to League rules, "*No Religion or Congruence shall be disseminated, no technique or theory shall be taught, no cultural set or pattern shall be exported, nor shall paraverbal speech be used with any non–Communicant high-intelligence lifeform, or any Colonial Planet*" (168, italics in original). Agat breaks those rules by communicating with Rolery through mindspeak, or paraverbal communications. Telepathy is an example of one of the elements that loosely links the *Hainish* texts. Here, the narrative suggests that lack of communication is a foolish corrective to imperialistic approaches to indigenous cultures because it is only in the equal, open exchange between Rolery and Agat that their two cultures are able to survive, and to become. The tenuous alliance that develops between the Terrans and the Tevarens is the first example of the provisional and complicated nature of peace in Le Guin's *Hainish Cycle*.

In *City of Illusion* (1967), Le Guin introduces a complicated Earth, or Terra, which is currently under the control of the Shing, the same threatening enemy from the previous two novels. The descendents of Rolery and Jakob Agat have sent a ship to Terra in an attempt to reestablish contact, but the Shing infiltrate the ship and erase the mind of the only adult survivor. This survivor is taken in by Terrans and named "Falk." The novel traces his existence on Terra as Falk, and his journey to find out what happened to him and who he really is. In the end, the Shing, who are anxious to find Werel (Rolery and Agat's world), tell Falk that his name was Remarren and that they can restore his memory, but only at the expense of the identity and memories of Falk. He undergoes the procedure, but manages to maintain both identities and thus becomes a hybrid: Falk-Ramarren. Fredric Jameson, interestingly, reads this moment in Le Guin's novel as a rendition of "that fundamental anxiety of Utopia [...] namely the fear of losing that familiar world in which all our vices and virtues are rooted (very much including the longing for Utopia itself) in exchange for a world in which all these things and experiences — positive as well as negative — will have been obliterated" (97). Read as a heterotopia rather than a struggle for utopia, the novel offers a different possibility. In the figure of Falk-Remarren, Le Guin answers such a reading with the possibility of the choice to fight (and he does have to fight) for the continuous, simultaneous existence of multiple realities.

As Falk-Ramarren, he is an alien to himself. At first, he finds this balance difficult to maintain:

> In those first fearful hours, he begged and prayed to be delivered sometimes from one self, sometimes from the other. Once when he cried out in anguish in his own native tongue, he did not understand the words he had spoken, and this was so terrible that in utter misery he wept; it was Falk who did not understand, but Ramarren who wept. In that same moment of misery he touched for the first

time, for a moment only, the balance-pole, the center, and for a moment ways *himself*: then lost again, but with just enough strength to home for the next moment of harmony [349].

The internal integration of two alien subjectivities is no simple task. Becoming-himself, for Falk-Remarren, means becoming-alien to himself and being able to maintain that state of becoming. There is no reconciled, stable, or single subject position. He is always and forever a nomadic subject in becoming. The romantic relationship between Rolery and Agat in *Planet of Exile* which works to unite while maintaining differences is here reworked to be embodied by a single character who is both self and other, human and alien. The plot of the novel hinges upon Falk-Remarren's ability to find a balance between the two subject positions so that he can access memories from both and find his way back to Werel. Le Guin portrays the hybrid figure of Falk-Remarren as one of potential and hope; his ability to retain two conflicting alien subject positions in simultaneous balance is Werel's hope for the future, and it marks an increasing emphasis on the positive potential of becoming in Le Guin's work.

The next major work in the *Hainish Cycle* is one of Le Guin's most highly regarded novels: *The Left Hand of Darkness* (1969). In it, the reader encounters a planet peopled by individuals who are, as a rule, neither male nor female, but who have the potential to be either during regular mating cycles, called Kemmer. Desire dictates sexual identity, since a male or female object of desire will elicit the opposite during Kemmer. The power dynamics and politics of the entire world of Gethen, or "Winter," are affected by the lack of an overriding gender division in the population. Indeed, as Adam Roberts puts it, "in *The Left Hand of Darkness* Le Guin has hit upon a means of exploring the ways that gender, and our assumptions about gender, shapes the world we live in" (109). The novel deconstructs gender so thoroughly that the very narrative structure does not function in terms of the kind of binary conflict that most readers might expect. Roberts points out that this lack of binary structure may have something to do with a certain amount of the negative response from critics (110). The plot evolves through journey and becoming as much as through conflict and resolution. The larger plot of *The Left Hand of Darkness* has to do with bringing Gethen into the Ekumen. Like *Planet of Exile*, this narrative involves the relationship between two people, an alien and a native person, which acts as both a catalyst and a microcosm of the larger provisional peace process between societies and worlds. Le Guin defamiliarizes sexual identity and recodes it as a function of desire through the Gethenians. As in the previous novels in the cycle, she also utilizes the figure of an alien visitor on Gethen. In this case, it is a male from the Ekumen (the League has advanced to a new stage in its history), called Genly Ai, who must find a way to exist among the typically gender-neutral Gethenians. In this way, Le Guin gives us a text that envisions a heterotopian unity between the sexes, but also highlights the intense negative response the male visitor has to that unity. It should also be noted that the Gethenians have a similar negative response to the male visitor. Unity, because it is a matter of heterotopian simultaneity, is never simple in these narratives.

Other formal qualities of this work are also pertinent to the concept of heterotopia. It begins, "I'll make my report as if I told a story, for I was taught as a child on my homeworld that Truth is a matter of the imagination" (1). Genly Ai's report is, the text announces through subtitle, part of the "Archives of Hain." Historical knowledge, what constitutes truth, and the role of personal memory are already laid out as issues of concern in the first sentence of the narrative. These are themes that come up over and over in all forms of revisionist fictions concerned with an ethics of becoming, and while they are more obviously important to the revised fairy tales and histories discussed in earlier chapters, they remain at the forefront of the space fiction texts discussed here as well. A bit later, Genly Ai continues, "The story is not all mine, nor told by me alone. Indeed I am not sure whose story it is; you can judge better. But it is all one, and if at moments the facts seem to alter with an altered voice, why then you can choose the fact you like best; yet none of them are false and it is all one story" (1–2). The multiple voices, perspectives, and possibilities in the text — while "all one" — are also divergent and even contradictory. It is deliberately constructed as a heterotopian text, in that sense. Robert Scholes writes of the novel, "We hear the bardic voices of folk-tellers, the cryptic voices of religious mysticism, and above all we hear the voices of the two main characters" (91). It is within this select group of diverse voices that Genly Ai's struggle with the alien other is set.

As the stranded human, Genly Ai is the primary focus of the narrative's exploration of becoming-alien. Through his personal relationship with a Gethenian, Estraven, Le Guin explores what it would take for a male to accept the possibility of subjectivity unmoored to ostensibly stable categories of biological sex: "And I saw then again, and for good, what I had always been afraid to see, and had pretended not to see in him: that he was a woman as well as a man. Any need to explain the sources of that fear vanished with the fear; what I was left with was, at last, acceptance of him as he was. Until then I had rejected him, refused him his own reality" (248). Genly Ai has lived among the Gethenians for months and months, but he has always interpreted them according to his own frames of reference and ways of seeing. This is the moment that marks Genly-Ai's becoming-alien. He not only accepts Estraven, but begins to think in Gethenian terms. Further, through the Gethenian model of provisionally gendered subjectivity, Genly Ai has to learn to think about subjectivity itself as something in flux rather than as fixed and stable. His becoming-alien is, in part, a coming to terms with nomadic subjectivity and with heterotopian simultaneity.

The overall plot of the novel, and Gethen's eventual integration into the Ekumen, hinges upon everyone's ability to learn to become-other, to think beyond the bounds of what had previously been constituted as the possible. Genly-Ai's becoming-alien is, then, an individual's experience of what the entire population of Gethen must do; people who have never thought of flight (there being no birds on their planet), who have assumed all people to be both male and female, and who have lived in stable, peaceful societies for millennia must confront the realities of aliens who bring difference and change. The novel insists on an ethics of becoming.

While *The Left Hand of Darkness* clearly develops the themes of heterotopia and becoming, *The Dispossessed: An Ambiguous Utopia* (1974) is in some ways the most obvious example of how the *Hainish Cycle* narratives depict the openness of possibility in productive and enabling ways. Shevek, a physicist working toward a temporal theory of unity between sequence and simultaneity, is the reader's guide through two worlds. On his home world of Anarres, an anarchist social structure both encourages and inhibits Shevek's work. Anarres is actually a moon of Urras, the large planet to which Shevek travels. The reader learns mainly about two of the countries on Urras, one capitalist and one communist. His personal experiences on both planets are examples of growth and transformation in fairly conventional ways. Interestingly, as Victor Urbanowicz has pointed out, Shevek's breakthrough in his temporal theory comes when he changes his methods (151). Instead of attempting to prove the theory through certainty as he has been taught to do, he employs the Terran "Ainsetain" model of hypothesis. By postulating simultaneity, Shevek is able to see how it works out, and thus to develop his temporal theory. It is this adjustment of perspective that marks Shevek's becoming-alien, and it is also an example of how Le Guin privileges a model of openness to possibilities in order to reconcile the seemingly irreconcilable, or heterotopia.

At the end of the novel, Shevek has escaped the capitalist/communist planet Urras to return to his anarchist Anarres and, with the help of the Hainish embassy, will provide his new knowledge to all worlds simultaneously. He chooses heterotopian possibility over any individual version of truth or good when he decides to give his work to everyone at once, rather than to his own planet or to the highest bidder. Keng, the Hainish representative helping

Shevek, is actually Terran, and she describes a fully dystopian Earth complete with environmental destruction, genocide, and war. The Hainish helped Terra to overcome some of its problems, but Keng is clear about the fact that she is in awe of the lush planet Urras. Shevek comes to understand that Keng is suffering from a lack of perspective, and from a lack of comprehension about becoming and time. He tells her,

> "You don't understand what time is.... You say the past is gone, the future is not real, there is no change, no hope. You think Anarres is a future that cannot be reached, as your past cannot be changed. So there is nothing but the present, this Urras, the rich, real, stable present, the moment now. And you think that is something which can be possessed! ... But it is not real you know. It is not stable, not solid — nothing is. Things change, change" [349].

He incorporates the ideas of simultaneity, transformation, and becoming in his description of time. The folly of attempting to stop time through ownership is contrasted with an ethics that embraces the openness of change and potential. Shevek's life's work has been to combine seemingly contradictory theories, and in so doing he brings instant communication across any distance to the Ekumen. A new kind of heterotopia is possible with the kind of technology he offers.

There is a difference of twenty-six years between the first publication of *The Dispossessed* and Le Guin's 2000 novel, *The Telling*.[6] In this novel a *female* envoy of the Ekumen, once again a human from Terra, Sutty, journeys to Aka in order to study the people there. Aka has recently undergone a dramatic political shift, and is now run by the Dovzan Corporation. Emphases on various models of nation-states and political organization in earlier novels are replaced by an exploration of the problem of corporate globalization. The Dovzan run a strict society of permits and checks, and they have outlawed the "old" ways, which are barely a generation in the past. Those old ways include a religion called The Telling, which Sutty comes to understand when she makes her requisite journey (echoing the various journeys of Rocannon, Falk, Genly Ai, and Shevek) out of the city and into the highlands. The Telling is essentially a religion based on and inclusive of all stories. It is a heterotopian religion that requires the acceptance of simultaneous contradictions. When faced with the multiplicity and richness that marks the texts of The Telling, Sutty is awed: "She knew now that all she would ever know of the Telling was the least hint or fragment of what there was to know. But that was all right; that was how it was. So long as it was here" (198). Its diversity is characterized as its strength. Through her connection to the Ekumen, Sutty is able to save The Telling library and to begin to work toward the decriminalization of the religion. The corporate need to reduce multiplicity by advancing metanarratives of progress and consumerism is contrasted with the heterotopian possibility of conflicting and proliferating discourses.[7]

The *Hainish Cycle* is itself a diverse and heterogeneous body of work. Read alongside the concept of heterotopia, these narratives can be seen to offer productive models of the simultaneous existence of conflicting possibilities. Le Guin's narrative strategy throughout the *Hainish Cycle* involves placing an alien other in a situation in which s/he must release old notions of knowledge and subjectivity so that new possibilities can be embraced in a process of becoming-alien. On a larger scale, Le Guin's Hainish universe is about various attempts to form peaceful and productive relationships with aliens' worlds in the name of the "League" or, later, the Ekumen. This strategy provides the connective tissue among the novels, and also presents an overall image of heterotopian coexistence.

Cosmic Genealogy: Canopus in Argos: Archives, *Doris Lessing*

Of the *Canopus in Argos: Archives* series, Doris Lessing wrote in 1978, "It was clear I had made — or found — a new world for myself, a realm where the petty fates of planets, let alone individuals, are only aspects of cosmic evolution expressed in the rivalries and interactions of great galactic Empires."[8] Lessing's space fiction series is set on a galactic scale, allowing for complex analyses of conflicting forces, each with its own goals and aims. Like Le Guin's *Hainish Cycle*, Lessing's series coheres only through a heterotopian model of simultaneous divergence. The "cosmic evolution" Lessing describes is, however, a different approach from Le Guin's that involves a long-term, historical understanding of development and change, and which foregrounds large systems of power.[9] While Le Guin's narratives tend to focus on one situation at a time from within the larger Hainish universe, each of which relates to larger questions, Lessing's space fictions approach from the perspective of larger questions and incorporate local situations. Lessing's novels explore questions of historical development and alien perspectives (*Shikasta*, 1979), creating social change (*The Marriages Between Zones*, 1980), confronting the alien Other and learning to adjust to a different way of existing in relation to the universe (*The Sirian Experiments*, 1981), accepting new realities in the wake of environmental disaster (*The Making of a Representative for Planet 8*, 1982), and of coping with political rhetoric (*The Sentimental Agents*, 1983). Each novel is, then, concerned with power relations and the conditions necessary for social change. This attention to power flows on a large scale and over long periods

Four. *Becoming-Alien in Feminist Space Fiction*

of time is coupled with more specific investigations into individual subjectivities in each text, producing a space fiction series that emphasizes analysis and critique, yet also offers something more by providing alternative models of power and production.

Shikasta, the first novel in Lessing's series, introduces the Canopean Empire and the planet initially known as Rohanda, and later as Shikasta. This planet is clearly a defamiliarized version of Earth, and the novel traces its development through the eyes of a highly advanced alien species: the Canopeans.[10] One Canopean agent, Johor, who is assigned to Shikasta at various points in his eons long career, narrates much of the novel. However, *Shikasta* also includes official reports from different alien agents and a long series of entries from a young woman's journal. *The Sirian Experiments*, the third novel in the series, offers the perspective of another alien agent representing another planetary power. Lessing's series offers an examination of large scale events, but through the varying individual perspectives that make up the narratives.[11]

The full title of the first text is *Canopus in Argos: Archives Re: Colonised Planet 5 Shikasta: Personal, Psychological, Historical Documents Relating to Visit by Johor (George Sherban), Emissary (Grade 9) 87th of the Period of the Last Days*. The archival documents that make up the text demonstrate that Canopeans value details that would be insignificant to more traditional histories. Johor records his thoughts and feelings as he becomes human, Rachel — the young woman whose journal is included in the text — details the increasingly dystopian conditions of life on Shikasta, other Canopean agents offer reports on their experiences of Shikasta, and the text even includes some documents written by enemy agents and intercepted by Canopean agents.[12] Recalling Colebrook's formula for a feminist genealogy discussed above, it is possible to see that the overall result is a genealogical depiction of Shikasta that foregrounds the instability of individual subjectivities in relation to social structures. The genealogical analyses of power flows and fluctuations in relation to individual subjectivities on Shikasta is combined with an exploration of an alternative model of power that privileges proliferation over linear progress and cooperation over dominance. This model is exemplified by the Canopeans, an alien race whose agents are able to become-alien; they can literally become members of an alien species in order to live among that species.

Shikasta begins with the following explanation: "Johor has been chosen as suitable to represent our emissaries to Shikasta — of whom there were many, carrying out a multiplicity of functions — in this compilation of documents selected to offer a very general picture of Shikasta for the use of first-year students of Canopean Colonial Rule" (2). The reader is positioned as a student from the first words of the narrative, and the text is constructed as a heterotopian collection of multiple perspectives. Johor relates the history of Canopean involvement on Earth, beginning with their establishment of a utopian society made up of natives and "Giants"; the Canopeans bring the Giants to Rohanda in order to aid in the development of both groups. This partnership is an immense success, and allows the Canopeans to establish a psychic link between Rohanda and the rest of the Canopean Empire (called the "Substance-of-We-Feeling," or "SOWF") that speeds up the intellectual and emotional development of both the natives and the Giants. However, planetary shifts weaken this link to the point of ineffectuality, and the inhabitants of Rohanda wind up open to attack by an enemy of the Canopean Empire, Shammat. While the Canopeans (Johor tells us) have only the best interests of Earth in mind, Shammat sets its designs on our planet in order to create chaos and pain, upon which the people of Shammat feed for strength and power. It is at this point in the history of Earth that the Canopeans begin to call it Shikasta, and the rest of the narrative traces Shikasta's battle with its unknown adversary, Shammat, as well as the attempts that Canopus makes to aid Shikasta. The most interesting aspect of this text in relation to the argument of this chapter has to do with the Canopean agents, particularly Johor, who become human in order both to observe and participate in life on this planet and thus provide a model of becoming in a literal form: becoming-alien.

In order to influence events on Shikasta, Canopean agents become-alien. They are born into humanity and live out lives as human beings, although their Canopean lives continue after their human deaths. The model of becoming in this novel is balanced with a continuity that can be read as an overarching heterotopian model. The Canopeans become-other and then return to their Canopean forms, yet they are altered by the experience of becoming-alien and continuously add to the possibilities available to the Canopean world view. For an agent to become human means that the agent must become-alien; there is no unified, integrated subject, but rather a nomadic one. Johor describes his experience of shifting to human form in terms that illustrate the fear that must accompany becoming-alien:

> At that moment it was necessary to collect oneself as at no other time. We had nothing to sustain us but the imprint of the Signature, which would emerge, like a brand on flesh that could show itself only in heat or under pressure. It was as if we had chosen deliberately to obliterate ourselves, trusting to an intangible we had no alternative but to trust [*Shikasta* 209–10].

The Signature will act as a kind of anchor during Johor's existence as a human being — called George Sherban — but it will not provide Johor with any substantial memories or sense of self beyond his existence as a human being.

Four. *Becoming-Alien in Feminist Space Fiction*

Johor is required to trust something he cannot possibly know before he becomes-alien. The choice "to deliberately obliterate" himself, his subjectivity, is described as both necessary and terrifying. He goes on to say, "I have to acknowledge — I can do no other — that this is a moment of fearful dismay. Even of panic. The terrible miasmas of Shikasta close around me and I send this report with my last conscious impulse" (210). Nomadic subjectivity is depicted as necessary but difficult, which is an apt description of the nature of an ethics of becoming. Johor is a Canopean agent trained to become-alien whenever necessary. *Shikasta* emphasizes that becoming-alien is a matter of subverting structures of self and other, of destroying the boundaries that keep subjectivity intact. However, the novel also provides a model of becoming in which the destruction of the subject is provisional, allowing for a balance between becoming-alien and returning to Canopean subjectivity, albeit having been altered by the experience of becoming.

In *Shikasta*, an official Canopean report describes the overriding characteristic of Earth as follows: "This planet is above all one of contrasts and contradictions, because of its in-built stresses. Tension is its essential nature. This is its strength. This is its weakness" (5). Shikasta is defined by its instability and conflict. Lessing's Canopeans find such indeterminacy creates tension that can either be harmful or productive. While the negative aspects of indeterminacy and tension are in constant evidence in the war, poverty, and suffering portrayed in the text, there are also places where the more positive possibilities of such turmoil are demonstrated. For an ethics that embraces openness and possibility, indeterminacy is a necessary condition. The Canopeans are able to incorporate contrast and tension into their indeterminate "worldview," which is based in provisionality and the acceptance of constant change. Johor's experience of becoming-alien is instructive not only because it provides a literal example of becoming, but also because it works through what such radical becoming might mean for an ethical stance.

From the beginning, the text slowly reveals details about the Canopean mindset, particularly through Johor's descriptions of his early visits to Shikasta. As he introduces himself to his readers (who, as stated above, are both his superiors and, later, first-year students of Canopean colonial rule), Johor explains his intentions as well as his limitations as an historian:

> In these notes I shall be trying to make things clear. There will be others, after me, and they will study this record as I have studied, so often, the records of those who came before. It is not always possible to know, when you make note of an event, or a state of mind, how this may strike someone perhaps ten thousand years later.
>
> Things change. That is all we may be sure of [3].

Johor's point is simply that he cannot know the significance, or insignificance, that his experiences will hold for future generations, and can only offer an attempt to "make things clear." Such moments of direct address position the reader as an observer of Canopean knowledge production. Specifically, the reader is offered an alternative history that functions as a version of the revisionist rewriting described in more detail in earlier chapters. Revision means becoming here.

The heterotopian nature of the universe of the novel is further emphasized by the way a human girl's diary takes over the narrative. Instead of providing the reader with George's account of his experiences as a human, Lessing chooses to work from Rachel's point of view. In doing so, Lessing allows the reader to view George's development, or construction, from the outside. Rachel is the first of many characters throughout the series who is engaged in a process of trying to understand the Canopeans. However, unlike most of the other characters who engage in this process, she is completely unaware of what she is actually attempting to understand. To her, George is simply a beloved brother, and her desire to understand him grows as she begins to see that he is somehow special, somehow significant to the course of history. Early in her journal, she writes that she has noticed George acting in strange ways at various times. For example, she notes, "But there were a lot of times I woke and George was awake. He was usually at the window. I did not pretend to be asleep. I knew he wouldn't be angry. I once asked him, Who are you talking to? He said he didn't know. A friend, he said. He seemed troubled. Not unhappy" (213). Presumably, George is experiencing some sort of contact with, or message from, the Canopeans during his late night vigils at the window. For Rachel, however, those occasions generate curiosity about her brother. She watches him learn from a series of people who seem to randomly appear in his life, develop into a young man who others seek in order to be taught, and become involved in an international political organization that she despises. Rachel is intensely aware of her brother's seemingly orchestrated development, and, through Rachel, Lessing's text offers an illustration of how subjectivity can be molded by outside forces. George/Johor is both a subject of genealogical analysis and an example of an alternative model of active becoming combined with a more enduring Canopean essence.

There is an abrupt shift in focus from the first to the second novel in Lessing's series. The second focuses more explicitly on exposing patriarchal myths that are too easily naturalized by pervasive power structures. In *The Marriages Between Zones Three, Four, and Five,* Lessing departs from the space fiction emphasis in the other novels and instead provides us with a fantasy text set in zones that encompass Shikasta.[13] The premise of the narrative is

Four. Becoming-Alien in Feminist Space Fiction

that two rulers of two different zones, Ben Ata and Al·Ith, are required to marry by an authority (perhaps the Canopeans) that remains mysterious throughout the novel. There is a romance plot here, similar to the one in Le Guin's *Planet of Exile*; romantic relationships are often fruitful ground for exploring boundaries between self and other, and marriages across groups, races, or species offer ways to develop heterotopian social structures. Ben Ata is the male ruler of a highly patriarchal and war-based society, while Al·Ith is a female ruler whose society is based on cultural exchange, story-telling, and cooperation. Through their marriage, each becomes something other than who/what they were, and, in turn, they influence their societies to change. In simplified terms, this narrative follows a development from male, warlike, and hierarchical versus female, caring, and cooperative, to a situation in which binary structures no longer suffice: a heterotopian model of simultaneously conflicting but mutually productive possibilities.

The marriage between Ben Ata and Al·Ith to highlights the social processes that create each of them; it is through their attempts to understand one another that they are able to view their own societies from the outside, and thus to understand how those societies construct individual subjects. Colebrook's terms of feminist genealogy are useful here, in part because the narrative analyzes large power structures and social processes in terms of how they create subjectivities. The relationship between this genealogical approach and the alternative possibility of becoming is clear in this text, since it is only through critical examinations of their own cultures that Ben Ata and Al·Ith are able to become-other. The individual is inextricably linked to the social, so that subjects-in-becoming forge the way for an overall ethics of becoming to take shape. The following passage, which comes from the end of the narrative, explains how their experiences of becoming transform their societies: "There was a continuous movement now, from Zone Five to Zone Four. And from Zone Four to Zone Three — and from us, up the pass. There was a lightness, a freshness, and an enquiry and a remaking and an inspiration where there had been only stagnation. And closed frontiers" (244–45). The truly compelling aspect of this narrative is the way in which it manages both to critique the patriarchal values of Ben Ata's society, and to avoid moralizing labels of "good" or "evil." Instead, it offers a heterotopian model based in an ethics of becoming.

The third novel in the *Canopus* series, *The Sirian Experiments*, brings the reader back to the Canopeans and to Shikasta, but through the perspective of the Sirians, a former enemy and current uneasy ally of the Canopeans. An overall heterotopian model continues to evolve as perspectives and possibilities proliferate. The narrator is a Sirian named Ambien II who describes her experiences in relation to Shikasta and the Canopean Empire. She explains, "Our technological development had reached a peak and had been established long enough for us to understand the problems it must bring. The chief one was this: there was nothing for billions upon billions of individuals to do. They had no purpose but to exist, and then die. That this would be a problem had not been foreseen" (13). Throughout Ambien II's narrative, she struggles to understand what it is that the Canopeans know that her own empire does not, and why they always have a purpose. At one point while Ambien II is visiting Shikasta along with another Sirian, Ambien I, and a Canopean, Klorathy, she is struck by the Canopean ability to fit into alien surroundings:

> But I recognized even then that the ability to become part of—I was going to say "to sink oneself into," but refrained, because of the invisible moral pressure of Canopus—an unfamiliar scene, a foreign race, even one considered (perhaps out of ignorance) inferior, is one to be admired, commended, and even emulated, if possible. I *did* try to behave as Klorathy did and as Ambien I was doing, as far as he was able. Klorathy feasted and even danced with them, told stories, in their tongue—and yet was able never to be less than Canopus [76].

While this is not a literal becoming-alien in the same sense that Johor's becoming is literal in *Shikasta*, it is a description of Ambien II's attempt to become-alien. She is unable to duplicate the Canopean's behavior, but she recognizes it as an ability she should cultivate; the desire to do so is what defines her relationship to the Canopeans throughout much of the text. Ambien II's need to understand the Canopeans makes her an engaging narrator; her position is similar to the reader's, as both attempt to develop a more full understanding of the Canopeans.[14]

Interestingly, Ambien II seems to come closest to understanding, or becoming–Canopean, when she is thinking through the struggles of her own empire, rather than when she is watching the Canopeans. The Sirian Empire shares Shikasta with the Canopeans at an early point in Shikasta's history, and the Sirians engage in a series of experiments on the South American continent. While Ambien II reflects upon these experiments, she writes,

> I can only put it like this: that it seems as if—I do not see how we can conclude anything else—when such deliberate, controlled experiments take place, to produce definitely envisaged stocks or strains, it is felt—most deeply and profoundly, and by the most responsible and evolved of our peoples—that some other possibility may have been lost. As if randomness and chance in themselves are a good and a blessing and even a means of acquiring something not yet defined. [...] I am stating my own personal opinion here, arrived at after much reflection [42].

Clearly, Ambien II's thinking here reflects the Canopean emphasis on fluidity and openness to change. Difference, change, and random combinations are the heart of heterotopian thinking. Efforts to control, even when well-intentioned, limit potential and close down possibilities.

While the text suggests that Ambien II develops a more complete understanding of the Canopeans during the course of the narrative, that understanding is never explained to the reader. Similarly, at no point does Lessing's series offer the reader a detailed look at Canopean society, or depict a Canopean home world. Carol Franko reads the absence of a Canopean home world as "utopia by innuendo," and argues that "this absence of a traditional exposition puts greater demands on readers; we must infer the principles that guide the Canopeans from the ambiguous things they do and say from other characters' ambivalent impressions of them" (25). The hints that Lessing does offer about the Canopeans come from cryptic remarks in Johor's reports, such as those examined above, the actions they take on Shikasta, and the observations of characters like Ambien II, so that the reader is constantly involved in a process of trying both to understand and to evaluate the Canopeans. Franko goes on to suggest that it is this required inference that makes the text utopian, since the reader is invited "to share in a utopian way of thinking — an ongoing process of negation and affirmation, doubt and hope" (25). While it is true that the reader is forced to negotiate a difficult conceptual ground, it is also the case that the Canopean "way of thinking" has more in common with heterotopian models of difference and simultaneity than it does with utopian metanarratives. In addition, Canopean perspectives remain largely inaccessible throughout the series, so that the reader is always only an observer of Canopean actions, rather than a collaborator in them. It is this distance between the reader and the Canopean texts (Johor's reports and the other official documents that make up most of the novels) that most clearly marks the reader's position.

The fourth and fifth novels in the *Canopus* series are shorter than the first three, and lack some of the detailed complexity that marks the earlier texts. Nevertheless, they do offer some interesting approaches to genealogical investigation in relation to an ethics of becoming. *The Making of the Representative for Planet 8* focuses on one man's experiences on a Canopean colony. It is not directly related to the plots of any of the other novels in the series, but it is another example of the emphasis on multiplicity and proliferation in the series. The narrator is one of "a species created by [the Canopeans] from stock originating on several planets" (11). Unfortunately, Planet 8 undergoes an unexpected climate change and the colony itself is destroyed. The novel offers one man's description of the months leading up to the end of the colony and, in so doing, provides yet another example of personal history. Additionally, like *The Sirian Experiments*, much of this text is about the narrator's attempts to understand Johor and the other Canopeans who visit the planet.

Johor is once again the most prominent Canopean character; he is usually the Canopean agent with whom the narrator discusses the situation of Planet 8. The narrative begins,

> You ask how the Canopean agents seemed to us in the times of The Ice.
> It was usually Johor who came, but whichever one of them it was, arrived without prior warning and apparently casually, stayed for a short or a long time, and during these agreeable visits — for we always looked forward to them — gave us advice, showed us how we could more effectively use the resources of our planet, suggested devices, methods, techniques. And then left without saying when we might expect to see Canopus again [11].

The narrator begins with a clearly approving view of the Canopeans, even if he suggests that he was occasionally frustrated by the lack of further information about their visits. At this point, the reader cannot be sure who has asked for this analysis of the Canopean agents on Planet 8, but since all of the texts in the series are part of the *Canopus in Argos: Archives*, the reader can assume that the Canopeans have found the analysis significant; it is part of their historical record. The novel ends with the destruction of the colony, and with a passage describing what the colonists experience through their deaths. The narrator explains, "We did not see wastes of snow or ice, no, but a perpetual shifting and changing — we were seeing our planet in a myriad guises, or possibilities" (159–60). Clearly, there is life after death for these colonists, as there is for a Canopean who becomes-alien but continues to exist as Canopean after the alien's death. As the passage continues, the narrator reasons that what he and the others are seeing are the potential versions of Planet 8, "what might have been or could have been" (160). Chance is integrated into the fabric of a universe that Lessing describes as infinite and therefore characterized by unlimited potential. Deleuze and Guattari argue that "becoming and multiplicity are the same thing" (*Thousand* 249), which suggests that the "myriad guises" the narrator sees can be read as describing a heterotopian universe that is based on multiplicity and becoming. The colonists exist in some form beyond the physical forms they occupied on the planet, implying that they, like the Canopeans, can become-other in a literal sense.

The Sentimental Agents, the fifth and final book in the *Canopus* series, brings an entirely new perspective. It is probably clear by now that the novels in the series build upon one another by offering alternative perspectives on what has come before; each text adds layers to the genealogical project of the whole. In this case, Lessing offers a perspective that the Canopeans consider

Four. *Becoming-Alien in Feminist Space Fiction*

to be mad. A young Canopean agent, Incent, has been diagnosed with a severe case of "Undulant Rhetoric," and another Canopean, Klorathy, is sent to help him recover. This novel foregrounds political critique, but it is an important critique in the context of feminist genealogy.[15] Rhetoric has overcome Incent's ability to think clearly, and becoming-alien only leaves him open to the propaganda that is political speech on Shikasta and other worlds in the text. Power is, here and elsewhere in the series, inescapable and potentially devastating. The model of becoming that Lessing offers in the earlier texts is a way of redirecting the power structures that contribute to subject construction in ways that are productive rather than destructive. Johor becomes George in *Shikasta* in order to exert a positive influence on the damaged planet, and when George becomes Johor once again, George's experiences have altered Johor so that he has a more complete and developed understanding of humanity. In *The Sentimental Agents*, Incent is unable to balance his enduring Canopean existence with the subjects he becomes. Therefore, in contrast with the radical model of becoming offered by Deleuze and Guattari, Lessing suggests that becoming is only a productive alternative when it is balanced with a more constant — yet still permeable and flexible — subjectivity. Johor balances provisional becoming with an enduring subject position. Incent is unable to do so.

Reading the *Canopus in Argos: Archives* series as a feminist genealogy that develops heterotopian possibilities allows for an exploration of the relationship between genealogical inquiry into knowledge production and active becoming. Johor's act of becoming-alien is the result of the long-term Canopean approach to Shikasta, which looks at history in genealogical terms. Ben Ata and Al·Ith become-alien through their interactions with one another and, in turn, effect long-term change in the zones they rule so that dystopian and utopian spaces become heterotopian. Other characters in the remaining books in the series learn of the need to embrace becoming, and of the potential dangers inherent in nomadic subjectivity. Through their genealogical investigations into power flows and subject construction, Lessing's space fiction texts set conditions through which it is possible for active becoming to take place, and an ethics of becoming realigns power relations.

Post-Human Potential: Xenogenesis Series, *Octavia E. Butler*

Butler's *Xenogenesis Series*, now published as a trilogy entitled *Lilith's Brood*, takes a post-apocalyptic Earth as its starting point and imagines a new society based on the intermingling of humans and an alien species, the

Oankali, which rescues some humans from nuclear disaster on Earth. The novels imagine a future in which humans must accept a species so alien that the mere sight of one of them is enough to drive a human being mad. Confronting otherness is perhaps the central theme of the series. In order to survive, Butler's human characters have no choice but to become-alien. There is both physical, literal transformation from human to alien, and, in the more strict sense of becoming as described by Deleuze and Guattari, learning to open to the transformative experience of altering understandings and perceptions in order to accommodate the understandings and perceptions of the aliens. As the trilogy develops, the two species create new, post-human generations that are hybrids of their human and Oankali parents, and these new generations are charged with developing new social structures and new ways of living that can incorporate aspects of both human and Oankali cultures. As humanity is replaced by children that are both human and alien, heterotopian social possibilities develop.

Dawn (1987), the first book in Butler's trilogy, describes a post-nuclear future in which humanity has destroyed Earth for human habitation and an alien species called the Oankali have arrived to offer the few survivors a kind of future. In other words, humanity has failed and the possibility of a future on Earth becomes necessarily post-human. The Oankali require new genetic material in order to continue to thrive. They evolve rapidly, but through a specific process of combining with other species; the Oankali wish to combine with the humans that they have rescued from Earth's ruins. None of this information is available to the protagonist of the first novel when it begins, however. Lilith — traditionally, Eve's precursor — wakes up in a room knowing only that she had been in a remote region of the Andes, and now was here.[16] Once she establishes that she is still alive, Lilith's thoughts are, "Awakening was hard, as always" (3), and Butler sets the tone for the narrative to come. Lilith will engage in a nearly continual process of awakening: first, to the reality that she is aboard a space ship; then, to the physical presence of the alien other; and, ultimately, to the knowledge that she herself is becoming-alien.

Lilith's first encounter with the alien other is a particularly potent moment in *Dawn*: "She did not want to be any closer to him. She had not known what held her back before. Now she was certain it was his alienness, his difference, his literal unearthliness. She found herself unable to take even one more step toward him" (11). His utter "alienness" is precisely what disturbs Lilith. She realizes that she is simply overwhelmed by the sheer otherness of the figure before her. Once she overcomes initial response to the alien, Lilith is confronted by an entirely new order of difference. The Oankali are made up of three genders rather than two: male, female, and ooloi. Ooloi make genetic trading possible because they are able to perceive and manipulate at a genetic level. The ooloi destabilize sexual identity in this novel, much like the Gethenians of Le Guin's *The Left Hand of Darkness*. Such destabilization is a first step toward developing an understanding of subjectivity as nomadic and open to becoming. The Oankali organize in family units comprised of male, female, and ooloi; the ooloi actually take part in the relationship between male and female. Later in the narrative, Lilith must find a way to have a relationship with a human male that is mediated by an ooloi. In a twist that helps the narrative explore the loss that accompanies becoming, the reader learns that once the Oankali become involved with humanity, it is no longer possible for men and women to have sexual relationships without the ooloi. Becoming-alien changes everything.

Yet, Lilith and the other humans have few choices. Not only are the Oankali responsible for rescuing Lilith and the other humans, they offer the potential for a post-human becoming that seems utterly necessary given the way humanity has managed to nearly destroy itself. The Oankali represent an alternative to human hierarchy, which is what they see as humanity's fatal flaw. In particular, the alternative they represent is one of symbiosis. This symbiotic rather than hierarchical existence is exemplified by their relationship to their living ship, which is actually another strain of the Oankali genetic tree from trades long past. The complicated relationship is explained to Lilith in the following terms: "'There is an affinity, but it's biological — a strong, symbiotic relationship. We serve the ship's needs and it serves ours. It would die without us and we would be planetbound without it. For us, that would eventually mean death'" (33). The Oankali need humanity's genes in order to continue; their existence depends upon genetic trade. Humanity has the opportunity to become something new through the Oankali. Deleuze and Guattari privilege symbiosis as a way of understanding becoming through alliance rather than filiation: "If evolution includes any veritable becomings, it is in the domain of *symbiosis* that bring into play beings of totally different scales and kingdoms, with no possibility of filiation" (*Thousand* 238, italics in original). The relationship between the Oankali and their ship could be understood in these terms. However, it is precisely the desire to merge with humanity in future generations that guides the Oankali. Lilith's perception of this desire is similar to Deleuze and Guattari's; she sees it not as an invitation to future potential but as a death sentence to humanity. Yet, to turn this way of thinking back on itself, the Oankali are a species that can only survive through genetic trading — symbiosis at a nuclear level — and that will evolve through *both* symbiosis and filiation. The Oankali, as a species, is always becoming-alien; their entire social structure is built upon the fabric of an ethics of becoming. Alison Tara Walker makes a similar argument: "through their gene trade and genetic manipulation, the Oankali are constantly becoming. Since becoming is never a fixed state but rather a constant process, the Oankali themselves are ephemeral, insofar as what defines them as a species relies on constant change" (113).[17] Their only true difficulty is making other species accept such an ethics. As one of the ooloi explains, "'Different *is* threatening to most species'" (186). The Oankali's need for difference puts them in a precarious position.

Lilith is eventually altered by an ooloi in preparation for the role she is to play in acclimating other humans to their new circumstances on the ship and among aliens. The alterations are genetic and are designed to bring out dormant abilities. In this way, Lilith becomes–Oankali. Deleuze and Guattari define becoming as molecular rather than molar; becoming-alien is a cellular change for Lilith and not a literal transformation into the form of the Oankali. The change is also largely unwelcome. Lilith fights against what she perceives to be the loss of her humanity for most of the text, and in the end, even though she is rejected by most of the other humans, some of whom display extreme brutality and violence, Lilith still hopes that humanity can find a way to survive on its own. Throughout the series, Lilith struggles with the loss of human identity and has difficulty embracing a heterotopian ideal. In many ways, Lilith's reactions seem utterly realistic given the shortage of choices open to her. Her becoming-alien is not of her own making, but rather a sacrifice endured for the sake of survival. Such a portrayal of becoming demands that the reader acknowledge not only the fear of the loss of the self (a kind of fear portrayed by both Le Guin and Lessing), but also the frustration and terror of the loss of the very categories that structure our understandings of ourselves. A post-human reality is more than one that embraces an ethics of becoming; it is also one that requires the acceptance of a massive loss.

The second novel in the *Xenogenesis* trilogy is *Adulthood Rites* (1988), and in it the issues of loss and becoming are explored in more detail. Lilith, who was impregnated by an ooloi who combined her DNA with a male human's and two Oanakli's, has given birth to Akin. As in *Dawn*, Butler utilizes third-person narration focusing on the protagonist, in this case, Akin. By shifting from a largely human perspective in the first novel to a human–Oankali hybrid perspective in the second, Butler alters the way in which humans, Oankali, and the trade between the two are viewed. The post-human hybrids, or "constructs," as they are called in the narratives, tend to look like their birth parents until the stage of metamorphosis, when they mature and become less human in appearance. At the beginning of *Adulthood*

Four. *Becoming-Alien in Feminist Space Fiction*

Rites, Lilith is still resistant to the entire situation and asks the ooloi who constructed Akin if "all the mismatched pieces of him fit together as best as they can," to which the ooloi replies: "Nothing in him is mismatched" (5). The new constructs are just that: new. They are both human and Oankali, and therefore are something different from either.

Akin is a particularly sensitive being, even as a baby; when he inadvertently causes Lilith pain while breastfeeding, he shares her physical discomfort and learns never to repeat his mistake: "he had learned an important lesson: He would share any pain he caused. Best, then, to be careful and not cause pain" (7). Butler returns to the idea of empathic transfer of pleasure and pain in the *Parable* novels (discussed in Chapter Three), but here she focuses on the Oankali's use of empathy as a way to temper human tendencies toward hierarchical organization and aggression, particularly in males. The Oankali tend to view human males as particularly dangerous—from a genetic standpoint—and therefore are wary of constructing males with human traits: "Before now, too many ooloi could not perceive the necessary mixture. They could have made mistakes and their mistakes could be monsters" (9). While Lilith's continued frustration at the loss of pure humanity permeates the second as well as the first text, there is also a persistent emphasis on humanity's shortcomings.

It is Akin who brings a different perspective into the trilogy—one that is able to see both the loss that Lilith feels and the desire for change that the Oankali embody. While the Oankali clearly see humanity as flawed, as a combined human/Oankali, Akin is able to understand why so many humans still wish for a chance to start over without being forced to "trade" with the Oankali. He takes on the task of convincing the Oankali to allow those humans who wish to do so to emigrate to Mars, where they will be allowed to begin again in a colony of their own making. The Oankali will provide them with necessary technologies and supplies for survival, but those humans who choose to leave will be free to preserve their species. Ultimately, Akin is successful in his pleas and humans are given an alternative to life with the Oankali. Akin represents the simultaneity of two divergent perspectives, and he is able to recognize the beliefs and needs of both the humans and the Oankali. He remembers Lilith explaining one of the central differences between humans and Oankalie, a difference that even she understood to be an example of humanity's flaws:

> "Human beings fear difference," Lilith had told him once. "Oankali crave difference. Humans persecute their different ones, yet they need them to give themselves definition and status. Oankali seek difference and collect it. They need it to keep themselves from stagnation and overspecialization. If you don't under-

stand this, you will. You'll probably find both tendencies surfacing in your own behavior." And she had put her hand on his hair. "When you feel a conflict, try to go the Oankali way. Embrace difference" [80].

Lilith's ethics of becoming teach Akin to embrace difference. In fact, he is the only Oankali who is able to embrace difference to the point of seeing beyond the need to collect it. As Naomi Jacobs points out, "Ultimately, it is not human agency, but posthuman agency that makes possible the survival of something like the human" ("Posthuman" 106). Akin argues that humanity should be allowed to continue to exist for its own sake because he is able to truly perceive the human position. A bit like Le Guin's Falk-Remarren, but created through genetic splicing rather than schizophrenic coexistence, Akin is a hybrid construct who is able to negotiate multiple possibilities, thereby creating a truly heterotopian universe. And, of course, Akin's achievement is what the reader is expected to desire. It is the embodiment of an ethics of becoming.

Imago (1989) is the final text in Butler's trilogy. It centers on yet another hybrid being; this time, it is the first ooloi to be born from the human/Oankali trade. Butler changes her narrative strategy in this third novel, so that the ooloi protagonist, Jodahs, is actually the first-person narrator. Jodahs, as ooloi, is neither male nor female; its existence was unintentional — a rare mistake among so many well-planned genetic creations. Much of the narrative is concerned with Jodahs's stages of metamorphosis, which involve tremendous risk, pain, and uncertainty. It is a creature in becoming throughout the text that, like Akin before it, challenges even the Oankali to accept further potential and change. As a construct ooloi, if Jodahs is allowed to mate it will effectively constitute the creation of a new species. Jodahs' task is to secure its future, and that of its human mate's. The Oankali resist Jodahs, just as they had Akin, but ultimately allow it to call for other mates among humans and Oankali, and to begin its own attempt at life on Earth. In this way, the trilogy ends with the birth of an entirely new, post-human species, one that is neither human nor Oankali, but that has been created by both.

It is necessary for Jodahs to start over on Earth because in *Imago* Butler throws one last curve into the narrative of Oankali/human existence. The ooloi, it turns out, will leave Earth a barren, lifeless place when it is time for them to seek out new genetic material once again, a mere few generations into the future. They gather the life that is Earth and take it with them. This can be read as a final condemnation of the Oankali as imperialistic, or it can be seen as Butler's ultimate challenge to accept that change is the only constant. Earth is not going to last forever, even in the "real" universe. In Butler's series, becoming is more than an ethics; it is a necessity.

Four. *Becoming-Alien in Feminist Space Fiction*

Heterotopian Alternatives

In feminist space fiction, contemporary women writers are able to create alternative worlds that work to defamiliarize our own world, thereby demystifying dominant discourses. The most ingrained assumptions readers have about everyday existence can be called into question by "escapist" space fiction narratives. Le Guin, Lessing, and Butler use the generic possibilities of space fiction not only to defamiliarize, but to suggest alternative possibilities. The situation of a human stranded on an alien planet or forced to accept an alien presence on Earth can, when developed carefully and thoughtfully, turn into a narrative that confronts the knowledge systems the reader takes for granted every day. These writers investigate what it would mean to conceive of a truly heterotopian universe, in which the radical knowledge of the instability of the subject plays out in various models of becoming-alien. Colebrook's formula for feminist genealogy links a critique of subjectivity to the conditions necessary for active becoming, and the narratives' attention to the subject construction of characters in relation to their becomings demonstrates how feminist genealogy can work. In the fantastic openings created by feminist space fiction, Le Guin, Lessing, and Butler create possibilities for alternative conceptions of subjectivity, knowledge, and power—for heterotopian universes.

Conclusion:
Becoming Powerful

In Margaret Atwood's *In Other Worlds: SF and the Human Imagination* (2011), she asks, "Are narratives a means to enforce social control or a means of escape from it?" (41). The particular narratives discussed in this project confront power, or "social control," and offer ways to resist it through a model of becoming. This project is about the power and potential of stories in the world today: the power they have to shape realities, and the potential they embody through the imaginative possibilities they offer. The preceding chapters have explored fictions that investigate, critique, and revise problematic power structures using fantastic literary forms. The readings of those texts have demonstrated how fantastic fictions can create an ethical response to power imbalances that are undergirded by concepts of linear time and stable identity.

The fantastic is a form of intervention into narrative that often accompanies other types of interventions that relate directly to social control. For example, revision of the kind described in Chapters One and Two is a way of interrupting assumptions about the past and its relationship to the present. The speculative narratives in chapters three and four also intervene into expectations by defamiliarizing the present and offering new ways of thinking about the future. Intervention, in this sense, means opening up the past, present, and future to possibilities that were once closed or ignored. Similarly, an emphasis on becoming is a way of intervening into notions of stable and coherent identities that limit subjects. The ethics of becoming that I have linked to contemporary women's fantastic writing is an intervention into the very notion of subjectivity, and, necessarily the relationship between an individual subject and the power relations that surround that subject.

One example of how confrontations with otherness operate to develop an ethics of becoming throughout this project is the way human experiences with alien others in Chapter Four mirror Beauty's first encounter with the Beast in different versions of the tale in Chapter One. Lilith's experience of the alien other in *Dawn* is a particularly good example. Like Beauty, Lilith is unprepared for what she encounters in the other; she is taken off guard but also required to come to terms with what she finds there. The Oankali are Lilith's Beast, not just in that first encounter, but because they hold her fate in their hands, provide her with a magical castle/ship in which to live, and, ultimately, require her to find the other sexually desirable.

Atwood's book on science fiction also claims, "Mythology, science fiction of the other-planetary kind, and modern technology: they all do fit together" (*In Other Worlds* 20). In fact, a look at the range of fantastic fictions discussed in this project makes it clear that mythology and science fiction do more than fit together; they can be read as occupying the same continuum of works that revise, remake and rethink the bounds of our social imaginaries. This project has focused on Atwood's dystopian narratives, but she has also written revised fairy tales and myths, such as *The Penelopiad*, a revision of Homer's *Odyssey*. Jeanette Winterson, whose works have always focused on revision, has now written a space fiction novel: *The Stone Gods*. Ursula K. Le Guin, who is known for her science fiction and fantasy, published *Lavinia*, a revision of *The Aeneid*. It is clear that revising the past and writing the future are more than related projects; they are part of the same process of intervention into contemporary culture.

Atwood also writes about the problem of genre categorization. She, like many of the writers discussed in this project, has resisted the label "science fiction" for her work in favor of more nebulous concepts like "speculative" or "space fiction." Atwood argues, "When it comes to genres, the borders are increasingly undefended, and things slip back and forth across them with insouciance" (*In Other Worlds* 7). Fantastic fictions that resist clearly defined genre categories destabilize narrative assumptions. Categories like genre can impede the work of analyzing contemporary literature, which is frequently directly concerned with destabilizing the boundaries created by genre distinctions. The narratives discussed here can productively be read as ethical responses to the way power operates in the contemporary world in part *through* their insistence upon crossing conventional literary boundaries. The fantastic can be read as a narrative performance of disruption that works to unsettle assumptions and to create the potential for new ways of being and thinking.

If, as Atwood states in *In Other Worlds*, "The myths of a culture are those stories it takes seriously—the ones that are thought to be key to its identity" (49), the task of myth unmaking and remaking in speculative fiction is crucial to creating narratives that work against social control. Those texts that are primarily concerned with the past — revised fairy tales, reinvented myths, and historical fiction — emphasize revisionist processes that work to reveal the underlying power structures operating in traditional narratives. They also provide examples of alternative narratives by producing new stories and centering previously marginalized forms of historical knowledge. The future-oriented texts — critical dystopias and space fictions — highlight their own alternative models; however, they also supply criticism of the present and past through revision and defamiliarization. All of the texts self-consciously consider how the past, present, and future might be better understood as interlinked areas of becoming rather than as distinct linear categories. Becoming can be understood as a way to destabilize subjectivity at its most fundamental level, allowing for reconfigurations of the categories upon which subjectivity is built. Fantastic fiction enables contemporary women writers to intervene into and unsettle expectations, and from there to offer an ethics that embraces indeterminacy and possibility.

At the heart of this project is the idea that literature itself can intervene. The critical and creative qualities of the texts described here address the realities of the world in unique and terribly important ways. In *Transpositions*, philosopher Rosi Braidotti argues for something like an ethics of becoming. Discussing contemporary power relations, she claims,

> The point is that the global economy does not function in a linear manner, but is rather web-like, scattered and poly-centered. It is not monolithic, but an internally contradictory process, the effects of which are differentiated geopolitically and along gender and ethnicity lines, to name only the main ones. This creates a few methodological difficulties for the social critic, because it translates into a heteroglossia of data which makes both classical and modernist social theories inadequate to cope with the complexities. We need to adopt non-linearity as a major principle and to develop cartographies of power that account for the paradoxes and contradictions of the era of globalization, and which do not take shortcuts through its complexities [31].

The fantastic fictions discussed here can offer precisely such cartography. They work against linear notions of time — and narrative — and help to address the complex, "web-like" nature of contemporary power.

The texts' resistance to stability operates on multiple levels. Coherent identity is rejected in favor of open, nomadic subjectivity. Braidotti argues, "a nomadic and post-humanistic vision of the subject can provide an alternative foundation for ethical and political subjectivity" (*Transpositions* 11). Such a vision is what fantastic fiction can offer. Angela Carter's "Beauty" turns into a beast in "The Tiger's Bride," Dana is physically and psychically altered by the past in Octavia Butler's *Kindred*, Margaret Atwood's Jimmy/Snowman in *Oryx and Crake* chooses to remake himself as a kind of mythical figure to the Crakers, and the human characters in Chapter Four are almost always engaged in processes of becoming-alien. Hybrid figures — a woman with wings in Carter's *Nights at the Circus*, a dog/cat mixture in *The Memoirs of a Survivor*, a genetically modified human in Butler's *Dawn*— constantly crop up requiring readers to remember that stable identities are fictions. Character development is replaced by character destabilization and becoming. Jordan's journeys in Jeanette Winterson's *Sexing the Cherry* are fantastic and historical, in the past and the present. Butler's empath (Lauren Olamina in the *Parable* novels) creates a religion and founds a community, but all in the service of allowing humanity to become by getting into space. Relationships between characters are complex and changing; fairy tale endings are hard to find, even in the fairy tales.

The emphasis on subjectivity in becoming in these texts is mirrored by their refusals of narrative closure. Doris Lessing's *The Memoirs of a Survivor* and Atwood's *The Handmaid's Tale* are both excellent examples of narratives that simply do not want to tie up the plot or leave readers with a clear sense of what must have happened. In fact, nearly all of the texts discussed in this project leave things open, unfinished, and/or unclear. Such endings can be frustrating to readers expecting the kind of simple, tied up conclusions typically found in contemporary narratives ranging from film to television to fiction. In some ways, the narrative openness which has been associated with the fantastic throughout this project is the key to seeing how they demonstrate an ethics of becoming. It is an ethics that *requires* resistance to closure: no simple categories, no unexamined boundaries.

Are there problems with an ethics of becoming? Certainly. The loss of essentialized identity structures is often terrifying for the characters discussed in this project, and many of them are forced into situations of becoming that they would never have chosen. Power in the contemporary world is forever at work assigning roles and slots, putting people, stories, relationships, experiences, and everything else into circumscribed and limiting categories. Resisting such control necessarily means resisting those categories. As Braidotti puts it, "The fast rate of change, as well as the paradoxical power relations of late postmodernity are such as to require more accurate cartographies and a higher degree of conceptual creativity on the part of critical thinkers" (*Transpositions* 19). Narratives populated by subjects-in-becoming, narratives that interrupt expectations, narratives that resist truncated endings — these are narratives that can offer readers new ways of thinking about living in the world. Braidotti writes, "The imaginary continues to be of relevance, providing the leverage we need to implement changes in the social realm, as well as in the depths of the subject" (*Transpositions* 87). Indeed, the imaginary seems to be indispensable to the project of addressing contemporary power structures. The fantastic fictions explored in this project may not create revolutions, but they do invite readers to reimagine their relationships to and with power. They expose dangerous assumptions, intervene into expectations, and offer an ethics that is capable of resisting and remaking our world.

Chapter Notes

Introduction

1. Todorov's theory of the fantastic is thoroughly explained in *The Fantastic*. Another important work that utilizes Todorov's basic structure is Rosemary Jackson's *Fantasy* (1981); she approaches the uncertainty of the fantastic from a psychoanalytic perspective but retains Todorov's central idea of uncertainty.

2. See "Octavia E. Butler on Coping with Power in Parable of the Sower, Parable of the Talents, and Fledgling," in Critique: Studies in Contemporary Fiction 49.4, Summer 2008.

Chapter One

1. Mlle. De Villeneuve's *Beauty and the Beast* (1740) is usually cited as the first version that embodies what we know as "Beauty and the Beast" today. There are several useful sources for information on the origins and historical development of the Beauty and the Beast tale. For an overview as well as complete texts of many of the variations, see *The Classic Fairy Tales*, ed. Maria Tatar (1999). The first chapter of Jack Zipes's *Fairy Tale as Myth/Myth as Fairy Tale* (1994) focuses on tales by Madam D'Aulnoy from the late seventeenth century and Madame de Villeneuve's version. Zipes's *Fairy Tales and the Art of Subversion* (1983, 2006) provides an even earlier history of the tale, ending with Beaumont's version; see pages 47–57. Betsy Hearne's *Beauty and the Beast: Visions and Revisions of an Old Tale* (1989) and Marina Warner's *From the Beast to the Blonde: On Fairy Tales and Their Tellers* (1994) also provide detailed accounts of the tale's origins, audiences, tellers/authors, and revisions over time.

2. There are at least two other prominent approaches to fairy tales, and to the Beauty and the Beast tale in particular. Bruno Bettelheim's *The Uses of Enchantment* (1976) is the most often-cited example of a psychoanalytic approach to the tale. Bettelheim argues that "Beauty and the Beast" is fundamentally a story to help children come to terms with leaving parental relationships for marital unions (306). Vladimir Propp's structuralist approach (see *Theory and History of Folklore* for an overview) is another method with wide appeal; his classifications have been taken up by folklorists and literary critics alike. Larry DeVries's "Literary Beauties and Folk Beasts," reprinted in Hearne's *Beauty and the Beast: Visions and Revisions of an Old Tale* (1989), takes up Propp's functional approach to the tale in order to examine it with a kind of detail that Propp himself does not provide. I agree with Zipes's evaluation of both approaches as universalizing, and therefore problematic. (See *Fairy Tales and the Art of Subversion*, 2006.)

3. "The Courtship of Mr. Lyon" was originally written for and published in the British edition of *Vogue* magazine. See Griswold 182.

4. In her discussion of early versions of the Beauty and the Beast tale, Warner describes variants in which "the beauty is the beast — at least she is also changed into a beast, and the metamorphosis leads to her escape from a tyrant father as well as a tyrant husband" (283). Contemporary revisions that explore the possibilities for a Beauty who is or becomes a Beast (see my discussions of Tanith Lee's "Beauty" and Carter's "The Tiger's Bride" below) thus have antecedents in seventeenth-century, and perhaps older, versions of the tale.

5. McKinley's choice of texts is interesting here. Rudyard Kipling's *Kim* (1901), a novel that is notable for its lack of women and emphasis on male relationships, seems a strange choice for Beauty's reading matter. It is, however,

possible to see Kipling's emphasis on Kim's double identity — both British and Indian — in relation to Beauty's dawning sense of a split life between the world of her family and the world of the Beast. Alternatively, the embedded critique of British colonialism in *Kim*, while problematic in its limited scope, could be linked to a comment upon Beauty's assumptions about the Beast being illiterate and/or stupid, both of which turn out to be far from the truth.

6. In contemporary revisions, the Beast's alliance with nature and a "heroic defiance of civilization" (Tatar 29) may be partly responsible for his appeal. Warner emphasizes the way in which the Disney film makes it obvious that the Beast is preferable to the prince who replaces him (313).

7. "Cupid and Psyche" dates to the second century C.E., when it emerged in Apuleius's *Transformations of Lucian, Otherwise Known as the Golden Ass*. Warner describes Apuleius's "Cupid and Psyche" as "a founding myth of sexual difference" (274). In the tale, which involves many elements of later incarnations of "Beauty and the Beast," Psyche is punished for disobedience and rewarded for extreme obedience. See Tatar pages 25–26 and Warner pages 273–76 for more on the relationship between "Cupid and Psyche" and later versions of "Beauty and the Beast."

8. Zipes connects the gambling father in "The Tiger's Bride" to a 1902 version of the tale — a poem by Guy Wetmore Carryl entitled "How Beauty Contrived to Get Square with the Beast." See *Fairy Tale as Myth*, page 41.

9. Sellers finds Tepper's emphasis on the concept of beauty to be the central focus of the text. Tepper contrasts the beauty of the fourteenth-century with a lack of beauty in the 1990s and the twenty-first century. Sellers demonstrates that the notion of beauty at work in Tepper's novel is more complex than it might seem, and involves "beauty as an effect of deliberate, accountable designation" (100). However, Sellers is unable to rescue the ending of the novel from its inaction. See pages 98–103 in Sellers.

Chapter Two

1. For more on PTSD and its implications for trauma theory, see Anne Whitehead and Joseph Flanagan, "The Seduction of History: Trauma, Re-Memory, and the Ethics of the Real" (2002).

2. Whitehead challenges LaCapra's notion of "working-through" in its application to literary texts, arguing that seeing literature as a way of representing, and healing, trauma could also lead to damaging neutralizing tendencies. She offers less realistic modes of literary production as a possible alternative, which I will discuss below.

3. While the novels examined in this chapter profit from being read in conjunction with certain aspects of trauma theory, they are not the works that are usually studied by theorists of trauma. There are developing sub-genres of "trauma fiction" and the "trauma novel" which include works like Toni Morrison's *Beloved* and Pat Barker's *Regeneration* trilogy, as well as various works by Dorothy Allison and Jamaica Kincaid. See Caruth, Flanagan, Vickroy, and Whitehead, as well as Leigh Gilmore's *The Limits of Autobiography: Trauma and Testimony* (2001). Gilmore includes an excellent chapter on Jeanette Winterson's *Written on the Body*.

4. Anne Whitehead has made a similar argument about how the experimental forms found in postmodernism and postcolonial writing have become important ways of representing trauma (87). One of the texts Whitehead focuses on is Pat Barker's *Another World*, the sequel to the *Regeneration* trilogy which has been given a great deal of attention by trauma theorists. Whitehead reads *Another World* as a ghost story in which the "ghosts embody or incarnate the traumas of recent history and represent a form of collective or cultural haunting" (7). In other words, she reads it as using fantastic literary modes to enact a confrontation between past and present.

5. Rufus is, in fact, a direct ancestor to Dana. Barr emphasizes that "rape makes Dana's life possible" (*Lost*, 100), since Dana has to keep Rufus alive long enough to father her grandmother, Hagar Weylin.

6. Many critics argue a link between Butler's portrayal of slavery in the past and marriage and/or domestic abuse in the present. Kevin does not abuse Dana, but her frequent bruises (from her trips to the past) are misinterpreted by her cousin. See Long, especially page 466. For discussions of marriage as oppressive and Kevin as oppressor, see Marc Steinberg's "Inverting History in Octavia Butler's Postmodern Slave Narrative" and Lucie Armitt's discussion of *Kindred* in *Contemporary Women's Fiction and the Fantastic*.

7. It is worth noting that it is difficult for Dana to make use of her knowledge of history from the present in her existence in the past. She brings a book on slavery to the past, but when Rufus finds it and is enraged by it, Dana realizes that along with creating positive

change, she could do irreparable harm in the past. See Steinberg for a more thorough discussion of this topic, especially pages 474–75. On the other hand, as Beverly Friend points out, it is Dana's knowledge of history that "stands her in good stead by preventing her from killing Rufus until he has raped her black great-grandmother, assuring the inception of Dana's family tree" (55).

8. Further discussions of Dana's attempts to educate/change/redirect Rufus can be found in Friend and Govan's "Homage."

9. Long goes into detail about the role of pain in *Kindred*, at times arguing that Butler uses it as an "ahistorical signifier of authenticity" (461). Since, as I argue above, I do not read the novel as an attempt to provide the reader with an "authentic" experience of slavery, Long's argument diverges from my own. Especially troubling is her assertion that Butler "impl[ies] that some African American women's bodies are particularly suited to endure a potent, reinvigorated history for all of us" (468). In no way do I read Dana as a representative figure, taking on the wounds of history for the rest of us.

10. Calling *The Passion* a novel may, in fact, be misleading. Winterson's revisionist rewriting includes literature as well as history and myth, and the lyrical nature of much of her work stems — at least in part — from the tendency to incorporate poetry as well as fiction into her writing. Judith Seaboyer lists some of the texts that are "repetitively woven into" *The Passion*: "the Book of Isaiah, *The Wanderer*, the poetry of Hardy, Auden, and Eliot [...] the poetic prose of Joyce [...] and references to Romantic poetry" (492).

11. Rosemergy points out that the inclusion of both male and female narrators is significant in Winterson's work (263).

12. Thomas Fahy focuses on the role of fractured bodies in *The Passion*, and points out that Henri's body — as well as the bodies of the men and boys around him in the army — are all damaged by the war; see "Fractured Bodies: Privileging the Incomplete in Jeanette Winterson's *The Passion*," especially page 101.

13. Susana Onega offers an account of further examples in which Henri and Villanelle use the same language, and occasionally even undertake the same actions. See pages 57–58.

14. For a detailed discussion of cross-dressing in *The Passion*, see Doan.

15. For more on the significance of Venice as the setting of the novel, see Seaboyer.

16. Fahy points to a later passage in the novel in which Villanelle tells Henri that a map of Venice will do him no good since it "is a living city. Things change" (*The Passion* 113). Reading this comment as producing a "contrast between the constructed and the organic," Fahy argues that "Venice can thus be read as a symbol for postmodern art with the continual (natural) changes it gives to meaning and life" (103). I am dubious of the constructed/organic distinction Fahy inserts here, even if he proceeds to deconstruct it, because it assumes a binary logic that I do not see in the text itself. One of the functions of the literary fantastic is to eliminate the need for such divisions. Like the time travel in *Kindred*, Venice's change-ablility is unexplained.

17. Seaboyer examines a variety of examples of mirroring and doubling in the text, but also finds the instance of the cook's reappearance to be related to trauma.

18. Armitt discusses the ways in which Dog-Woman is read as a politically conservative figure, but concludes that "though purportedly fighting for the King, [Dog-Woman] actually fights for herself" (*Contemporary* 20).

19. Her attempts at heterosexual relationships are failures, but Dog-Woman does not engage in any sexual relationships with women in the text. Nevertheless, Farwell argues that Dog-Woman is actually a lesbian subject as a result of her excessive size, which "constitutes the disruptive agency that is only possible with a lesbian subject" (185).

20. Jago Morrison further notes that the particular figures of Preacher Scroggs and Firebrace, the victims of Dog-Woman's violence at the brothel, serve to create an "implicit conflation of male homosexuality with beastiality and necrophilia" (179).

21. "The Shoes That Were Danced to Pieces" is tale #133 in the final, 1857, edition of *Children's and Household Tales* by Jacob and Wilhelm Grimm. Any number of English translations are now available, but Jack Zipes's *The Complete Fairy Tales of the Brothers Grimm* (1987) is a particularly comprehensive source.

22. It is worth noting that Robin McKinley has also rewritten "The Twelve Dancing Princesses" in her collection entitled *The Door in the Hedge* (1981). In McKinley's version, the "old soldier" is the main character and hero, but the princesses are not caught naughtily enjoying themselves every night. Rather, they are under a spell that the soldier must break in order to free them from the horrible fate of having to spend each night dancing in the arms of evil princes who wish to take over their kingdom. The princesses are, then, rewritten

as victims rather than transgressors who need to be put back into place.

23. Morrison gestures to the fact that Jordan and Dog-Woman "appear in different bodily guises in the seventeenth and twentieth centuries" (175) in order to claim that those embodiments could tempt readers to read the novel in Foucauldian terms, "as an archaeology of the body, as study of its changing historical production" (175). I, of course, agree; Morrison, however, wishes to make the point that such a reading is not reflective of the primary subject matter of the novel, which has more to do with New Scientific discourses than it does with "historically specific, regulatory regimes of hetero-normativity" (175). While Winterson may not always offer precisely the critique of normative discourses that every critic hopes for, the genealogical/traumatic nature of the inquiry into history that her text enacts is evident. A reading of her treatment of New Scientific discourses need not contradict other approaches. Indeed, the more the better, from the perspective of an ethics of becoming.

24. Farrell points out that "the ends of the nineteenth and twentieth centuries have in common a pervasive insecurity about systems of heroic value. Trauma has provided one mode of coping" (23). Nicolas, at the end of the twentieth century, attempts to understand what a hero is. This is a link to the Carter novel discussed below which is set in 1899 and troubles the concept of a public figure, or hero.

25. Blodgett provides a clever reading of Fevvers as a parody of the nineteenth-century angel in the house (52). As the "new woman" who is supposed to usher in the twentieth-century, Fevvers is the antithesis of her idealized private-sphere upper-middle class predecessor.

26. Carter's use of the circus in the text is intriguing. Michael argues that "fantasy and material situation meet head on in the world of the circus. The set divisions and hierarchies between humans and animals and between men and women in the Western world at large break down in Carter's circus" (194).

27. One of the complicating factors in Fevvers's story to Walser is her assertion that she was "hatched" (7). Like Jordan in *Sexing the Cherry*, Fevvers is a foundling.

28. It seems likely that Carter's reference to "authentic history" might also be meant to evoke Georg Lukács's argument in *The Historical Novel*, where he claims that an historical novel should be faithful to its historical time period.

29. Michael points to Mignon as an example of a "potential solution" to the "male-dominated system" because she eventually finds love in a lesbian relationship (188–89). Mignon's case is offered as an alternative, but there is an important distinction between "alternative" and "solution." Carter clearly offers hopeful possibilities, but no single simplistic answers.

30. One of the recurrent themes in the criticism on *Nights at the Circus* is just how much control Fevvers has over her own story. For example, Laurie J.C. Cella writes, "Fevvers constructs herself as an object to be admired, but her posture and attitude reinforce the notion that she is the mistress of her own image, aware of herself as spectacle and controlling the way this image is understood and publicized" (56). Fevvers is in no way a victim of history.

31. One aspect of the text that many critics point to is that it actually ends with Fevvers's triumphant statement that she was able to fool Walser into believing in her virginity. Blodgett, for example, writes that "Her joy redeems the world" (54). Fevvers is, in the end, surprised by her own ability to control the images of herself.

Chapter Three

1. In Moylan's work, critical dystopias are historically situated in the late 1980s and 1990s. He reads them as responding to earlier utopian and anti-utopian texts, as well as traditional dystopias. Lessing's *Memoirs* does not figure in his scheme, however, and Atwood's *The Handmaid's Tale*, as I will explain, registers as a problem in his formulation of what constitutes a politically correct critical dystopia.

2. Examples of classic dystopian narratives include Yevgeny Zamyatin's *We* (1924), Aldous Huxley's *Brave New World* (1932), and George Orwell's *Nineteen Eighty-Four* (1949).

3. The social disintegration Lessing describes in *Memoirs* can be productively read in Marxist terms. As Mona Knapp writes, "The collapse is not due to any particular cataclysm, rather Western capitalist society simply rots from the inside out, as Marx predicted it eventually would" (122). It is, however, tricky to ascribe Marxist thinking to Lessing at this point; *Memoirs* was published a full twenty years after Lessing broke with the Communist movement.

4. Aaron S. Rosenfeld argues that *Memoirs* is actually an example of genre mixing rather than a dystopia that incorporates elements of other texts. Rosenfeld's argument is interesting in that he manages to define four different science fictional genres in Lessing's novel (apocalypse, dystopia, utopia, and arcadia), all of

which he asserts are actually incorporated within a "realistic" (his quotation marks) frame. He makes the point that such genre blending can work to "fuse truth and fiction" (47), which is in keeping with the larger claim this project makes concerning the genealogical inquiry into the production of knowledge.

5. Jeanne Murray Walker offers a different, but convincing, reading of "it" as "the exhausting demand that individuals place on the social structure, their need, and their inability to be satisfied" (97). There are moments in the text to support such a reading, yet the Survivor herself is far from a gorging consumer — and since it is she who uses the term "it," Walker's definition seems only partially correct.

6. Young characters are often more aware of and prepared for social disintegration than their adult counterparts in dystopian fiction, which is the case in Butler's *Parable of the Sower* as well as Lessing's *Memoirs*. Betsy Draine sees Emily's "pioneering spirit" (135) in *Memoirs* as evidence of underlying Marxist assumptions in the text. She argues that Emily is "able to shuck off old assumptions, decadent habits of behavior, and outmoded social relationships and assist a new social system to develop" (135). While that may be true, the text ultimately leads Emily into the Survivor's alternative behind the wall, and not the other way around.

7. Draine, as it turns out, believes that the ending of the novel is a failure and so always chooses to read the rest of the novel as though for the first time.

8. Draine identifies the six-sided room as a Jungian symbol, representing the union of the ego with the non-ego (9).

9. "Griot" is a word for a West African storyteller. (Thank you to Winifred Morgan for pointing out that important fact.)

10. For example, Magali Cornier Michael develops an argument about the specific ways in which the society in *The Handmaid's Tale* parallels "less overt" examples of the way women were treated in 1980's American society: "As an exaggeration of existing relations of power, Gilead has truth value at the same time as it exists as a fiction. Indeed, to a certain degree, Gilead contains 1980s America culture" (138).

11. The fact that Offred's narrative is in the present tense has occasioned a range of responses from critics. For example, Karen F. Stein points out that "her use of the present tense for recollection of the past suggests fiction, perhaps even trickery, deceit" (274), while Dominick M. Grace argues that by speaking in the present tense, Offred "discourages us from seeing her narrative as fixed, final, and anterior; it is, instead, ongoing, and it unfolds for us as it does for her" (484). Atwood's use of the present tense for Offred's narrative is closer to Butler's use of the journal form in the *Parable* novels than it is to Lessing's dystopian novels. I agree with Grace's assessment of the use of the present tense as encouraging a sense of openness; it works to engage the reader in the process and potential of Offred's story.

12. Many critics have shown how Atwood actually works quite closely with the standard formula of more traditional dystopian narratives. Offred is a typical outsider protagonist caught within an overwhelming and dictatorial system, there is a resistance movement and a love affair, constant worry over the possibility of spies, overarching surveillance, and so on. See Davidson, Feuer, and Ketterer. As one might expect from a text that embraces indeterminacy and potential, the narrative structure itself can be read in multiple ways.

13. For a thorough treatment of the role of language in relation to power and authority in *The Handmaid's Tale*, see Ildney Cavalcanti.

14. The narrator's memories of her husband's reactions to the power shift in their relationship are read by Michael as evidence of the fact that the Gileadean regime's rise to power was enabled by underlying patriarchal modes of thinking, so that the novel is criticizing "Western modes of thought themselves" (142–43).

15. Moylan, who describes Atwood's text as an "ambiguous" rather than strictly "critical" dystopia, emphasizes that there is a "counter-narrative" to Gilead within the text developed around the "the culture of resistance practiced by the Handmaids," which includes "sexual transgression," "spying," "language itself," and "the direct action of the Mayday Underground" (163). For Moylan, it is imperative that the "utopian horizon" of a critical dystopia be available within the textual frame, so that what he reads as the ultimate triumph of Gilead in the narrative prevents him from classifying the text as a critical dystopia. The emphasis on critical analysis of power structures and the engendering of space for new possibilities is my definition of the term, and Atwood's text fulfills my requirements. Moylan's emphases on the various moments of resistance in the text that do not necessarily come to satisfying conclusions only enhance the point that Atwood includes a variety of counter-discourses within the text.

16. There is a wide range in the way critics approach the "Historical Notes." Some of the more remarkable readings include Ketterer,

who states that "the 'Notes' strongly imply that Atwood cannot have intended *The Handmaid's Tale* only as the typical dire dystopian warning or call to rebellion if she envisages Gilead either passing away naturally in the fullness of time or being dramatically overthrown" (212). The fact that Gilead is eventually overturned leads Ketterer to argue that the entire cautionary function of the text is no longer valid. Clearly, Atwood suggests that the eruption of a regime such as Gilead, even for a day or a week, should never be allowed to occur.

Another—opposing—reading of the "Historical Notes" section comes from Murphy, who argues that the use of the "Historical Notes actually reduces "the dystopian distance" (35) of the text. He sees the "pseudo-documentary" style of the Notes as "more verisimilitudinous" (27) than the rest of the text, so that the inclusion of the Notes makes the entire narrative seem more plausible.

17. Recognizing that the *Parable* novels explicitly critique dominant power structures, critics often emphasize the complexity of the ways they respond to power. In her discussion of how the novels represent utopian possibilities, Melzer points out that "The struggle of power relations is at the center of [Butler's] writing and informs the manifestations of the utopian desire that run through her narratives" (par. 13). Moylan, who finds a useful utopian model in *Sower* but not in *Talents*, argues, "Butler's willingness to explore the empowering force of a spirituality motivated but materially transcendent vision that is rooted in difficulty and difference allows her to posit a politicizing process that produces a vulnerable but viable utopian alternative by the end of this first book in the series" (237). Any movement toward positive change in Butler's texts is accompanied by a deeply ingrained awareness of power relations, both in terms of recognizing the dominant forces which will have to be confronted (as Melzer describes), and in relation to finding ways of gaining power in order to effect change (as Moylan specifies).

18. For a detailed discussion of Butler's use of community in *Sower*, see Dubey, who contrasts Butler's urban approach to community with the privileging of rural folk communities in texts by other African-American women writers, arguing that Butler emphasizes journey and change rather than a specific location in her definition of community through most of the novel.

Chapter Four

1. The history of the relationship of women writers to science fiction, which has implications for what constitutes revision and what is simply science fiction, has been the subject of a number of recent studies. See Brian Attebery's *Decoding Gender in Science Fiction*, Justine Larbalestier's *The Battle of the Sexes in Science Fiction*, Joanna Russ's *To Write Like a Woman: Essays in Feminism and Science Fiction*, and Pamela Sargent's *Women of Wonder the Classic Years*.

Ursula Le Guin, for example, has published science fiction since the middle of the twentieth-century and is perhaps one of the best known authors of the genre; it is difficult to claim that she is both a major figure within the genre and an outsider who revises it. On the other hand, writers like Le Guin, Joanna Russ, and Marge Piercy are often considered to have changed the direction of science fiction in significant ways. The important point in the context of this project is simply that the space fiction of Butler, Le Guin, and Lessing demonstrates a tendency to rewrite patriarchal themes that were dominant in earlier examples of the genre.

2. Critical dystopian narratives, which clearly operate less as static models and more as dynamic explorations, could be classified as heterotopias in Pordzik's schematic. The inclusion of utopian possibilities within critical dystopias makes them hybrid cases, much like the space fiction narratives discussed here.

3. In particular, Rocannon's journey and concurrent induction into telepathy prefigure Genly Ai's journey with Estraven in *The Left Hand of Darkness*.

4. Much of the imagery, particularly the descriptions of alien species (sentient and otherwise) in *Rocannon's World* is drawn from Norse mythology. Le Guin, in later years, is rather critical of her own attempt here for being "too timid to make up her own" images. See Lefanu pp. 133–4 and Le Guin's introductions to later reprints of the novel for such statements. I suggest, however, that her use of mythological creatures can be read as an example of revisionist writing that she simply fine-tuned in later works.

5. For example, see Elizabeth Cummins Cogell's "Setting as Analogue to Characterization in LeGuin."

6. Le Guin published a number of short stories set in the Hainish universe during the years between *The Dispossessed* and *The Telling*, as well as a novel about colonial occupation

and environmental destruction, *The Word for World is Forest*. However, in this context it is useful to jump ahead in order to look at how Le Guin has positioned the *Hainish Cycle* in recent work.

7. Moylan characterizes *The Telling* as "a critical dystopia with a strong utopian presence" ("'The Moment'" 150), and argues that the novel may be part of the beginning of a shift toward a necessary revival of "eutopian narratives that speak a directly transformative truth to global, capitalist power" (151). I do not share the reading of a shift since the earlier texts seem to me to offer similar moments of potential; the power dynamics have changed, and with them the specific responses embedded in the texts. However, the overall response is still an ethics of potential and becoming that embraces heterotopian possibilities.

8. In remarks at the beginning of *Shikasta*.

9. Others have read Lessing's space fiction in these terms as well. Barbara Dixson, for example, reads the *Canopus* series as unified through both form and content. She argues that the "imperial novels" (those that specifically emphasize perspectives of power — *Shikasta*, *The Sirian Experiments*, and *The Sentimental Agents*) "offer different perspectives on the workings of power" (17).

10. For more on the function of defamiliarization in the text, see Susan Rowland who argues that "the novel through its structure and Shikastan perspective defamiliarizes Earth history and its 'alien' reality" (45). The use of space fiction to investigate the production of historical knowledge is another way to consider Lessing's approach in *Shikasta*.

11. Fishburn offers a detailed account of narration and perspective in the *Canopus* series in *The Unexpected Universe of Doris Lessing*.

12. The relationship between Shikasta and Canopus is explored in detail by Phyllis Sternberg Perrakis, who argues that the inner world of Shikasta and the outer world of Canopus are put into a productive tension in the novel that, eventually, leads to the growth of both human and Canopean characters. See "The Marriage of Inner and Outer Space in Doris Lessing's *Shikasta*."

13. Critics have paid substantial attention to the very rich fantastic second text in the *Canopus* series, *The Marriages Between Zones Three, Four, and Five*. Some of the approaches to the text include a utopian model, postcolonial interpretations, religio-symbolic readings, and psychoanalytic analysis: Naomi Jacobs reads the novel as a new type of utopia; Mona Knapp focuses on the novel's depiction of "the struggle to go beyond domestic borders and adopt the ways of the 'other'" (158); Perrakis applies Lessing's knowledge of Jungian philosophy and Sufism to the text; and Virginia Tiger uses Lacan and Irigaray to investigate the ways the text employs a range of literary strategies. I see this wide range of productive analyses as further evidence of the heterotopian nature of the text.

14. M. Patricia Mosier elaborates upon the role Ambien II plays as a student of Canopean teachers. She reads *The Sirian Experiments* through the lens of Sufi tradition, in which the teacher/disciple relationship is central.

15. Knapp finds fault with what she perceives to be Lessing's condemnation of all rhetoric in *Sentimental Agents*. For a more detailed discussion of *Sentimental Agents* and Lessing's emphasis on political language in the novel, see "Canopuspeak: Doris Lessing's *Sentimental Agents* and Orwell's *1984*."

16. In an article focusing on religion in Butler's work, including the *Xenogenesis* trilogy, Sarah Wood makes the point that "Butler's fiction repeatedly admonishes unquestioning reliance on religious myths. Significantly, however, she does not entirely abandon such epistemological frameworks of belief. Instead, employing strategies of revision through the inclusion of alternate belief systems, she begins a process of subversion grounded in the concept of inclusivity" (96). Similarly, Alison Tara Walker argues "Butler alters the Lilith myth in order to reenvision positive, most importantly generative, possibilities for such a negative narrative (109). Here is yet another example of how revisionist rewriting supports an ethics of becoming.

17. Walker's article presents a fascinating Deleuzian reading of the *Xenogenesis* trilogy. Her specific emphasis, however, is on the way Butler constructs Lilith's "origin story" (109) as a becoming rather than a strictly genealogical narrative. (Genealogical in this sense means line of genetic descent and not Foucauldian historiography.)

Works Cited

Amis, Kingsley. *New Maps of Hell: A Survey of Science Fiction*. New York: Harcourt, 1960.

Armitt, Lucie. *Contemporary Women's Fiction and the Fantastic*. New York: St. Martin's Press, 2000.

———. "The Fragile Frames of *The Bloody Chamber*." *The Infernal Desires of Angela Carter*. Ed. Joseph Bristow and Trev Lynn Broughton. London: Longman, 1997. 88–99.

Attebery, Brian. *Decoding Gender in Science Fiction*. New York: Routledge, 2002.

Atwood, Margaret. *The Handmaid's Tale*. 1985. New York: Anchor, 1998.

———. *In Other Worlds: SF and the Human Imagination*. New York: Doubleday, 2011.

———. *Oryx and Crake*. New York: Doubleday, 2003.

———. *The Year of the Flood*. New York: Doubleday, 2009.

Bacchilega, Cristina. *Postmodern Fairy Tales: Gender and Narrative Strategies*. Philadelphia: University of Pennsylvania Press, 1997.

Baccolini, Raffaella. "Gender and Genre in the Feminist Critical Dystopias of Katherine Burdekin, Margaret Atwood, and Octavia Butler." *Future Females, The Next Generation: New Voices and Velocities in Feminist Science Fiction Criticism*. Ed. Marleen S. Barr. Lanham: Rowman, 2000. 13–34.

———, and Tom Moylan. "Introduction. Dystopia and Histories." *Dark Horizons: Science Fiction and the Dystopian Imagination*. Ed. Rafaella Baccolini and Tom Moylan. New York: Routledge, 2003. 1–12.

Barr, Marleen S. *Alien to Feminity: Speculative Fiction and Feminist Theory*. Contributions to the Study of Science Fiction and Fantasy 27. New York: Greenwood Press, 1987.

———. *Feminist Fabulation: Space/Postmodern Fiction*. Iowa City: University of Iowa Press, 1992.

———. *Lost in Space: Probing Feminist Science Fiction and Beyond*. Chapel Hill: University of North Carolina Press, 1993.

Barthes, Roland. *Mythologies*. Trans. Annette Lavers. New York: Hill and Wang, 1972.

Bettelheim, Bruno. *The Uses of Enchantment*. New York: Knopf, 1976.

Blodgett, Harriet. "Fresh Iconography: Subversive Fantasy by Angela Carter." *Review of Contemporary Fiction* 14 (1994): 49–55.

Bollinger, Laurel. "Models for Female Loyalty: The Biblical Ruth in Jeanette Winterson's *Oranges Are Not the Only Fruit*." *Tulsa Studies in Women's Literature* 13 (1994): 363–380.

Braidotti, Rosi. *Metamorphoses: Towards a Materialist Theory of Becoming*. 2002. Cambridge: Polity, 2005.

———. "Teratologies." *Deleuze and Feminist Theory*. 2000. Ed. Ian Buchanan and Claire Colebrook. Edinburgh: Edinburgh University Press, 2001. 156–72.

Bristow, Joseph, and Trev Lynn Broughton. Introduction. *The Infernal Desires of Angela Carter*. Ed. Joseph Bristow and Trev Lynn Broughton. London: Longman, 1997. 1–23.

Bryant, Sylvia. "Re-Constructing Oedipus through 'Beauty and the Beast.'" *Critical Essays on Angela Carter*. Ed. Lindsey Tucker. New York: G.K. Hall, 1998. 83–95.

Burns, Christy L. "Fantastic Language: Jeanette Winterson's Recovery of the Postmodern Word." *Contemporary Literature* 37 (1996): 278–306.

Butler, Octavia E. *Adulthood Rites*. New York: Aspect Warner, 1988.

———. *Dawn*. New York: Aspect Warner, 1987.

———. *Imago*. New York: Aspect Warner, 1989.

———. "An Interview with Octavia E. Butler." *Across the Wounded Galaxies: Interviews with Contemporary American Science Fiction Writers*.

Ed. Larry McCaffrey. Urbana: University of Illinois Press, 1990.

———. *Kindred*. 1979. Boston: Beacon Press, 1988.

———. *Parable of the Sower*. New York: Warner, 1993.

———. *Parable of the Talents*. 1998. New York: Warner, 2000.

Carter, Angela. *The Bloody Chamber*. 1979. New York: Penguin, 1993.

———. *Nights at the Circus*. 1984. New York: Penguin, 1993.

Carter, Theresa. "Temporal Temptations in Lessing's *Mara and Dann*: Arriving at the Present Moment." *Doris Lessing Studies* 23.2 (2004): 17–20.

Caruth, Cathy. *Unclaimed Experience: Trauma, Narrative, History*. Baltimore: Johns Hopkins University Press, 1996.

Cavalcanti, Ildney. "Utopias of/f Language in Contemporary Feminist Literary Dystopias." *Utopian Studies* 11(2000): 152–80.

Cella, Laurie J.C. "Narrative 'Confidence Games': Framing the Blonde Spectacle in *Gentlemen Prefer Blondes* (1925) and *Nights at the Circus* (1984)." *Frontiers* 25 (2004): 47–62.

Cogell, Elizabeth Cummins. "Setting as Analogue to Characterization in Ursula Le-Guin." *Extrapolation* 18: 131–41. 1977.

Colebrook, Claire. "A Grammar of Becoming: Strategy, Subjectivism, and Style." *Becomings*. Ed. Elizabeth Grosz. Ithaca: Cornell University Press, 1999. 117–40.

Davidson, Arnold E. "Future Tense: Making History in *The Handmaid's Tale*." *Margaret Atwood Vision and Forms*. Ed. Kathryn Van Spanckeren and Jan Garden Castro. Carbondale: Southern Illinois University Press, 1988. 113–121.

Day, Aidan. *Angela Carter: The Rational Glass*. Manchester: Manchester University Press, 1998.

Deleuze, Gilles. *Negotiations, 1972–1990*. Trans. Martin Joughin. New York: Columbia University Press, 1995.

Deleuze, Gilles, and Félix Guattari. *A Thousand Plateaus: Capitalism and Schizophrenia*. Trans. Brian Massumi. Minneapolis: University of Minnesota Press, 1987.

Dixson, Barbara. "Structural Complexity in Doris Lessing's Canopus Novels." *Journal of the Fantastic in the Arts* 2.3 (1990): 14–22.

Doan, Laura. "Jeanette Winterson's Sexing the Postmodern." *The Lesbian Postmodern*. Ed. Laura Doan. New York: Columbia University Press, 1994. 137–55.

Doerksen, Teri Ann. "Octavia E. Butler: Parables of Race and Difference." *Into Darkness Peering: Race and Color in the Fantastic*. Ed. Elisabeth Anne Leonard. Contributions to the Study of Science Fiction and Fantasy 74. Westport, CT: Greenwood Press, 1997. 21–34.

Draine, Betsy. *Substance Under Pressure: Artistic Coherence and Evolving Form in the Novels of Doris Lessing*. Madison: University of Wisconsin Press, 1983.

Dubey, Madhu. "Folk and Urban Communities in African-American Women's Fiction: Octavia Butler's *Parable of the Sower*." *Studies in American Fiction* 27 (1999): 103–28.

Fahy, Thomas. "Fractured Bodies: Privileging the Incomplete in Jeanette Winterson's *The Passion*." *Mosaic* 33.3 (2000): 95–106.

Farrell, Kirby. *Post-Traumatic Culture: Injury and Interpretation in the Nineties*. Baltimore: Johns Hopkins University Press, 1998.

Farwell, Marilyn R. *Heterosexual Plots and Lesbian Narratives*. New York: New York University Press, 1996.

Feuer, Louis. "The Calculus of Love and Nightmare: *The Handmaid's Tale* and the Dystopian Tradition." *Critique: Studies in Contemporary Fiction* 38 (1997): 83–95.

Fishburn, Katherine. *The Unexpected Universe of Doris Lessing: A Study in Narrative Technique*. Contributions to the Study of Science Fiction and Fantasy 17. Westport, CT: Greenwood Press, 1985.

Flanagan, Joseph. "The Seduction of History: Trauma, Re-Memory, and the Ethics of the Real." *Clio* 31 (2002): 387–402.

Foucault, Michel. *Discipline and Punish: The Birth of the Prison*. Trans. Alan Sheridan. 1977. New York: Vintage, 1995.

———. *The History of Sexuality, Volume I: An Introduction*. Trans. Robert Hurley. 1978. New York: Vintage, 1990.

———. "Nietzsche, Genealogy, History." *Language, Counter-Memory, Practice: Selected Essays and Interviews*. Trans. Donald F. Bouchard and Sherry Simon. Ed. Donald F. Bouchard. Ithaca: Cornell University Press, 1977. 139–64.

———. "Of Other Spaces." 1967. Trans. Jay Miskowiec. 14 February 2004. http://foucault.info/documents/heteroTopia/foucault.heteroTopia.en.html.

———. *The Order of Things: An Archaeology of the Human Sciences*. 1971. New York: Vintage, 1994. Trans. Of *Les Mots et les choses*. Paris: Editions Gallimard, 1966.

———. "Two Lectures." *Power/Knowledge: Selected Interviews and Other Writings 1972–1977*. Trans. Colin Gordon, Leo Marshall,

John Mepham, Kate Soper. Ed. Colin Gordon. New York: Pantheon, 1980. 78–108.
Franko, Carol. "Dialogic Narration and Ambivalent Hope in Lessing's *Shikasta* and Le Guin's *Always Coming Home.*" *Journal of the Fantastic in the Arts* 2.3 (1990): 23–33.
Friend, Beverly. "Time Travel as a Feminist Didactic in Works by Phyllis Eisenstein, Marlys Millhiser, and Octavia Butler." *Extrapolation* 23 (1982): 50–55.
Gamallo, Isabel C. Anievas. "Subversive Storytelling: The Construction of Lesbian Girlhood Through Fantasy and Fairy Tale in Jeanette Winterson's *Oranges Are Not the Only Fruit.*" *The Girl: Constructions of the Girl in Contemporary Fiction by Women*. Ed. Ruth O. Saxton. New York: St. Martin's Press, 1998. 119–34.
Gilbert, Sandra M., and Susan Gubar. *The Madwoman in the Attic: The Woman Writer and the Nineteenth-Century Literary Imagination*. New Haven: Yale University Press, 1979.
Gilmore, Leigh. *The Limits of Autobiography: Trauma and Testimony*. Ithaca: Cornell University Press, 2001.
Grace, Dominick M. "*The Handmaid's Tale*: 'Historical Notes' and Documentary Subversion." *Science Fiction Studies* 25 (1998): 481–94.
Granofsky, Ronald. *The Trauma Novel: Contemporary Symbolic Depictions of Collective Disaster*. New York: Peter Lang, 1995.
Greene, Gayle. *Doris Lessing: The Poetics of Change*. Ann Arbor: University of Michigan Press, 1994.
Grimm, Jacob, and Wilhelm Grimm. *The Complete Fairy Tales of the Brothers Grimm*. Trans. and ed. Jack Zipes. New York: Bantam, 1987.
Griswold, Jerry. *The Meanings of "Beauty and the Beast": A Handbook*. Peterborough, ON: Broadview Press, 2004.
Gottschall, Jonathan. "Quantitative Literary Study: A Modest Manifesto and Testing the Hypotheses of Feminist Fairy Tale Studies." *The Literary Animal: Evolution and the Nature of Narrative*. Ed. Jonathan Gottschall and David Sloan Wilson. Evanston, IL: Northwestern University Press, 2005. 199–224.
Govan, Sandra Y. "Connections, Links, and Extended Networks: Patterns in Octavia Butler's Science Fiction." *Black American Literature Forum* 18 (1984): 82–87.
———. "Homage to Tradition: Octavia Butler Renovates the Historical Novel." *Melus* 13 (1986): 79–96.
Haffenden, John. "Angela Carter." *Novelists in Interview*. New York: Methuen, 1985.

Haggis, Jan. "White Women and Colonialism: Towards a Non-Recuperative History." *Feminist Postcolonial Theory*. Ed. Reina Lewis and Sara Mills. New York: Routledge, 2003. 161–89.
Hanson, Clare. "'The Red Dawn Breaking Over Claphan': Carter and the Limits of Artifice." *The Infernal Desires of Angela Carter*. Ed. Joseph Bristow and Trev Lynn Broughton. London: Longman, 1997. 59–72.
Harvey, David. *Spaces of Hope*. Berkeley: University of California Press, 2000.
Hearne, Betsy. *Beauty and the Beast: Visions and Revisions of an Old Tale*. Chicago: University of Chicago Press, 1989.
Hutcheon, Linda. *A Poetics of Postmodernism: History, Theory, Fiction*. New York: Routledge, 1988.
Jacobs, Naomi. "Beyond Stasis and Symmetry: Lessing, Le Guin, and the Remodeling of Utopia." *Extrapolation* 29 (1988): 34–45.
———. "Posthuman Bodies and Agency in Octavia Butler's *Xenogenesis*." *Dark Horizons: Science Fiction and the Dystopian Imagination*. Ed. Rafaella Baccolini and Tom Moylan. New York: Routledge, 2003. 91–111.
Jameson, Fredric. *Archaeologies of the Future: The Desire Called Utopia and Other Science Fictions*. London: Verso, 2005.
Kennedy, Maev. "Mystery of the Tudor Banana." *The Guardian* 15 June 1999. Web. 8 May 2013.
Ketterer, David. "Margaret Atwood's *The Handmaid's Tale*: A Contextual Dystopia." *Science Fiction Studies* 16 (1989): 209–17.
Knapp, Mona. *Doris Lessing*. New York: Frederick Ungar, 1984.
———. "Canopuspeak: Doris Lessing's *Sentimental Agents* and Orwell's *1984*." *Neophilologus* 70.3 (1986): 453–61.
Lacey, Lauren. "Octavia E. Butler on Coping with Power in *Parable of the Sower*, *Parable of the Talents*, and *Fledgling*." *Critique: Studies in Contemporary Fiction* 49.4 (2008): 379–394.
Larbalestier, Justine. *The Battle of the Sexes in Science Fiction*. The Wesleyan Early Classics of Science Fiction Series. Middletown, CT: Wesleyan University Press, 2002.
Le Guin, Ursula K. *The Dispossessed*. 1974. New York: Harper Prism, 1994.
———. *The Left Hand of Darkness*. New York: Ace Books, 1969.
———. *The Telling*. New York: Harcourt, 2000.
———. *Three Hainish Novels*. Garden City, NY: Nelson Doubleday, 1967.
Le Prince de Beaumont, Jeanne-Marie. "Beauty and the Beast." *The Classic Fairy Tales*. Trans.

and ed. Maria Tatar. New York: Norton, 1999. 32–42.
Lee, Tanith. "Beauty." *Red as Blood, or Tales from the Sisters Grimmer*. New York: Daw Books, 1983. 149–186.
Lefanu, Sarah. *Feminism and Science Fiction*. 1988. Bloomington: Indiana University Press, 1989.
Lessing, Doris. *Documents Relating to The Sentimental Agents in the Volyen Empire*. 1983. New York: Vintage, 1984.
———. *The Making of the Representative for Planet 8*. 1982. London: Granada, 1983.
———. *Mara and Dann: An Adventure*. New York: HarperPerennial, 1999.
———. *The Marriages Between Zones Three, Four, and Five*. 1980. New York: Vintage, 1981.
———. *The Memoirs of a Survivor*. 1974. New York: Vintage, 1988.
———. *Re: Colonised Planet 5: Shikasta. Canopus in Argos: Archives*. 1979. New York: Vintage, 1981.
———. *The Sirian Experiments*. 1981. New York: Vintage, 1982.
———. *The Story of General Dann and Mara's Daughter, Griot and the Snow Dog*. 2005. New York: Harper Perennial, 2006.
Leys, Ruth. *Trauma: A Genealogy*. Chicago: Chicago University Press, 2000.
Long, Lisa A. "A Relative Pain: The Rape of History in Octavia Butler's *Kindred* and Phyllis Alesia Perry's *Stigmata*." *College English* 64 (2002): 459–83.
Lukács, Georg. *The Historical Novel*. New York: Humanities Press, 1965.
Maass, Vera Sonja. *The Cinderella Test: Would You Really Want the Shoe to Fit?* Santa Barbara: Praeger, 2009.
Mahoney, Elisabeth. "Writing So to Speak: The Feminist Dystopia." *Image and Power: Women in Fiction in the Twentieth Century*. Ed. Sarah Sceats and Gail Cunningham. London: Longman, 1996. 29–40.
Makinen, Merja. "Theorizing Fairy-Tale Fiction, Reading Jeanette Winterson." *Contemporary Fiction and the Fairy Tale*. Ed. Stephen Benson. Detroit: Wayne State University Press, 2008. 144–177
Margalit, Avashai. *The Ethics of Memory*. Cambridge: Harvard University Press, 2002.
McKinley, Robin. *Beauty: A Retelling of the Story of Beauty and the Beast*. 1978. New York: HarperTrophy, 1993.
———. *The Door in the Hedge*. 1981. New York: Firebird, 2003.
———. *Rose Daughter*. 1997. New York: Ace, 1998.
———. "The Story Behind *Rose Daughter*." 10 March 2007. http://www.robinmckinley.com/Essays/RoseDaughter.html.
Melzer, Patricia. "'All that you touch you change': Utopian Desire and the Concept of Change in Octavia Butler's *Parable of the Sower* and *Parable of the Talents*." *Femspec* 3.2 (2002). 27 May 2004. http://www.femspec.org/samples/butler.html.
Michael, Magali Cornier. *Feminism and the Postmodern Impulse, Post-World War II Fiction*. Albany: State University of New York Press, 1996.
Moraru, Christian. *Rewriting: Postmodern Narrative and Cultural Critique in the Age of Cloning*. Albany: State University of New York Press, 2001.
Morrison, Jago. "'Who Cares About Gender at a Time Like This?' Love, Sex and the Problem of Jeanette Winterson." *Journal of Gender Studies* 15.2 (2006): 169–80.
Mosier, M. Patricia. "A Sufi Model for the Teacher/Disciple Relationship in *The Sirian Experiments*." *Extrapolation* 32 (1991): 209–21.
Moylan, Tom. "'The moment is here ... and it's important': State, Agency, and Dystopia in Kim Stanley Robinson's *Antarctica* and Ursula K. Le Guin's *The Telling*." *Dark Horizons: Science Fiction and the Dystopian Imagination*. Ed. Rafaella Baccolini and Tom Moylan. New York: Routledge, 2003. 135–53.
———. *Scraps of the Untainted Sky: Science Fiction, Utopia, Dystopia*. Boulder: Westview Press, 2000.
Onega, Susana. *Jeanette Winterson*. Contemporary British Novelists. Manchester: Manchester University Press, 2006.
Peach, Linden. *Angela Carter*. Modern Novelists. New York: St. Martin's Press, 1998.
Perrakis, Phyllis Sternberg. "The Marriage of Inner and Outer Space in Doris Lessing's *Shikasta*." *Science Fiction Studies* 17 (1990): 221–36.
———. "Sufism, Jung and the Myth of Kore: Revisionist Politics in Lessing's *Marriages*." *Mosaic* 25.3 (1992): 99–120.
Pordzik, Ralph. *The Quest for Postcolonial Utopia: A Comparative Introduction to the Utopian Novel in the New English Literatures*. New York: Peter Lang, 2001.
Propp, Vladimir. *Theory and History of Folklore*. Ed. Anatoly Liberman. Trans. Ariadna Y. Martin and Richard P. Martin. *Theory and History of Literature* Vol. 5. Ed. Wlad Godzich and Jochen Schulte-Sasse. Minneapolis: University of Minnesota Press, 1984.

Raschke, Debrah. "Cabalistic Gardens: Lessing's *Memoirs of a Survivor*." *Spiritual Explorations in the Works of Doris Lessing*. Contributions to the Study of Science Fiction and Fantasy 81. Ed. Phyllis Sternberg Perrakis. Westport, CT: Greenwood Press, 1999.

Rigney, Barbara Hill. *Margaret Atwood*. Women Writers. Totowa, NJ: Barnes & Noble, 1987.

Roberts, Adam. *Science Fiction*. The New Critical Idiom. London: Routledge, 2000.

Rosemergy, Jan. "Navigating the Interior Journey: The Fiction of Jeanette Winterson." *British Women Writing Fiction*. Ed. Abby H.P. Werlock. Tuscaloosa: University of Alabama Press, 2000. 248–69.

Rothberg, Michael. *Traumatic Realism: The Demands of Holocaust Representation*. Minneapolis: University of Minnesota Press, 2000.

Rowland, Susan. "'Transformed and Translated': The Colonized Reader of Doris Lessing's *Canopus in Argos* Space Fiction." *British Women Writing Fiction*. Ed. Abby H.P. Werlock. Tuscaloosa: University of Alabama Press, 2000. 42–55.

Rusk, Lauren. *The Life Writing of Otherness: Woolf, Baldwin, Kingston and Winterson*. New York: Routledge, 2002.

Russ, Joanna. *To Write Like a Woman: Essays in Feminism and Science Fiction*. Bloomington: Indiana University Press, 1995.

Sargent, Pamela. *Women of Wonder the Classic Years: Science Fiction Writing by Women from the 1940s to the 1970s*. San Diego: Harcourt Brace, 1995.

Scholes, Robert. *Structural Fabulation. An Essay on Fiction of the Future*. University of Notre Dame Ward-Phillips Lectures in English Language and Literature 7. Notre Dame: University of Notre Dame Press, 1975.

Seaboyer, Judith. "Second Death in Venice: Romanticism and the Compulsion to Repeat in Jeanette Winterson's *The Passion*." *Contemporary Literature* 38 (1997): 483–509.

Sellers, Susan. *Myth and Fairy Tale in Contemporary Women's Fiction*. New York: Palgrave, 2001.

Smith, Angela Marie. "Fiery Constellations: Winterson's *Sexing the Cherry* and Benjamin's Materialist Historiography." *College Literature* 32 (2005): 21–50.

Stein, Karen F. "Margaret Atwood's *The Handmaid's Tale*: Scheherazade in Dystopia." *University of Toronto Quarterly* 61 (1991–2): 269–79.

Steinberg, Marc. "Inverting History in Octavia Butler's Postmodern Slave Narrative." *African American Review* 38 (2004): 467–476.

Tatar, Maria, ed. *The Classic Fairy Tales*. New York: Norton, 1999.

Tepper, Sheri S. *Beauty*. 1991. New York: Bantam, 1992.

Tiger, Virginia. "'The Words Had Been Right and Necessary': Doris Lessing's Transformations of Utopian and Dystopian Modalities in *The Marriages Between Zones Three, Four, and Five*." *Style* 27.1 (1993): 63–81.

Todorov, Tvetan. *The Fantastic*. Trans. Richard Howard. Ithaca: Cornell University Press, 1975.

Urbanowicz, Victor. "Personal and Political in 'The Dispossessed.'" *Ursula K. Le Guin*. Ed. Harold Bloom. New York: Chelsea House, 1986.

Vickroy, Laurie. *Trauma and Survival Theory in Contemporary Fiction*. Charlottesville: University of Virginia Press, 2002.

Walker, Alison Tara. "Destabilizing Order, Challenging History: Octavia Butler, Deleuze and Guattari, and Affective Beginnings." *Extrapolation* 46 (2005): 103–19.

Walker, Jeanne Murray. "Memory and Culture within the Individual: The Breakdown of Social Exchange in *Memoirs of a Survivor*." *Doris Lessing: The Alchemy of Survival*. Ed. Carey Kaplan and Ellen Cronan Rose. Athens: Ohio University Press, 1988. 93–114.

Walker, Nancy A. *Feminist Alternatives: Irony and Fantasy in the Contemporary Novel by Women*. Jackson: University Press of Mississippi, 1990.

Warner, Marina. *From the Beast to the Blonde: On Fairy Tales and Their Tellers*. London: Chatto & Windus, 1994.

Watkins, Susan. "Writing in a Minor Key." *Doris Lessing Studies* 25.2 (2006): 6–10.

Whitehead, Anne. *Trauma Fiction*. Edinburgh: Edinburgh University Press, 2004.

Wilson, Sharon Rose. *Myths and Fairy Tales in Contemporary Women's Fiction: From Atwood to Morrison*. New York: Palgrave Macmillan, 2008.

Winterson, Jeanette. *Oranges Are Not the Only Fruit*. 1985. New York: Atlantic Monthly Press, 1987.

―――. *The Passion*. New York: Grove Press, 1987.

―――. *Sexing the Cherry*. New York: Grove Press, 1989.

Wood, Sarah. "Subversion through Inclusion: Octavia Butler's Interrogation of Religion in *Xenogenesis* and *Wild Seed*." *Femspec* 6.1 (2005): 87–99.

Zipes, Jack. *Breaking the Magic Spell: Radical Theories of Folk and Fairy Tales*. Rev. ed. Lexington: University Press of Kentucky, 2002.

_____. *Fairy Tales and the Art of Subversion. The Classical Genre for Children and the Process of Civilization.* 2nd ed. New York: Routledge, 2006.

_____. *Fairy Tale as Myth / Myth as Fairy Tale.* Lexington: University Press of Kentucky, 1994.

_____. *Relentless Progress: The Reconfiguration of Children's Literature, Fairy Tales, and Storytelling.* New York: Routledge, 2008.

_____. *Why Fairy Tales Stick: The Evolution and Relevance of a Genre.* New York: Routledge, 2006.

Index

Adulthood Rites 170–172
agency 23, 126, 133
alien 20, 43–47, 143, 144, 149, 154, 158, 159, 168, 170–172, 173, 175
Amis, Kingsley 143
anarchy 115, 156
Armitt, Lucie 11–12, 31, 87n18, 90, 98
Atwood, Margaret 2, 6, 15, 19, 22, 26, 104, 133, 134, 135, 136, 140, 175; *The Handmaid's Tale* 105, 106, 108, 122–130, 132, 140, 141, 177; *In Other Worlds* 174, 175; *Oryx and Crake* 9, 105, 130–133, 140, 141, 176–177

Bacchilega, Cristina 26, 27, 46–47, 51
Baccolini, Rafaella 19, 106–109, 119, 122, 125, 133, 135
Barr, Marleen S. 9–10, 145
Barthes, Roland 18; *Mythologies* 25–26, 34
Beauty 39, 40–41, 51–55, 62–63
"Beauty" 42–47, 51, 62
"Beauty and the Beast" 13, 17, 27–51, 56–57, 63
becoming 1, 2, 15–17, 18, 22, 40, 41, 47, 60, 61, 63, 71, 84, 93–94, 95, 101, 105–106, 120, 128, 133, 140, 141, 154, 162, 167, 169, 176–177; becoming-alien 142, 144, 148, 151, 154, 155–156, 158, 159–161, 164, 167, 168–170; becoming-animal 50, 119–120, 148; becoming-other 37, 42, 50–51, 74, 75, 90, 100, 117, 127, 139, 147, 148, 149, 152, 163; and trauma 68
"La Belle et La Bête" 28–30
binary logic 60–61, 63, 76, 88, 96, 125, 163
Bollinger, Laurel 57, 60
Braidotti, Rosi 1, 71, 105, 141, 142, 147, 176, 177–178; on becoming 16, 17, 148; on ethics 14–15
Bristow, Joseph 31
Broughton, Trev Lynn 31
Bryant, Sylvia 32, 38, 48–49
Burns, Christy L. 78–79, 84
Butler, Octavia E. 2, 6, 11, 18, 19, 22, 64, 70, 102, 104, 122, 140, 145, 147, 173; *Adulthood Rites* 170–172; *Dawn* 144, 168–170, 175, 177; *Imago* 172; *Kindred* 8, 18–19, 66, 69, 71–78, 80, 81, 93, 176; *Parable of the Sower* 105, 133–140, 141, 177; *Parable of the Talents* 105, 133–140, 141; *Xenogenesis*, or *Lilith's Brood* 142, 145, 167–172

Canopus in Argos: Archives 117, 142, 145, 147, 158–167
Carter, Angela 2, 6, 11, 15, 18, 21, 30–31, 64, 70, 102; "The Courtship of Mr. Lyon" 31–38, 50, 62; *Nights at the Circus* 17, 66, 69, 71, 94–101, 102, 177; "The Tiger's Bride" 47–51, 63, 176
Carter, Theresa 120, 121
Caruth, Cathy 67, 69, 73
"Cinderella" 23, 52, 54
City of Illusion 153–154
class (economic) 25, 29, 30, 32–33, 39, 131
Colebrook, Claire 147–148, 159, 163, 173
control societies 13, 15, 132
"The Courtship of Mr. Lyon" 31–38, 50, 62

Davidson, Arnold E. 129
Dawn 144, 168–170, 175, 177
Day, Aidan 33, 36, 38
defamiliarization 135, 144, 149
Deleuze, Gilles 1, 13, 15–16, 147, 148, 166–170; on ethics 14, 105, 120, 138–139
DiMarco, Danette 132
Disney 31, 43, 45, 54
The Dispossessed 156–157
Doan, Laura 60, 92
Doerksen, Teri Ann 135
Draine, Betsy 112, 117
dystopia 10, 19, 52, 103–141, 142, 147; critical 19, 106–109, 110

ethics 7, 113, 140; and history 74; as resistance 13–15
ethics of becoming 13–17, 18, 19, 21, 22, 24, 26, 28, 32, 58, 62, 65, 70, 71, 77, 82–83,

87–88, 89, 93, 100, 102, 115–117, 119, 120, 123, 142, 145, 147, 149, 156, 161, 163, 170, 172, 174–178; as collective 122; and storytelling 118

fairy tales 10, 18, 21–63, 91–92, 97
the fantastic 1, 2, 6, 7–10, 14, 15, 71–72, 79, 82, 86, 103, 108, 112, 117, 123, 132, 143, 174, 175, 177; and becoming 16, 90; in fairy tales 27; fantastic [fi]ction 13; and history 64–67, 70, 89; and violence 91
fantasy (as genre) 7; feminist fantasy 10; and history 86, 94, 102
Farrell, Kirby 67–68, 69, 95, 102
Farwell, Marilyn R. 90
femininity 30, 37
feminism 10, 23–24, 26, 93, 95
feminist genealogy 147–148
Feuer, Louis 127
Fishburn, Katherine 112, 117
Foucault, Michel 10–13, 14, 15, 67, 68, 77, 98–99, 100, 102, 131, 133, 137; on heterotopia 145–147; *The History of Sexuality* 12; "Nietzsche, Genealogy, History" 65–66
Franko, Carol 165
future 40, 43, 53, 63, 65, 97–98, 103, 127, 129, 135, 140, 168

Gamallo, Isabel C. Anievas 60
gender 30, 39, 82, 83, 90–92, 126–127, 140, 144, 154–155, 169
genre 6–7, 20, 107–108, 119, 122–123, 133, 175; hybrid 17; multiple 60, 98, 110n4; subversion of 125
Gilbert, Sandra M. 21
Glover, Jayne 131–132
Gottschall, Jonathan 23–24
Govan, Sandra Y. 74, 77
Granofsky, Ronald 108–111
Greene, Gayle 112
Griswold, Jerry 28, 29, 33
Guattari, Félix 1, 15–16, 120, 138–139, 147, 148, 166–170
Gubar, Susan 21

Haffenden, John 98
Haggis, Jane 65
Hainish Cycle 142, 145, 148–158
The Handmaid's Tale 105, 106, 108, 122–130, 132, 140, 141, 177
Hanson, Clare 98
Harvey, David 146–157
heterotopia 145–147, 148, 149, 151–153, 155, 156, 157–158, 162, 163, 164–165, 166, 173
history 20, 64–103, 108, 125, 129, 159, 162
The History of Sexuality 12
Hutcheon, Linda 18, 81; historiographic meta[fi]ction 18, 69–70
hybridity 16–17, 41–42, 46–47, 101, 153–154, 168, 170–172

identity 8, 50, 60, 177
Imago 172
In Other Worlds 174, 175

Jameson, Fredric 153

Kindred 8, 18–19, 66, 69, 71–78, 80, 81, 93, 176
Knapp, Mona 109n3, 112

LaCapra, Dominick 68, 84
Lee, Tanith 2, 17, 18, 21, 42; "Beauty" 42–47, 51, 62
Lefanu, Sarah 143–144
The Left Hand of Darkness 154–156, 169
Le Guin, Ursula K. 2, 5, 6, 20, 22, 145, 147, 170, 172, 173, 175; *City of Illusion* 153–154; *The Dispossessed* 156–157; *Hainish Cycle* 142, 145, 148–158; *The Left Hand of Darkness* 154–156, 169; *Planet of Exile* 151–153, 154, 163; *Rocannon's World* 149, 150–151; *The Telling* 149, 157–158
Le Prince de Beaumont, Jeanne-Marie 28; "La Belle et La Bête" 28–30
Lessing, Doris 2, 6, 8, 19, 22, 26, 104, 122, 123–124, 133, 134, 135, 136, 140, 145, 149, 170, 173; *Canopus in Argos: Archives* 117, 142, 145, 147, 158–167; *The Making of a Representative for Planet 8* 158, 165–166; *Mara and Dann: An Adventure* 105, 117–122, 125, 140; *The Marriages Between Zones* 158, 162–163; *The Memoirs of a Survivor* 17, 105, 106, 108, 109–117, 118, 122, 128–129, 140, 141, 177; *The Sentimental Agents* 158, 166–167; *Shikasta* 20, 142, 144, 158, 159–162; *The Sirian Experiments* 158, 159, 163–165; *The Story of General Dann* 105, 117–122, 140, 141
Long, Lisa 73, 77n9

Maas, Vera Sonja 23
Mahoney, Elisabeth 125
Makinen, Merja 8
The Making of a Representative for Planet 8 158, 165–166
Mara and Dann: An Adventure 105, 117–122, 125, 140
Margalit, Avishai 70, 76, 79
The Marriages Between Zones 158, 162–163
Marxism 96, 97–98, 122
McKinley, Robin 2, 18, 21, 38–39, 91n22; *Beauty* 39, 40–41, 62; *Rose Daughter* 39, 41–42, 46, 47, 62
Melzer, Patricia 138
The Memoirs of a Survivor 17, 105, 106, 108, 109–117, 118, 122, 128–129, 140, 141, 177
memory 79–80, 81, 96–97, 125–126, 130–131, 153
Michael, Magali Cornier 98, 100, 102, 122n10, 125, 127
morality 113, 124–125, 129, 140

Moylan, Tom 19, 106–109, 117, 122, 128*n*15, 133, 158*n*7
multiplicity 59
myth 7, 21, 25–26, 28, 62, 175; and history 76
Mythologies 25–26, 34

"Nietzsche, Genealogy, History" 65–66
Nights at the Circus 17, 66, 69, 71, 94–101, 102, 177

Onega, Susan 84
Oranges Are Not the Only Fruit 8, 55–62, 63, 79, 85, 91, 92
Oryx and Crake 9, 105, 130–133, 140, 141, 176–177

pain 77, 80, 134
Parable of the Sower 105, 133–140, 141, 177
Parable of the Talents 105, 133–140, 141
The Passion 66, 69, 78–84, 86, 91
past 20, 43, 63, 64, 129; and present 76, 85, 87, 92–94; representations of 69–70
Peach, Linden 98
Planet of Exile 151–153, 154, 163
Pordzik, Ralph 147
post-human 20, 46, 142, 148, 168, 169, 170, 172
postmodernism 26, 56, 59, 69–70, 81, 102; postmodern parody 57
power 6, 8, 9, 12, 24, 33, 82, 110–114, 122–128, 133, 135–137, 138, 140, 145, 158–159, 167, 174; and Foucault 10–13, 99; global 130, 131; and history 77; patriarchal 10, 26, 29, 34, 39, 51, 87, 162–163; and trauma 68

quantitative analysis of literature 23–24
quest 58, 59–60

race 73, 74, 75–76, 138
Raschke, Debrah 117
resistance 9, 84, 125, 128, 176, 177–178; ethics as 13–15, 16, 25
revision 22, 81, 126, 138, 143, 155, 162, 175–176; of fairy tales 24–63, 91–92, 97; and genre 107; of history 64–103; of the present 104–106, 126, 130, 135
Rigney, Barbara Hill 126
Roberts, Adam 154
Rocannon's World 149, 150–151
Rose Daughter 39, 41–42, 46, 47, 62
Rosemergy, Jan 59–60, 78*n*11, 83
Rusk, Lauren 60

Scholes, Robert 155
science [fi]ction 20, 42, 45, 42, 119, 143–145, 175
Seaboyer, Judith 83
Sellers, Susan 25–26, 53*n*9
The Sentimental Agents 158, 166–167
Sexing the Cherry 16, 66, 69, 84–94, 177
sexuality 49, 92, 140, 154–155, 169
Shikasta 20, 142, 144, 158, 159–162
The Sirian Experiments 158, 159, 163–165
Smith, Angela Marie 92, 93
socialization 23, 26, 50
space fiction 142–173
The Story of General Dann 105, 117–122, 140, 141
subjectivity 15, 57, 59, 88, 103, 105, 147, 162; and history 65–66; nomadic 17, 23, 41–42, 50, 62, 76, 78, 80, 82, 93, 109, 126, 139, 151, 154, 161; and power 141; and time 70–71; unitary 35, 38, 41
Suvin, Darko 119

Tatar, Maria 34–35
The Telling 149, 157–158
Tepper, Sheri S. 18, 21; *Beauty* 51–55, 63
Tiger, Virginia 119, 121
"The Tiger's Bride" 47–51, 63, 176
time 6, 20, 40, 63, 70–71, 96, 99–100, 157
Todorov, Tzvetan 7–8, 9, 14
trauma 18, 67–69, 70, 73, 74, 84, 87, 97, 102–103, 111, 130

Urbanowicz, Victor 156
utopia 131, 132, 138, 147, 153, 165

Vickroy, Laurie 68, 74
violence 74–75, 83, 90–91

Walker, Alison Tara 170
Walker, Nancy A. 10
Warner, Marina 28, 45, 47, 51
Watkins, Susan 118–119
Wilson, Sharon Rose 26
Winterson, Jeanette 2, 6, 8, 22, 64, 70, 71, 97, 102, 175; *Oranges Are Not the Only Fruit* 8, 55–62, 63, 79, 85, 91, 92; *The Passion* 66, 69, 78–84, 86, 91; *Sexing the Cherry* 16, 66, 69, 84–94, 177

Xenogenesis, or *Lilith's Brood* 142, 145, 167–172

Zipes, Jack 8–9, 22, 32, 60; on "Beauty and the Beast" 28–29, 30